Language-Sensitive Teaching and Learning

Richard Rossner • Rod Bolitho

Language-Sensitive Teaching and Learning

A Resource Book for Teachers and Teacher Educators

Richard Rossner
Cambridge, UK

Rod Bolitho
Wymondham, UK

ISBN 978-3-031-11338-3   ISBN 978-3-031-11339-0 (eBook)
https://doi.org/10.1007/978-3-031-11339-0

© The Editor(s) (if applicable) and The Author(s), under exclusive licence to Springer Nature Switzerland AG 2022

This work is subject to copyright. All rights are solely and exclusively licensed by the Publisher, whether the whole or part of the material is concerned, specifically the rights of translation, reprinting, reuse of illustrations, recitation, broadcasting, reproduction on microfilms or in any other physical way, and transmission or information storage and retrieval, electronic adaptation, computer software, or by similar or dissimilar methodology now known or hereafter developed.

The use of general descriptive names, registered names, trademarks, service marks, etc. in this publication does not imply, even in the absence of a specific statement, that such names are exempt from the relevant protective laws and regulations and therefore free for general use.

The publisher, the authors, and the editors are safe to assume that the advice and information in this book are believed to be true and accurate at the date of publication. Neither the publisher nor the authors or the editors give a warranty, expressed or implied, with respect to the material contained herein or for any errors or omissions that may have been made. The publisher remains neutral with regard to jurisdictional claims in published maps and institutional affiliations.

This Palgrave Macmillan imprint is published by the registered company Springer Nature Switzerland AG.
The registered company address is: Gewerbestrasse 11, 6330 Cham, Switzerland

To our wives, Natasha and Annick, with thanks for their love and support.

Acknowledgements

The authors would like to thank the following people for the support of different kinds they generously offered at various stages of the writing process:

Lukas Bleichenbacher
Klaus-Börge Boeckmann
Carla Carnevale
Lyn Dawes
Maaike Hajer
Maria Heron
Frank Heyworth
Jens Loescher
Josef Leisen
Neil Mercer
David Newby
Gerda Piribauer
Nataša Pirih Svetina
Ben Rampton
Daniela Rotter
Caroline Schwarz
Christian Sinn
Anna Schröder-Sura
Jason Skeet
Belinda Steinhuber
Gerald van Dijk

Contents

1 Unit 1: The Nature and Purposes of Language as Communication .. 1
  1.1 Introduction 1
  1.2 Section 1: Users of a Language as 'Social Agents' 1
      1.2.1 Task 1 1
      1.2.2 Commentary 2
      1.2.3 Task 2 2
      1.2.4 Task 3 3
      1.2.5 Task 4 3
      1.2.6 Commentary 3
      1.2.7 Task 5 4
      1.2.8 Commentary 5
      1.2.9 Task 6 5
      1.2.10 Commentary 5
      1.2.11 Task 7 6
      1.2.12 Commentary 6
      1.2.13 Task 8 7
      1.2.14 Commentary 7
      1.2.15 Summary 8
      1.2.16 Some Questions for Reflection 9
  1.3 Section 2: Variations in Language Use 9
      1.3.1 Task 9 9
      1.3.2 Commentary 10
      1.3.3 Task 10 10
      1.3.4 Commentary 10
      1.3.5 Task 11 11
      1.3.6 Commentary 11
      1.3.7 Task 12 12
      1.3.8 Commentary 12
      1.3.9 Task 13 12
      1.3.10 Commentary 13

		1.3.11	Summary	13
		1.3.12	Some Questions for Reflection	14
	1.4	Section 3: Identity and Culture in Language Use		14
		1.4.1	Task 14	14
		1.4.2	Commentary	15
		1.4.3	Task 15	15
		1.4.4	Task 16	16
		1.4.5	Commentary	16
		1.4.6	Task 17	18
		1.4.7	Commentary	18
		1.4.8	Task 18	19
		1.4.9	Commentary	19
		1.4.10	Task 19	20
		1.4.11	Commentary	20
		1.4.12	Summary	20
		1.4.13	Some Questions for Reflection	21
	1.5	Section 4: Language and Power		21
		1.5.1	Task 20	21
		1.5.2	Commentary	22
		1.5.3	Task 21	23
		1.5.4	Commentary	23
		1.5.5	Task 22	24
		1.5.6	Commentary	24
		1.5.7	Task 23	25
		1.5.8	Task 24	25
		1.5.9	Commentary	26
		1.5.10	Summary	26
		1.5.11	Some Questions for Reflection	26
	1.6	Conclusion		27
	References			27
2	**Unit 2: Language and Communication in Education 1**			**29**
	2.1	Section 1: Language and Learning		29
		2.1.1	Task 1	29
		2.1.2	Task 2	30
		2.1.3	Commentary	30
		2.1.4	Task 3	31
		2.1.5	Task 4	31
		2.1.6	Commentary	31
		2.1.7	Summary	32
		2.1.8	Questions for Reflection	33
	2.2	Section 2: Context and Communication		33
		2.2.1	Task 5	33
		2.2.2	Commentary	33
		2.2.3	Task 6	34
		2.2.4	Task 7	34

		2.2.5	Commentary	35
		2.2.6	Task 8	36
		2.2.7	Commentary	36
		2.2.8	Task 9	37
		2.2.9	Commentary	38
		2.2.10	Task 10	38
		2.2.11	Commentary	39
		2.2.12	Summary	39
		2.2.13	Some Questions for Reflection	41
	2.3	Section 3: The Uses of Language in Teaching		41
		2.3.1	Task 11	41
		2.3.2	Commentary	42
		2.3.3	Task 12	42
		2.3.4	Commentary	42
		2.3.5	Task 13	43
		2.3.6	Task 14	43
		2.3.7	Commentary	43
		2.3.8	Summary	44
		2.3.9	Questions for Reflection	46
	2.4	Section 4: Learning Talk and Context		46
		2.4.1	Task 15	46
		2.4.2	Commentary	47
		2.4.3	Task 16	47
		2.4.4	Commentary	48
		2.4.5	Task 17	49
		2.4.6	Commentary	49
		2.4.7	Task 18	50
		2.4.8	Commentary	52
		2.4.9	Summary	53
		2.4.10	Some Questions for Reflection	54
	2.5	Conclusion		54
	References			54
3	**Unit 3: Language and Communication in Education 2**			**57**
	3.1	Section 1: The Language Repertoires of Individual Students		57
		3.1.1	Task 1	57
		3.1.2	Commentary	58
		3.1.3	Task 2	59
		3.1.4	Commentary	59
		3.1.5	Task 3	60
		3.1.6	Commentary	60
		3.1.7	Task 4	60
		3.1.8	Task 5	61
		3.1.9	Commentary	61
		3.1.10	Task 6	62

		3.1.11	Commentary	63
		3.1.12	Task 7	63
		3.1.13	Commentary	64
		3.1.14	Task 8	65
		3.1.15	Commentary	66
		3.1.16	Task 9	66
		3.1.17	Commentary	67
		3.1.18	Summary	67
		3.1.19	Questions for Reflection	69
	3.2	Section 2: Language and Subjects		69
		3.2.1	Task 10	70
		3.2.2	Commentary	71
		3.2.3	Task 11	71
		3.2.4	Commentary	72
		3.2.5	Task 12	73
		3.2.6	Commentary	73
		3.2.7	Task 13	74
		3.2.8	Commentary	74
		3.2.9	Summary	75
		3.2.10	Questions for Reflection	76
	3.3	Section 3: Scaffolding		76
		3.3.1	Task 14	76
		3.3.2	Commentary	77
		3.3.3	Task 15	78
		3.3.4	Commentary	79
		3.3.5	Task 16	80
		3.3.6	Commentary	81
		3.3.7	Task 17	82
		3.3.8	Commentary	82
	3.4	Task 18		83
		3.4.1	Commentary	84
		3.4.2	Task 19	84
		3.4.3	Commentary	86
		3.4.4	Task 20	86
		3.4.5	Commentary	87
		3.4.6	Summary	88
		3.4.7	Questions for Reflection	89
	3.5	Section 4: The Impact of 'Teaching' Language and Questions on Learning and Language Development		89
		3.5.1	Task 21	89
		3.5.2	Commentary	90
		3.5.3	Task 22	90
		3.5.4	Commentary	91
		3.5.5	Task 23	91
		3.5.6	Commentary	92

		3.5.7	Task 24	92
		3.5.8	An Art Teacher Might Say	93
		3.5.9	Commentary	94
		3.5.10	Task 25	95
		3.5.11	Commentary	96
		3.5.12	Summary	96
		3.5.13	Questions for Reflection	97
	3.6	Conclusion		97
	References			98
4	**Unit 4 Language and Communication in Education 3**			**99**
	4.1	Section 1: The Impact of Schooling on the Development of a Student's Language Repertoire		99
		4.1.1	Task 1	99
		4.1.2	Task 2	100
		4.1.3	Commentary	100
		4.1.4	Task 3	100
		4.1.5	Commentary	101
		4.1.6	Task 4	102
		4.1.7	Commentary	103
		4.1.8	Task 5	103
		4.1.9	Commentary	104
		4.1.10	Task 6	104
		4.1.11	Commentary	104
		4.1.12	Summary	105
		4.1.13	Some Questions for Reflection	105
	4.2	Section 2: Aspects of Literacy and Oracy		106
		4.2.1	Task 7	106
		4.2.2	Commentary	106
		4.2.3	Task 8	107
		4.2.4	Commentary	107
		4.2.5	Task 9	108
		4.2.6	Commentary	108
		4.2.7	Task 10	108
		4.2.8	Task 11	109
		4.2.9	Commentary	109
		4.2.10	Task 12	109
		4.2.11	Commentary	110
		4.2.12	Task 13	111
		4.2.13	Task 14	111
		4.2.14	Commentary	113
		4.2.15	Task 15	114
		4.2.16	Commentary	115
		4.2.17	Summary	115
		4.2.18	Some Questions for Reflection	118

	4.3	Section 3: The Range of Genres which Children should be able to Understand and Reproduce in Different Subject Areas 118
		4.3.1 Task 16 118
		4.3.2 Task 17 119
		4.3.3 Commentary 119
		4.3.4 Summary....................................... 120
		4.3.5 Some Questions for Reflection 121
	4.4	Section 4: A Teacher's Language Repertoire and its Impact on the Development of Learners' Literacy and Oracy 121
		4.4.1 Task 18 121
		4.4.2 Commentary 122
		4.4.3 Task 19 123
		4.4.4 Commentary 123
		4.4.5 Summary....................................... 124
		4.4.6 Some Questions for Reflection 125
	4.5	Conclusion.. 125
	References... 125
5	**Unit 5: Building Language Sensitivity into Teacher Education and Training** 127
	5.1	Introduction 127
	5.2	Section 1: Improving the Current Situation in Teacher Education and Training 128
		5.2.1 Task 1 128
		5.2.2 Task 2 128
		5.2.3 Commentary 129
		5.2.4 Task 3 129
		5.2.5 Commentary 130
		5.2.6 Task 4 133
		5.2.7 Task 5 134
		5.2.8 Commentary 134
		5.2.9 Task 6 134
		5.2.10 Commentary 135
		5.2.11 Task 7 135
		5.2.12 Commentary 136
		5.2.13 Task 8 137
		5.2.14 Commentary 137
		5.2.15 Task 9 138
		5.2.16 Commentary 139
		5.2.17 Task 10 140
		5.2.18 Commentary 140
		5.2.19 Task 11 141
		5.2.20 Commentary 142
		5.2.21 Summary....................................... 144

5.3	Section 2: Tasks for Teacher Training		144
	5.3.1	Introduction	144
	5.3.2	Task 12	144
	5.3.3	Commentary	145
	5.3.4	Task 13	146
	5.3.5	Commentary	147
	5.3.6	Task 14	147
	5.3.7	Commentary	148
	5.3.8	Task 15	148
	5.3.9	Commentary	149
	5.3.10	Task 16	150
	5.3.11	Task 17	150
	5.3.12	Task 18	151
	5.3.13	Commentary	151
	5.3.14	Summary	152
5.4	Section 3: Drawing on Good Practice		152
	5.4.1	Introduction	152
	5.4.2	Germany	152
	5.4.3	Austria	153
	5.4.4	Task 19	153
	5.4.5	Commentary	153
	5.4.6	Task 20	154
	5.4.7	Task 21	155
	5.4.8	Commentary	155
	5.4.9	Switzerland	156
	5.4.10	Task 22	156
	5.4.11	Task 23	156
	5.4.12	Task 24	157
	5.4.13	Commentary	157
	5.4.14	Netherlands	158
	5.4.15	Task 25	159
	5.4.16	Commentary	160
	5.4.17	Task 26	160
	5.4.18	Commentary	160
	5.4.19	Task 27	162
	5.4.20	Commentary	163
	5.4.21	Summary	164
5.5	Section 4: Building Language-Sensitive Teaching and Learning Systematically into all Teacher Education		164
	5.5.1	Task 28	165
	5.5.2	Commentary	166
	5.5.3	Task 29	167
	5.5.4	Commentary	168
	5.5.5	Task 30	170
	5.5.6	Commentary	171

		5.5.7	Task 31	172
		5.5.8	Commentary	173
		5.5.9	Task 32	174
		5.5.10	Commentary	174
		5.5.11	Task 33	175
		5.5.12	Commentary	176
		5.5.13	Summary	177
	5.6	Language-Sensitive Education: Taking Action		178
	5.7	Conclusion		179
	References			180

Appendix: Inventory of Task Types for Teacher Education and Training 185

Index ... 189

List of Figures

Fig. 1.1	The Four Sides Model (JazzyJulius, public domain, via Wikimedia Commons)	4
Fig. 1.2	Extracts from Indian news media. https://english.deepika.com/Index.aspx (accessed 28 January 2022)	16
Fig. 1.3	Political slogans	23
Fig. 2.1	Communication in context	40
Fig. 3.1	Page from a UK science textbook (from Gardom Hulme et al. 2017, p.48)	70
Fig. 3.2	Page of a history textbook (from Wilkes 2014, p. 23)	72
Fig. 3.3	The Eagle by Alfred Lord Tennyson (1809–1892)	80
Fig. 3.4	How to search the Internet (from an article by Nicky Levine MFA provided by wikiHow) (a wiki building the world's largest, highest quality how-to manual. Please edit this article and find author credits at wikiHow.com. Content on wikiHow can be shared under a Creative Commons License)	85
Fig. 3.5	A challenging text	87
Fig. 4.1	'In a Whispering Garden' by Thomas Hardy	102
Fig. 4.2	Sample B a literacy assessment tool recommended by the National Council of Teachers of English in the USA. (Source: Kathryn Mitchell Pierce. 'Listening In on Student Learning.' Blog post on behalf of the NCTE Standing Committee on Literacy Assessment. October 4, 2019)	112
Fig. 4.3	A typical task for assessing basic adult literacy (freely adapted from an Internet source)	113
Fig. 4.4	Genre-based curriculum cycle (Hammond 2001, p. 28, cited in Beacco et al. 2016)	120
Fig. 5.1	Issues from lesson observation	141
Fig. 5.2	Diagram of photosynthesis	143
Fig. 5.3	Parasites	146
Fig. 5.4	Making Maps	149
Fig. 5.5	**Characteristics of words and phrases** (from van Dijk et al., 2021)	161

List of Tables

Table 1.1	Roles and purposes in language use	2
Table 1.2	Sample SMS exchange	6
Table 1.3	A four-dimensional model of language and communication	7
Table 1.4	Extract from census form	19
Table 2.1	Example of classroom language use	36
Table 2.2	Two ways in which teachers use language in class	37
Table 2.3	Repertoire of learning talk (based on Alexander 2018, p. 8)	47
Table 3.1	Thinking about your language repertoire	58
Table 3.2	Percentage proportion of children in a selection of local authority areas in the UK whose first language is not English	61
Table 3.3	Possible difficulties with language at school	64
Table 3.4	Situations where scaffolding may be useful	76
Table 4.1	Literacy and Oracy Activities	110
Table 4.2	Sample A (to assess writing at different levels) (freely adapted and simplified from an Internet source)	111
Table 4.3	Oracy Framework © Voice 21, 2022. Developed in partnership with Oracy Cambridge, University of Cambridge	114
Table 5.1		131
Table 5.2	Factors to consider when designing a teacher education module on language sensitivity	133
Table 5.3	Some factors to consider when designing an in-service training course on language sensitivity	134
Table 5.4	Language-related subskills needed for subject specialist teacher	150
Table 5.5	Appropriate and inappropriate teacher language	154
Table 5.6	Statements about beliefs	165
Table 5.7	Steps towards language-sensitive teacher education	170

Introduction

What Is Language-Sensitive Teaching?

The teaching and learning of any subject involve using language most of the time. It is therefore very important that teachers at all levels in education think carefully about how best to use the language effectively, and how to ensure that their students are able to use this language to advance their learning and cognitive and social development. The issue of language in education has become even more urgent as schools, especially those in Europe, have become linguistically and culturally more heterogeneous due to migration and the need for some students to adapt to using a language other than their first language in education. But many students for whom the language used at school is their first and only language, especially those from more deprived backgrounds, also have challenges when it comes to language and literacy.

The Aim of the Book

The purpose of the book is to offer teachers and student teachers of any subject, including teachers of the language of schooling and of foreign languages, opportunities to become more familiar with the workings of language in everyday use and especially in classroom and online teaching and learning. The book also offers ideas which can be used or adapted for modules in teacher education courses or in planning professional development activities for practising teachers, and the last unit is aimed specifically at those working in the field of teacher education, including curriculum development for teacher education, and in-service development.

While the book is written in English, most of the tasks and commentaries are relevant for teachers working in other language contexts and the tasks selected can be adapted and/or translated for different environments.

What Does the Book Contain?

There are five overlapping units. The units are divided into sections containing several tasks each focusing on an aspect of the uses of language in education or, in Unit 1, in everyday situations. Each task or group of tasks is followed by a commentary with suggested answers and/or discussion of relevant issues. Every section ends with a brief summary and two or three questions for reflection.

Using the Book

There is no set pathway through the tasks and commentaries in the book. The first four units can be worked through from beginning to end, but a more flexible approach may be to select topics from the contents page and to identify tasks in the relevant sections that will be useful for you as a teacher or for given purposes in teacher education or professional development. It is advantageous to do the tasks, where possible, with someone else or in a group, so that issues and answers can be discussed, but the tasks are also designed to be useful to those working alone, for example as assignments that are part of a teacher education course.

Unit 5 is designed specifically for teacher educators and those supporting practising teachers, but teachers may also find tasks there which are relevant to their needs. The unit also contains a suggested 'core syllabus', which can serve as a menu for teacher education modules or for individual and collective professional development.

Chapter 1
Unit 1: The Nature and Purposes of Language as Communication

1.1 Introduction

'Language' is a catch-all term for a means of communication. It is generally regarded as an essentially human characteristic, though there is evidence of highly developed patterns of communication in animals and birds. 'Language' is also used as a specific term, to describe the accepted norm of communication in a particular homogeneous group of speakers. In this specific sense, the language used by one group is not available to all speakers in another group, and so its use as an effective means of communication is restricted. Within the 'home' group of a particular language, however, it is usually the main means of establishing social cohesion, of intelligible daily exchanges at every level of society and, importantly, of affirming aspects of identity. In this opening unit, we explore some of the dimensions of language in communication as a way of providing a wider context for our discussion of the educational issues that we address in the rest of the book.

1.2 Section 1: Users of a Language as 'Social Agents'

1.2.1 Task 1

If we accept that users of any language are potentially 'social agents', i.e. members of society who have tasks to perform, we also recognise that these tasks are differentiated and that each contributes in a different way to the functioning of society as a whole. To see this more clearly, we invite you to complete Table 1.1, either individually or in discussion with a colleague. We have provided an example.

Table 1.1 Roles and purposes in language use

Language user	Main role and context	Purposes in using language
A taxi driver	To carry customers safely from place to place; in a car	Clarifying destination; asking for the fare; perhaps social chat
A nurse		
A waiter		
A TV newsreader		
A teacher		

1.2.2 Commentary

This simple task illustrates some important requirements of any language, for example the need for the avoidance of misunderstandings, a capacity for flexibility and adaptability to new situations and demands, scope to express shades of meaning and emotions, reliance on shared and accepted cultural and societal norms and ways of avoiding ambiguity in instructions or explanations. Each of the jobs mentioned above has a recognised place in any society, but none of them could be carried out successfully without the focused, and sometimes specialised, use of language. Some involve dialogue with another person, the nurse for example, whereas others, the newsreader for instance, are more monologic in nature, at least for part of the time. All will have a social niche outside their job role, with family or friends, and in that context they will use language in different ways and with different purposes. Native speakers of any language will usually switch easily and comfortably from one social context to another, though sometimes boundaries are crossed. I recently heard an annoyed wife saying to her husband, 'Don't use your football coach tone to me!'

But communication doesn't always go smoothly, even between speakers of a shared language, as the following extracts and tasks illustrate.

1.2.3 Task 2

In this first example, what role does the parent adopt? And how does the child bring him back on track?

Child: Why are Batman and Robin called the dynamic duel?
*Parent: Du*o*. It means two people together.*
Child: Yes, but why are they called the dynamic duo?
Parent: Dynamic means exciting, full of action.
Child: Like dynamite, 'cos they're dynamite
data from Sealy (1996)

1.2.4 Task 3

In this example, starting with a short phone call, what is the probable cause of the husband's last response?

> *Wife: Hello, darling. I'm staying a bit later at work then going for a drink with some of the team. Is that OK with you?*
> *Husband: OK, fine. See you later.*
> *(....)*
> *Wife (arriving home after the children's bedtime): Hi, darling. Is everything OK?*
> *Husband: No, everything is definitely **not** OK ....*

1.2.5 Task 4

What could have been done to avoid the misunderstanding expressed in this exchange of email messages?

Supplier to recipient of goods: *We delivered your order in three days as agreed. That was two weeks ago and we still haven't received payment from you.*

Recipient to supplier: *We settle all invoices within thirty days. You can expect payment soon.*

1.2.6 Commentary

Misunderstandings and miscommunications like these happen all the time, in professional as well as personal interactions, and it may be useful for those involved in language education to understand why. The Four Sides Model, developed by Schulz von Thun (1981), may be helpful here. He postulates that there are potentially four aspects to any message sent by one person to another, and the same four elements are present in the way in which a listener receives the message, though there may be differences between the speaker's intentions and the listener's understanding. The model is captured in Fig. 1.1:

In Task 2, the parent assumes a teacher role, but the child uses emphasis to focus his parent on what he wants to know...The parent's listening ear at first focuses on a detail of the message rather than on exactly what the child wants to know, and the child has to 're-send' the message in order to get the response he is looking for. The parent's second response resolves the query to the child's satisfaction and enables him to create a mnemonic that he can use to remember the new word and its meaning.

In Task 3, the husband simply assumes that his wife wouldn't be very late, and he doesn't check on her expected return time. When she comes home later than he expected, he is annoyed, perhaps because she is normally at home at the children's bedtime. Her initial *appeal* to him is based on their personal relationship. She obviously feels comfortable about *revealing* her plans and gives some factual

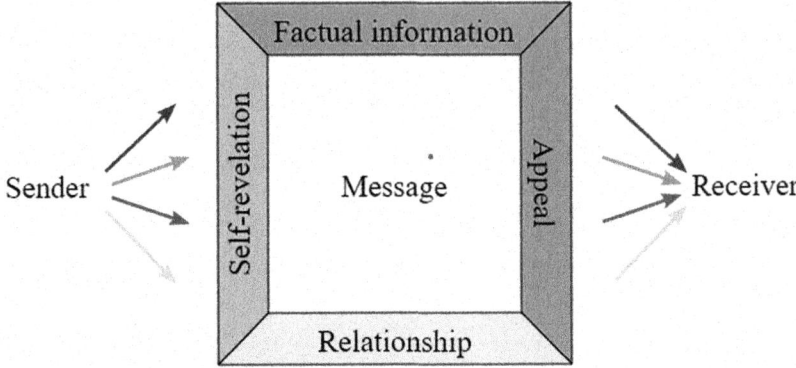

Fig. 1.1 The Four Sides Model (JazzyJulius, public domain, via Wikimedia Commons)

information to explain them. The husband's listening ear picks all of this up but he doesn't reveal any of his expectations or assumptions, and this leads to the annoyance he experiences when she comes home.

In Task 4, there is a mismatch between the recipient's and the supplier's understanding of the terms of business, something that it would have been better to clear up when the order was placed. There is no evidence of face-to-face contact in the exchange, and so Schulz von Thun's model is not directly relevant here.

1.2.7 Task 5

Communication between people who know each other usually takes place on the basis of shared assumptions. These may involve issues of status, accepted traditions or behaviour norms, cultural factors or even the right to initiate or conclude an interaction. When a journalist interviews a politician on television, for example, the interaction usually starts with an exchange of courtesies, but quickly progresses to a series of prepared questions from the interviewer to the politician, which the politician will try to answer on her/his own terms rather than those of the questioner. This extract, freely adapted from a real source, is not untypical:

> *Interviewer:* I'd like to talk to you about the latest crime figures. They show a worrying increase in knife crime, particularly among teenagers. Why is this happening?
>
> *Politician:* I agree that it's worrying but, with the police, we are urgently exploring ways of tackling the problem.
>
> *Interviewer:* That's good to hear, but don't you need to find out what's causing it?
>
> *Politician:* We are committed to eradicating knife crime completely and we are recommending an amnesty for people to hand in their knives without fear of arrest. We believe this will ....
>
> *Interviewer:* Forgive me for interrupting, but don't you need to address the causes and not just the crime itself.
>
> *Politician:* We think the figures you mentioned may be misleading, and they certainly vary in different locations around the country. Take London, for example ....

> *Interviewer:* But the fact is that more and more people—often young people—are being killed and injured in knife attacks. Why is that happening?
> *Politician:* To come back to my earlier point, before you interrupted me ... London has a higher incidence of knife crime than some other cities and we are focussing on towns and cities that show rising trends ....
> *Interviewer:* And will you be looking into the reasons behind this?
> *Politician:* If you'll just let me finish my point, I'll try to answer ...:

The interviewer and the politician both have defined roles to play in this exchange. What are these roles, and how do they play out during the interview?

1.2.8 Commentary

This kind of interchange is very rarely about misunderstanding. It is about two different and conflicting agendas or purposes: the interviewer exercising his right to push for answers in the public interest and the politician trying to alter the course of the interview in order to make party political points. Each of the protagonists knows exactly what the other is trying to achieve, and so the real issue here is one of control. Successful interviewers try to remain courteous but they do not, on the whole, defer to powerful politicians. In many cultures and contexts, but by no means in all, this is seen as a legitimate holding to account of political leaders. The same behaviour in most business negotiations or round a family dinner table would be regarded as highly unusual and even unacceptable except in the context of a real argument.

1.2.9 Task 6

What is going on in this everyday exchange? To what extent do mother and daughter understand each other?

> *Mother:* Julia, you're definitely going to miss the bus!
> *Daughter:* Oh no! I can't find my sports bag. Where have you put it?
> *Mother:* I haven't touched it. Your lunch box is on the kitchen table.
> *Daughter:* Can't you turn the radio down? Anyway, I have to run.
> *Mother:* Have a good day. Love you!
> *Daughter:* Bye
> (adapted from personal experience)

1.2.10 Commentary

Again, there are no real misunderstandings here despite the superficial evidence that mother and daughter are talking past each other in the heat of the moment and have different preoccupations. Here, we are looking at an exchange that is probably repeated in one form or another on a daily basis, and each of the speakers has a different and possibly conflicting immediate agenda while moving towards the same further goal, which is for Julia to catch the bus.

When misunderstandings or conflicting agendas do arise in spoken interaction, the immediacy of speech allows them to be explored and put right if both parties are committed to resolving the situation. This has until recently been much less easy to achieve in written exchanges. Over many centuries, people came to regard the written word as permanent and powerful, and written communication between two people, usually by letter, was always subject to time delay before an answer was composed and received. Letter writing was also regarded as something of a literary form and collected correspondence was evidence of the thought processes and philosophical positions of the writers, as well as valuable chronicles of the age in which they lived. That era does seem to be coming to an end as more immediate, informal and ephemeral means of written communication have become such a regular feature of our lives. People in offices complain about the number of email messages in their inbox, and often set about replying to them as though an instant response is inevitable. This is even more the case with text messaging and online chats, which have even developed their own shorthand and, like quick spoken exchanges, often rely on shared assumptions as a basis for successful communication.

1.2.11 Task 7

Try to decode this example of chat between two friends (Table 1.2):

Table 1.2 Sample SMS exchange

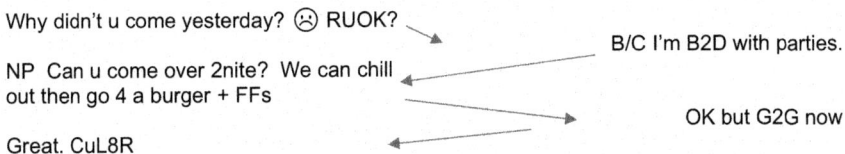

Why didn't u come yesterday? ☹ RUOK?

B/C I'm B2D with parties.

NP Can u come over 2nite? We can chill out then go 4 a burger + FFs

OK but G2G now

Great. CuL8R

1.2.12 Commentary

It's easy to see why some adults are baffled by this sort of exchange, but that is part of the point! Friends use devices like these as part of a well-established communication code within their peer group, and parents are not supposed to belong to this group. It is easy to see, though, why some linguists and education professionals have begun to express concern about the impact of texting and the language used in social media chat on the general level of literacy among young people. Ashley Campbell summed it up in these terms:

> There have been suggestions from both media sources and educators that texting may have a negative effect on the literacy skills of students. Perhaps the biggest problem is that stu-

dents do not distinguish between times when they need to write formally without using 'textisms', and when they are writing informally and the use of textisms is acceptable. With more long term studies on the same group of individuals, it may be possible for researchers to determine if the use of textisms does indeed have negative effects on literacy. With long term studies, it may be possible to see if individuals carry the textisms that they use in their personal correspondences into their formal writing in a workplace environment. Until the time that concrete results are acquired to suggest that texting has deleterious effects, it may be wise to encourage students to lessen their use of textisms, and to instead use proper grammar and spelling while they are using texting as a form of communication. (Campbell 2014)

However, this view is far from universal, as this extract from an interview with the novelist Margaret Atwood shows:

You get a lot of nonsense about, 'Won't Twitter destroy English language?' Well, did the telegram destroy the English language? No .... So it is a short form communication method, like writing on washroom walls. Or like Romans writing graffiti back in Rome, or Vikings writing runes on the walls of tombs they had broken into. You weren't going to write a novel on the wall of a tomb. But you were going to write 'Thorfeld was here,' which is pretty much what they wrote. 'Found no treasure. Shit.' (Slone 2013)

1.2.13 Task 8

Here you may find it useful to make a few notes on both sides of the argument. Do you agree with the last sentence in the quote from Campbell or are you more in favour of Atwood's more liberal view? Reasons?

1.2.14 Commentary

With developments in modes of communication like these in mind, it may be useful to refer to a four-dimensional, socially rooted model of language and communication such as the one in Table 1.3, offered here with no claim to comprehensiveness but with examples, which you may want to add to.

Table 1.3 A four-dimensional model of language and communication

	Insider/Internal (within an established social, educational or professional group)	External (beyond an established group, with 'outsiders')
Informal	For example • Talk within a family or peer group (e.g. friends or workplace colleagues) • Online chat • Social media interaction	For example • Talk with distant relatives, friends of friends, newcomers to a group, etc. • Blogs • Posts on social media
Formal	For example • Manager < >employee talk • Talk in internal meetings • Teacher < >pupil talk in class settings • Emails, letters	For example • Talk in meetings with business partners • Talk with officials and authorities • Interviews for jobs, grants, etc.

Clearly, there are different degrees of formality and informality in different situations, and skilled communicators draw on their pragmatic competence to make the necessary adjustments in speech more or less spontaneously, and in writing usually in a more conscious and considered way.

Technology, as the examples above show, has had a profound influence on the way we all communicate, and a consequence has been for us all to be much more conscious of the need to identify the purpose behind the messages we read and the news we are exposed to on a day-to-day basis. People (and there are many) who have very active social media accounts with lots of followers are now described as 'influencers', an epithet which has only recently come into common use. Handling the information explosion is now a priority for children at school, and it is seen in curriculum documents as a key twenty-first century skill. Personal identity associated with email accounts, social media and even the posting of news items can all too easily be concealed in ways that make it very difficult to trace the originators of financial scams, fake news and malicious messaging. Where once bullies plied their hateful trade face to face, they can now do it online without necessarily having to face the consequences. Where fraudsters once had to confront their victims at the front door, they can now approach vulnerable people anonymously online or by telephone. And where journalists were once visibly accountable for everything they wrote or reported, it is now possible for anybody with malign intent to spread fake news and propaganda without even being identified as the original authors. It is clearly essential for the present and future generations of school children to learn how to recognise fraud, malice and false information quickly and effectively.

1.2.15 Summary

In this section, we have looked at some ways in which we are all social agents, using language, with all its imperfections, for a wide range of purposes according to our priorities in life and our various roles in society. The decisions we make about communication affect those around us most immediately, but technology now enables us to reach far beyond the inner circle of our family, friends or workplace colleagues and to do good or ill to those we are able to contact. As many of us found out during the COVID pandemic, the power of technology has also been harnessed to the cause of education, keeping schooling and university studies going at distance while so many people have been unable to meet face to face in normal educational settings. Some of these developments would undoubtedly have happened anyway, but the exigencies of the global health emergency certainly accelerated the process.

In the next section, we will look more closely at the choices we make when using language, according to our intentions as communicators, and at the ways in which we tune our communication strategies to reflect these intentions and our awareness of the people we interact with.

1.2.16 *Some Questions for Reflection*

(a) Think of an example of a miscommunication which you have experienced. Try to recreate the language that was used and make notes about how the misunderstanding could have been cleared up.
(b) What kind of 'insider talk' have you taken part in? In what settings, with whom and for what purposes?

1.3 Section 2: Variations in Language Use

As we mature, most of us become more and more sensitive to the people we are with and the situations in which we find ourselves, and consequently more and more able to vary and tune the language we use accordingly. Let's start by considering a couple of examples.

1.3.1 *Task 9*

What changes from the first exchange to the second in this example? Why does Margaret make those changes?

> *Margaret: How did my father's operation go?*
> *Surgeon: As well as could be expected, but he had respiratory problems and we decided on a tracheotomy as a temporary measure.*
> *Margaret: Oh dear! That sounds bad. Is he going to recover?*
> *Surgeon: In cases like this, the prognosis is generally good, but we'll know more when the effects of the anaesthetic have worn off.*
> *Margaret: When will that be?*
> *Surgeon: Later this evening ... maybe around 10. You could call again then.*
> *Margaret: I will. And thanks for all you've done.*
> ....
> *(5 minutes later)*
> *Margaret: I've just spoken to the hospital, darling.*
> *Anna (daughter, aged 10): How's Grandpa?*
> *Margaret: He's resting after his operation. They're helping him to breathe more easily.*
> *Anna: But he's going to get better, isn't he?*
> *Margaret: They think so. Most people do after an operation like that. We'll know better when he wakes up.*

1.3.2 Commentary

Here there is evidence of a speaker adjusting her language according to who she is speaking to (her interlocutor). Margaret understands the medical terms the surgeon uses, but knows very well that Anna, at her age, would struggle with them and might even be scared by them. For this reason, she explains things in a way which she knows Anna will understand and perhaps be reassured by. This is a kind of mediation of information which parents often use when explaining something to their children. This kind of versatility in a language user is learned behaviour, built up over a long period of time starting in childhood. In the next task, there is an example of a very early stage in that kind of development.

1.3.3 Task 10

Look through these short exchanges between family members. How old would you say Emily is? What has she learned to do with language? What might she still need to learn?

> *Emily: I want more jelly beans!*
> *Mother: So how do you ask nicely?*
> *Emily: Can I have jelly beans?*
> *Mother: ... and one more word?*
> *Emily: ... pleeeeease!*
> *Mother: Good girl. Here you are. Now go and share them with your brother.*
> ....
> *Jake: Oooh! You've got jellybeans!*
> *Emily: They're mine! You can't have any!*
> *Jake: But Mummy said to share them.*
> *Emily (after thinking): You can have two! But only if you ask nicely.*
> *Jake: Can I have my jellybeans, please?*
> *Emily: Here you are..!. I want to play with Teddy.*
> *Jake: You can't! He's mine!*
> ....
> *Emily: Mummy, Jake won't give me Teddy. It's not fair!*
> *Mother: Did you ask him nicely?*
> *Emily (after thinking): No, but I still want to play with Teddy.*
> *Mother: Well ... you know how to ask.*

1.3.4 Commentary

In this extract, Emily (aged 4) is reminded by her mother about how to ask for something she wants. She obviously wants the jellybeans (a kind of sweet) very badly and so she is motivated to comply. She then applies the same condition to her little brother, as often happens between siblings. However, she clearly associates this kind of polite request with jellybeans, and she fails to transfer her newly acquired linguistic know-how to a slightly new situation and has to rely on her mother to remind her again about how to ask politely for what she wants. Children need this kind of reinforcement constantly, and it comes from parents, teachers, other adults and older siblings in everyday situations like the one illustrated in the extract.

The next task is based around a dialogue in which we see that even adults sometimes struggle to cope in commonplace situations.

1.3.5 Task 11

Look at this exchange between a car mechanic and his customer. Why do you think the customer is so ready to accept the mechanic's estimate?

> *Customer: Have you had time to look at my Toyota?*
> *Mechanic: Yes, I have. It's in quite a state to be honest.*
> *Customer: Oh dear, tell me the worst.*
> *Mechanic: Well, to start with, the distributor needs replacing, the track rod ends are clapped out and you're going to need a new starter motor soon.*
> *Customer: Anything else?*
> *Mechanic: Yes, the suspension is about to collapse and the exhaust manifold is blowing. It shouldn't really be on the road.*
> *Customer: Hmmm! Can you give me an estimate for the work?*
> *Mechanic: I'm afraid spares don't come cheap for such an old Toyota. You're looking at more than £600 plus VAT, I'm afraid.*
> *Customer: Phew! That's a bit of a shock. But I don't have a choice, so please go ahead and do what needs to be done!*

1.3.6 Commentary

The obvious answer to the task is that the customer needs the car and can't repair it himself. The mechanic knows this and so feels quite free to list all the defects in technical terms, adding a warning intended to scare the customer just a little. The customer probably doesn't understand all the technical terms and simply feels unable to challenge the mechanic's obvious expertise. This creates a dependency relationship that leads to the customer's unquestioning acceptance of the estimate, even though it is clearly approximate. This might be seen as a failure on the customer's part to ask for a breakdown of the costs or a more comprehensible explanation of the work that is needed. However, what is also missing here is any attempt by the mechanic to mediate by explaining the problems in lay terms, either because it is not in his interests to do so or because he simply hasn't mastered the linguistic flexibility this would require.

1.3.7 Task 12

What kind of linguistic flexibility does the business reporter need in order to do what the television audience needs from him?

> Newscaster: *Here, to explain more about the so-called TTIP agreement and its significance, is our senior business editor Tom Cannon.*
> Cannon: *OK, let's start at the beginning. TTIP stands for the Transatlantic Trade and Investment Partnership. It's an agreement which is being negotiated between the U.S. and the E.U. The advantages of TTIP are evident. Greater growth would create jobs and prosperity for both areas because there is an existing basis of investment in both directions. It would require a fair amount of norming of standards, especially in food industries and car production, but most economists agree that the benefits are there for all to see.*
> Newscaster: *Aren't there any downsides?*
> Cannon: *There are. The White House is worried about increased competition for American businesses and the dangers of unemployment as a consequence. EU member states are particularly concerned about the impact on farmers and agriculture of the import of cheaper American foodstuffs and genetically modified crops. But as in all these kinds of negotiations, the devil is in the detail, and negotiators are wrestling with issues around tariffs, those standards that I mentioned, and other market access issues such as licensing. There's a long way to go.*
> Newscaster: *Thank you, Tom. This is clearly something we'll be returning to again and again.*

1.3.8 *Commentary*

The draft TTIP agreement is a long and detailed document which includes a lot of legal and economic language to pin down the detail. A general public TV audience doesn't want to hear about the detail and so Tom Cannon's role is to give a very brief, broad brush-strokes summary of the main points under negotiation. In order to do this, he has to master the detail and boil it down to the required length using straightforward language which makes it accessible to his audience. In doing so, he is mediating between the document and the negotiators on the one hand and an interested but non-specialist public. This is a skill which is needed in many walks of life.

1.3.9 *Task 13*

Explain the differences between these two accounts of cheesemaking.
Account 1:
https://www.youtube.com/watch?v=wxm8jTzU_8o (listen to the first 4½ minutes with the woman's voice).
Account 2

Pasteurised cheese is produced with milk that has been heated to a temperature of 72 °C for 15 seconds. Pasteurisation normally occurs between 70°C and 72°C, but methods vary and in some processes the temperature and the duration of heating are changed. For example, some cheesemakers prefer a method in which the milk is heated to 69°C for up to 40 minutes. This lower temperature process is preferred because it ensures that the natural enzymes and bacteria needed in cheesemaking are not lost.

Another common process in cheesemaking is sometimes referred to as 'cooking' cheese. In this method, the curds are heated or 'cooked' for a short time at a temperature between 40°C and 49°C, which makes the cheese firm enough but also soft and pliable. Many Italian cheeses, such as Mozzarella are made in this way. (text freely adapted from an Internet source)

1.3.10 Commentary

The first account is delivered orally and in a relatively informal way, characterised by the use of 'we' to describe the steps in the process. The visual support brings the speaker's account to life in a very immediate way, and her emotional involvement in the process also shines through. There are several moments when the main speaker reveals her feelings (using first-person singular) about the job and about the cheese she is making. The second written account is much more dispassionate, sticking to the facts and describing the process objectively and impersonally through the use of verbs in the passive voice. This is one more example of the versatility of language, which enables us to make adjustments to an account like these according to personal attitude, purpose, audience and medium of communication.

1.3.11 Summary

In this section, we have drawn attention to just a few ways in which we adapt our use of language to different situations and for different purposes. Individual language users develop the skills involved needed to make these adaptations to different degrees, and as society has become more complex and multi-layered, they have become more subtle and sophisticated. A police officer making an arrest will caution a suspect with a standardised and legally acceptable form of words, but the same officer will need to keep notes on her/his procedures, explain them to a senior officer, use them as a basis for interrogating the suspect and later in order to give evidence in court. Each of these contexts is slightly different and will require adjustments to the way she/he makes use of language in order to meet the different needs of each situation. This kind of transition from one medium to another is not always easy, even for native speakers of a language, but most professions require it to a greater or lesser degree. However, languages which have matured over centuries, and which have long-established written forms are able to accommodate adaptations such as these and will continue to respond to any demands which are placed on them in a fast-changing world. It could be argued, conversely, that minority languages such as those used by tribes in Papua New Guinea or in the Amazon jungle are likely to be less capable of this kind of adaptation because of the restricted social context in which they need to operate. As civilisation (and with it more established languages) encroaches on areas like these, speakers of these less flexible languages will be forced to start to adapt in order to survive. Pinker (2003) describes human language as 'an adaptation to the cognitive niche'.

1.3.12 Some Questions for Reflection

(a) Write a 'language diary' to record the variations in the way you receive and use language on a typical day. Make notes on what you learn from doing this.
(b) Think of a process that you are familiar with (e.g. making an omelette; changing a wheel on a car). Record yourself telling someone how to do it if he/she is physically present. Then write down simple instructions for the same process to be read by someone who is not present. What differences do you notice in the language choices you make in each case? Why is it important for children to be able to master both ways of describing a process?

1.4 Section 3: Identity and Culture in Language Use

We all use language to a greater or lesser extent to help to identify ourselves. This kind of self-identifying may have a number of different triggers, for example the need to be seen to belong to a particular region or city, the pressure to be accepted in a particular social or professional group or a strong desire to represent oneself in terms of cultural heritage or ethnicity. In this chapter, we will look at examples of this.

1.4.1 Task 14

Read this extract from an essay about the Liverpool accent and, if possible, find an example of the accent on the Internet to listen to. (i) How do you account for the negative attitude towards some urban and regional accents? (ii) How do you explain this statement by an exiled Liverpudlian: *'When I'm back on Merseyside I quickly drop back into Scouse.'* (the name for the accent)?

> *The Liverpool English accent has been regarded in society as being ill-educated and low prestige. This stereotypical view could well be influenced by the media's representation of Liverpudlians, who are often portrayed in a negative or criminal way. In 2004, the BBC*

conducted an online poll to determine attitudes towards the accents and languages in the British Isles. The poll, of which there were 5000 participants, concluded that Asian, Liverpool and Birmingham accents were "unpleasant to listen to and lacking in social status" (BBC, 2004). In addition to this, participants were asked to rank celebrities by how pleasant their accents are. The Liverpudlian accents of celebrities Cilla Black and Paul O'Grady were received negatively by participants. Another survey of 1000 participants conducted by Bury Technologies (BBC, 2009), also concluded that the accent is unpopular, as Liverpool came out at the bottom of the poll of British accents. One third of Liverpudlians who took part in the nationwide survey admitted to changing or calming down their accent whilst being interviewed for a job in order to benefit their career. from: UKEssays. (November 2018). Attitudes Towards Accents: The Scouse Accent. Retrieved from https://www.ukessays.com/essays/languages/liverpool-accent.php?vref=1 (used with permission)

1.4.2 Commentary

Prejudice against some urban accents still exists in the UK, and there is no doubt that people's job prospects improve in inverse proportion to the strength of their accents. Urban accents such as Scouse, Geordie and Brummie are markers of belonging which their users value. There seems to be an association with a kind of emotionally rooted tribal identity, when speakers of these varieties of English confront each other, for example at football matches. The same kinds of emotions come to the fore, for example, when England play Australia in cricket matches. Accents are generally the result of differences in the way the language is pronounced and they usually remain comprehensible to speakers of the same 'parent' language, but dialects may not be, as we shall see in the tasks that follow.

1.4.3 Task 15

In this video, a Malaysian English speaker checks whether her American friend can understand some short samples of the dialect that has come to be known as 'Manglish'.
   https://www.youtube.com/watch?v=GyKBBdITXoo
   (i) Why is 'Manglish' usually seen as a dialect or a Creole variety of English rather than just an accent? (ii) What has influenced the development of 'Manglish' as a dialect of English? (iii) Which aspects of 'Manglish' cause most difficulty to a native English speaker?

1.4.4 Task 16

Consider the short extracts from an Indian news website in Fig. 1.2 below. Which aspects of the language used show divergence from the 'standard' English which you would expect to find in a British newspaper article?

(i) An estimated 17 lakh pilgrims visited the Vaishno Devi shrine in 2020 despite the Covid-19 pandemic.

(ii) CEC Sushil Chandra, along with his various other deputies, held a comprehensive review of present status and projected trends of the pandemic with special focus in the five poll-going states.

(iii) The Speaker stressed on ensuring that sanitation and other arrangements are in place at all places, as per official guidelines He also directed that adequate arrangements for COVID positive officers and employees of Parliament may also be made. This comes as Parliament heads toward Budget Session, even as the dates have not been announced yet.

(iv) "Based on specific input generated by the Police regarding presence of terrorist in Harwan/Shalimar area, a search operation was launched by Srinagar Police and CRPF in the said area. During the search operation, the search party was fired upon indiscriminately by hiding terrorist, which was effectively retaliated upon leading to a brief shootout & elimination of a dreaded terrorist Saleem Parray, linked with proscribed terror outfit LeT," a police statement said. Soon after the said operation, a second encounter erupted at Gasu in which a foreign militant was killed

---

Fig. 1.2 Extracts from Indian news media. https://english.deepika.com/Index.aspx (accessed 28 January 2022)

1.4.5 Commentary

While 'Manglish', as a dialect, is widely understood right across Malaysia, there are aspects of it, both lexical and grammatical, which would not be easily comprehended by other speakers of English. It is, however, essentially a vernacular, spoken variety of English, not usually written down except in transcripts of spoken exchanges. It has developed to its present state as a direct result of the blend of cultures, languages and ethnicities in the population of Malaysia, with borrowings from Mandarin and Cantonese, from Tamil and from Bahasa Melayu. It has also made 'economies' in everyday expressions compared with most other varieties of English, for example, the ubiquitous 'Can!' or 'Can?' which is a shortening of, respectively 'Yes, I can do that' or 'Can I do that?'

1.4 Section 3: Identity and Culture in Language Use

The Indian variety of English is underpinned and maintained by a huge media industry as well as by the widespread consumption of 'Bollywood' movies. In a 2016 *Guardian* article, Kavitha Rao goes so far as to suggest that certain features of Indian English ('prepone' and 'needful' are the examples in the title of the article) could usefully be adopted by other varieties of the language, mainly because they express something in a short and clear way which other varieties don't have available. Indian English has well-established written as well as spoken conventions, and these have historical and cultural roots. Interestingly, it is sometimes only variations in pronunciation, stress and intonation that hinder intelligibility in Indian speakers of English.

In these extracts, the references which other users of English would find difficult or unusual are mainly in items of vocabulary such as 'lakh' in the first extract (a short and convenient term for a hundred thousand), or 'poll-going' in the second extract, which is a neat coinage to avoid a whole clause. The use of a preposition after 'stress', as in extract 3, is common in almost all South Asian varieties of English. In the same extract, you may be struck by the use of 'even as' to introduce a clause where British English would use 'even though'. The omission of articles before nouns in the fourth extract is typical of Indian journalese, and it is also a common phenomenon in spoken Indian English. Some vocabulary choices in this extract also stand out, for example 'said' (slightly anachronistic and more formal than is usual in British newspaper English), and 'shootout' and 'erupted' which are both rather informal but very graphic as word choices. You may also have noticed the rather unusual embedded clause 'which was effectively retaliated upon', probably also an economy in the number of words needed to express the message. None of these features effectively inhibit understanding and that is almost always the case with written Indian English.

Other languages also have their dialects. There are several Creole varieties of French in Africa, and also in Louisiana in the south of the USA. These all arose in the aftermath of the colonial era. The situation in Switzerland with the Swiss dialect of German is different. High German speakers have difficulty understanding Swiss German, but all educated Swiss German speakers can also speak and write High German. The dialect has developed over centuries, and is mainly characterised by deviations in pronunciation, but there are also lexical differences. There is a written form of Swiss German, appearing mainly in works of literature that are not well known outside the region.

In all of these cases, and as with accents, people identify very closely with the dialect or variety they use. It helps to define who they are, to give them a sense of belonging and to give them a sense of their local, regional or national roots. But all of these features derive from the culture in which individuals grow up and are immersed in from birth onwards, as we shall see in the tasks that follow:

1.4.6 Task 17

Consider these short exchanges and explain the speakers' choices of language in each case:

Case 1 Two British males in their twenties:

"Hello, mate. How've you been?"
"Can't complain. You? Still out of work?"

Case 2 Two British teenage girls.

"Hey, Laura. Not speaking to me, then?"
"Course I am, silly! I just didn't see you. We're still good."
"Even after last night?"
"It's all good! I'm over it."

Case 3 British female shop assistant and immigrant customer after a transaction.

"Thanks, darling. See you later!"
"Thank you!"
(afterwards, to a friend) *"Why does she always call me darling? It's embarrassing."*
"Oh, don't worry. They all do that."

1.4.7 *Commentary*

In Case 1, we see immediately that the two speakers are known to each other, probably friends. 'Mate' is a very common mode of address between males, most often adults. The reduced reply and the single word question in the second speaker's reply are a further sign of informality, as is the enquiry about the first speaker's employment status. All these features are in keeping with the unspoken cultural norms among British men. There is no awkwardness between them.

Case 2 is an example of teenage culture in action. The first speaker immediately engages her friend with a question about their relationship, which is clearly important to her. The second speaker is quick to put her mind at rest, reinforcing her reassuring message, and then dealing in a similar way with the follow-up question, repeating her informal use of 'good'. The language used in this exchange is rooted in teenage culture and the accompanying norms of a friendly relationship. The uncertainty in the mind of the first speaker is connected with her concern about the status of her friendship, but she addresses her worry in a direct and uninhibited way, which may also be normal in the teenage peer group that they both belong to.

Case 3 is an example of a cultural misunderstanding. The female shop assistant probably routinely addresses her customers (possibly both male and female) as 'Darling' and this may seem completely strange to a non-British customer, who might easily misinterpret it. The uncertainty that characterises this kind of misunderstanding can be disturbing for any outsider to a particular culture. In this case, the customer checks it out with a friend who puts his mind at rest.

Hofstede defined culture as 'the collective programming of the mind that distinguishes the members of one group or category of people from others' (2012), and this is very clearly expressed in the language used in the first two cases, but obviously not in Case 3 where the speakers come from different cultural backgrounds.

In the next task we shall see how identity and culture sometimes come together and cause difficulties.

1.4.8 Task 18

In the 2011 census in Northern Ireland, respondents were asked to tick a box to define their ethnicity. The options are listed in Table 1.4. What difficulty might someone of mixed race, e.g. with mixed-race parents and grandparents, have with this form?

Table 1.4 Extract from census form

What is your ethnic group?
>>> Tick one box only

Ethnicity	
White	☐
Chinese	☐
Irish Traveller	☐
Indian	☐
Pakistani	☐
Bangladeshi	☐
Black Caribbean	☐
Black African	☐
Black Other	☐

Mixed ethnic group, write in
[   ]

Any other ethnic group, write in
[   ]

1.4.9 *Commentary*

This is typical of problems with forms designed by people of one culture to be filled in by people of many different ethnicities. It also illustrates the limitations of the language we have available to define ethnicity. Our mixed-race respondents may have three or four different ethnicities in their background and may be at a total loss as to how to put this into words in the space available. Irish Travellers may prefer to describe themselves as 'White' and may suspect discrimination of some kind. And why is colour used to define some ethnicities but not Chinese, Pakistanis, Indians or

Bangladeshis? In fact, these descriptors impact on a person's identity, and may cause disorientation or even dysphoria in someone completing the form, who may not fully comprehend the reasons why this kind of categorisation is important to a government.

1.4.10 Task 19

Read this personal account of an experience dating back to the writer's student days. Why was the writer in two minds about the experience? Also, why do some speakers of a foreign or second language aspire to native-speaker levels of proficiency?

> *I got to see much of Germany and Central Europe in the sixties by hitch-hiking around, as was common in those days among students like myself. I was lucky to meet with so much kindness and companionship among the drivers who picked me up and helped me on my way. They were often glad to have someone to talk to to relieve the monotony of long spells at the wheel. I had extra curiosity value for some of them because I was English, and for me it was a chance to practise my German. They often bought me coffee or a snack when we stopped along the way. On one occasion, I was picked up near Freiburg by a driver heading south, to Basel, and he shocked me by asking what life was like in North Germany. I asked him why he had asked. 'Don't you come from Hamburg, then?' he asked by way of reply. At first, I was flattered that he had taken me for a German, but when I began to think about it later, I wasn't so sure.* (personal anecdote)

1.4.11 Commentary

Of course, the writer was initially pleased to be identified as a German (North German spoken varieties are closer to English than those in South Germany), but when he thought about it, perhaps he was happy about his 'curiosity value' as an Englishman, which possibly also encouraged German drivers to treat him to coffees and snacks! Being identified as an Englishman who speaks German was probably closer to the self-image he wanted to project. Nonetheless, native-speaker proficiency in a language remains an aspiration for many language learners, particularly for immigrants who want to be accepted in the country they now call home.

1.4.12 Summary

In this section, we have but scratched the surface of some of the issues surrounding the ways in which language is intertwined with identity and culture. There are many other aspects which could be considered in much more depth in a more specialised work than this one. However, we hope we have raised some awareness in our readers of the complexity of these interrelationships, and how they can potentially affect us in everyday life, in encounters with strangers and acquaintances in an increasingly globalised world, and ultimately in how we define ourselves both publicly and privately. Language itself is a cultural artefact and yet it is needed to describe all aspects of the culture it has sprung from. How this characteristic impacts on language in education will be explored later in this book.

Meanwhile, in the next section, we will move on to consider some of the factors which can make language and its users powerful.

1.4.13 Some Questions for Reflection

(a) To what extent is your personal identity expressed through your language? If you also have a second or foreign language, how does speaking it affect your sense of identity?
(b) How can you, as a teacher, acknowledge and value language and cultural differences in your learners?

1.5 Section 4: Language and Power

> *Language is power, life and the instrument of culture, the instrument of domination and liberation.* (Angela Carter)

Angela Carter's words, quoted in a posthumous edition of her writing (1997), resonate just as much now as when she wrote them. The all-pervasive power of language is with us every single day of our lives, whether we always recognise it or not. In this chapter, we look at some ways in which this power is wielded for different purposes and with varying degrees of clarity or subtlety. We start with a short and simple task.

1.5.1 Task 20

Read these short extracts and identify their provenance and purpose. What linguistic clues enabled you to do this?
Extract 1.

> '.... have inherited many characteristics that continue to set them apart from their contemporaries—superb performance, ergonomic design features, longevity and award-winning reliability. Along with powerful suction, and a five-year parts guarantee, these features are among many that make ...'

Extract 2[1]

... ever since 401 years ago, the reason we could never be who we dreamed of being was you kept your knee on our neck. We were smarter than the underfunded schools you put us in but you had your knee on our neck. We could run corporations and not hustle in the street, but you had your knee on our neck. We had creative skills, we could do what anybody else could do, but we couldn't get your knee off our neck. What happened to Floyd happens every day in this country, in education, in health services and in every area of American life. It's time for us to stand up in George's name and say, 'Get your knee off our necks.'

Extract 3[2]

1. *The public hallways, stairways, and fire escapes of the building may not be obstructed. DO NOT leave bicycles, toys, garbage bags or any debris in the public halls at any time!*
2. *Garbage should be tied up in bags and carried out to the garbage cans at the street curb. DO NOT place garbage in the hallways or under the stairs.*
3. *Do not throw garbage out the windows into the yard. The yard is to be kept clear of garbage and debris at all times.*
4. *The roof shall not be used for storage. Tenants should not go to the roof for any purpose.*
5. *Children shall not be allowed to play in the public hallways or stairs.*
6. *Quiet hours shall be between 11 pm and 8 am on weekdays, and 11 pm and 11 am on weekends. During these hours, tenants may not play loud music, operate heavy machinery, or make any loud noises which may disturb their neighbors.*
7. *Tenants are responsible for the behavior of their guests. A violation of the house rules by a guest will be treated as a violation by that tenant.*
8. *Tenants shall maintain their apartments in a condition that does not create fire and/or health hazards, including noxious odors.*

Tenants who wish to make any alteration in their apartments must first seek official approval.

1.5.2 Commentary

The first extract is from an advertising leaflet for vacuum cleaners. Its purpose is to sell. The power needed to sell or promote products lies in the language chosen, here as so often, through adjectives and through the description of unique selling points: 'five-year guarantee', 'ergonomic design features', etc.

The second extract is taken from a eulogy by the Rev. Al Sharpton for George Floyd, a black man who was killed by police in Minneapolis in June 2020. The power in his address comes from his use of the rhetorical device of repetition, here

---

[1] Al Sharpton's Eulogy for George Floyd, Houston Texas 4 June 2020.
 https://www.yahoo.com/lifestyle/rev-al-sharpton-americans-knee-222300657.html.
[2] freely adapted from an Internet source

used to stir emotions by recalling the way in which George Floyd was killed, by the knee of a policeman on his neck, making it impossible for him to breathe, and used here as a metaphor for the repression that many African Americans experience. Repetition is a rhetorical device commonly used by politicians and preachers to drive home a point to an audience or congregation.

The third extract is from a set of house rules intended for tenants to abide by. The power here can be seen in the writer's use of modal verbs: 'may not', 'shall', 'shall not', 'is to', 'should not', 'must', as well as in the use of imperative verbs, some of them capitalised for particular emphasis. These choices have been typical of written rules and regulations ever since the ten commandments first appeared in English in Tyndale's translation in 1534.

1.5.3 Task 21

Look at the slogans from recent political campaigns in Fig. 1.3 and also at the quote from Fairclough below them. How are they related? What part does language play in each message?

The exercise of power in modern society, is increasingly achieved through ideology, and more particularly through the ideological workings of language. (Fairclough 2014)

FOR THE MANY NOT THE FEW (Labour)

BY THE PEOPLE AND FOR THE PEOPLE

GET BREXIT DONE! (UK Conservative Party)

MAKE AMERICA GREAT AGAIN! (US Republican Party)

Fig. 1.3 Political slogans

1.5.4 Commentary

Slogans are powerful, as any political spin doctor will tell you. They can make the difference between victory and defeat in any election. But the most effective ones are short and pithy, expressing ideology in a very concise and convincing way.

The Labour Party slogan expresses one of the core ideas of socialism and targets the perceived gulf between rich and poor. 'By the People and for the People' is also an egalitarian slogan which echoes Lincoln's words in his famous Gettysburg Address. 'Get Brexit Done' cleverly appealed to the many people in the UK who were tired of all the argument about leaving the European Union. The last slogan, used in the Republican presidential election campaign in 2017, is designed, to strike a chord with the large number of voters who were unhappy with Barak Obama's presidency and who wanted the USA to 'recover' economically and reputationally. All the slogans are underpinned by ideology and are designed to influence voters' thinking at a crucial time. Their conciseness appeals to a significant proportion of any population who don't want to listen to long speeches and arguments, and who want political messaging to be short, clear and targeted.

Fairclough argues in several of his publications that critical discourse analysis should be part of the national curriculum and taught in schools so that citizens are not susceptible to ideological manipulation and can make up their own minds about what politicians tell them. This seems to have become even more important now that so many messages are spread on social media, and in an era when ideologies can all too easily become the basis for radicalisation and ultimately acts of terror. The next task invites you to look at part of a speech with a critical eye.

1.5.5   Task 22

Cicero was famous for his powers of oratory. What makes this commonly quoted, translated extract from one of his speeches so powerful? Who is he appealing to? What do you notice about the language he uses?

> *Do not blame Caesar, blame the people of Rome who have so enthusiastically acclaimed and adored him and rejoiced in their loss of freedom and danced in his path and gave him triumphal processions. Blame the people who hail him when he speaks in the Forum of the 'new wonderful good society' which shall now be Rome, interpreted to mean 'more money, more ease, more security, more living fatly at the expense of the industrious.'* ~ Marcus Tullius Cicero https://www.azquotes.com/author/2894-Marcus_Tullius_Cicero

1.5.6   Commentary

This extract is in part a reproach to Julius Caesar himself, with whom Cicero had fallen out, and partly an attempt to make Roman citizens aware of the way in which Caesar had 'bought' their loyalty. Some commentators have seen it as one of the first anti-capitalist speeches. His use of imperatives and his choice of the word 'blame' invite the audience to collude with him. He also strikes a sensitive chord by referring to 'loss of freedom' which is a core value for his fellow citizens, and cleverly implies that they have inflicted this loss on themselves in a kind of Mephistophelian pact with Caesar. Cicero was famous for his ability to sway the mood of his audiences in the Forum and elsewhere simply through the power of his words. The struggle he was often engaged in is captured neatly in this additional quotation from Fairclough's 'Language and Power':

Broadly speaking, inculcation is the mechanism of power-holders who wish to preserve their power, while communication is the mechanism of emancipation and the struggle against domination (2014, p. 75)

Small wonder that present-day politicians strive to attain Cicero's levels of oratorial proficiency and to find ways of encapsulating key messages as economically and effectively as he did!

In the tasks that follow, we look at how power is wielded in interpersonal terms, and how it is expressed in language.

1.5.7 Task 23

In this dialogue between a chief executive and one of his senior managers, comment on the power relationship and how language is used to reinforce it.

> *"You have been guilty of gross negligence and you are dismissed with immediate effect."*
> *"But I ...."*
> *"No ifs, no buts. You have 20 minutes to get your things together, clear your desk and vacate your office."*
> *"You'll be hearing from my solicitor!"*
> *"I'll look forward to it."*
> *(freely adapted from a literary source)*

1.5.8 Task 24

In this extract, what linguistic and non-linguistic means does the teacher use to exert his power over the students?

> *Father Arnall came in and the Latin lesson began and he remained still, leaning on the desk with his arms folded. Father Arnall gave out the theme-books and he said that they were scandalous and that they were all to be written out again with the corrections at once. But the worst of all was Fleming's theme because the pages were stuck together by a blot: and Father Arnall held it up by a corner and said it was an insult to any master to send him up such a theme. Then he asked Jack Lawton to decline the noun 'mare' and Jack Lawton stopped at the ablative singular and could not go on with the plural.*
>
> *"You should be ashamed of yourself," said Father Arnall sternly. "You, the leader of the class!"*
>
> *Then he asked the next boy and the next and the next. Nobody knew. Father Arnall became very quiet, more and more quiet as each boy tried to answer it and could not.* (from *Portrait of the Artist as a Young Man* by James Joyce)

1.5.9 Commentary

In each of the extracts above, a power relationship is enacted with the help of language. In the first extract, the chief executive delivers his message with a minimum of words, but clearly and unmistakably. He goes on to cut short his manager's response by interrupting him and setting a time limit for him to clear his office. He responds to the threat from the manager ironically, to show that he is not concerned about the consequences of his decision.

In the second extract, the teacher initially imposes his presence on the class by standing still. Then he accompanies the handing out of the theme books (exercise books that students write in) by using the strong word 'scandalous', by holding up one of the books and describing the owner's behaviour as an 'insult'. The switch by Joyce to direct speech in the account brings the encounter to life as Father Arnall uses his power to shame the class leader because he is unable to decline a Latin noun. The fearful atmosphere is intensified by the teacher's silence as the class proceeds.

In interpersonal encounters like these, people use language in different ways in order to exert power and influence. In both of these rather dramatic cases, status and physical dimensions like seating or standing and body language also play a part in determining where the power lies, but power games are carried out every day in a smaller, often less consequential way, in playgrounds, in workplaces, round family dinner tables and on sports fields everywhere as people seek influence over others. Language is always a key part of such processes.

1.5.10 Summary

In this section, we have looked at just a few instances of the relationship between language and power. We are not always aware of the extent to which these types of uses of language can affect our thinking and decision-making, and there is a strong case for raising awareness of the relationship in children from an early age, so that they can exercise their rights as citizens more effectively when they reach adulthood. This may seem to be a fundamental democratic value, though it has never been a popular one with autocrats or in systems where the state wants to control and manipulate its citizens.

1.5.11 Some Questions for Reflection

(a) In what ways can you, as a teacher, raise your learners' awareness of the ways in which language is used to wield power?

(b) In your own educational context, or in a context you are familiar with, how much importance is given to this kind of critical awareness? What factors might prevent it from being prioritised?

1.6 Conclusion

In this introductory unit, we have examined some of the language-related issues which may concern us all, whether at home, in our communications with others, and in spoken and written language. In the next unit we will look more closely at some of the key concepts in language and how they are interpreted in educational settings.

References

BBC. (2004). Online Poll on Regional Accents. http://www.bbc.co.uk/voices/yourvoice/poll_results.shtml

BBC. (2009). News Report on Survey of Accents by Bury Technologies. http://news.bbc.co.uk/1/hi/business/7843058.stm

Campbell, A. (2014). The Effects of Text Messaging on Students' Literacy. Retrieved April 15, 2020, from https://thescholarship.ecu.edu/handle/10342/4582

Carter, A. (1997). *Shaking a Leg: Collected Writings*. Penguin Group USA.

Essays, UK. (2018, November). Attitudes Towards Accents: The Scouse Accent. https://www.ukessays.com/essays/languages/liverpool-accent.php?vref=1

Fairclough, N. (2014). *Language and Power* (3rd ed.). Longman.

Hofstede, G. (2012). Hofstede's fifth dimension: new evidence from the World Values Survey. *Journal of Cross-Cultural Psychology, 43*(1), 3–14.

Joyce, J. (2008). *Portrait of the Artist as a Young Man*. Oxford University Press.

Pinker, S. (2003). Language as an Adaptation to the Cognitive Niche,' in Christensen, M. and S. Kirby (pp. 16–37).

Rao, K. (2016, January 4). Don't Prepone It—Do the Needful. 10 Indianisms We Should All Be Using In *The Guardian*. https://www.theguardian.com/commentisfree/2016/jan/04/indian-english-phrases-indianisms-english-americanisms-vocabulary

Schulz von Thun InstitutDas Kommunikationsquadrat. http://www.schulz-von-thun.de n.d. accessed 21.10.2022

Sealy, A. (1996). *Learning about Language*. Open University Press.

Slone, I. B. (2013). "Who Survives, Who Doesn't?" An Interview with Margaret Atwood. Retrieved April 15, 2020, from https://hazlitt.net/feature/who-survives-who-doesnt-interview-margaret-atwood

Chapter 2
Unit 2: Language and Communication in Education 1

Unit 1 was concerned with the general nature and purposes of language as communication in society. This unit is the first of three focusing on language as used in the more specific context of learning and teaching. It deals with the ways in which a person's cognitive development is aided by language, by the use of language by teachers and by the materials used for teaching and learning.

The unit also explores the factors that guide teachers' choices in their use of language in the classroom, and the ways in which the use of language varies depending on the intentions of teachers and learners.

2.1 Section 1: Language and Learning

2.1.1 Task 1

Think of the following formal or informal learning situations:

(a) Learning to drive.
(b) Finding out about the history of a place you are visiting.
(c) Learning why bees and other insects are important.
(d) Playing chess for the first time.

In each case:

– How does a person use oral and/or written communication in the learning process?
– To what extent can non-linguistic means of learning be useful?

2.1.2 Task 2

Children depend on language to acquire new concepts. Read through the following transcript of part of a lesson with a pre-school class of children aged 4–5. What language and other forms of communication is the teacher using to teach the mathematical concept of 'taking away' (subtraction)? How does she build on the children's existing knowledge of maths?

> *Teacher (T): Now our special maths word of the week is 'take away'. We're going to be learning all about taking away. When we take away, we are finding less. Everybody show me the sign for less* (children use their arms and hands to show sign for minus). *If I'm finding one more, is that adding or is it taking away?* (teacher uses arms to show plus sign and minus sign). *I'm going to ask ... Oliver.*
> *Oliver:* (boy shows plus sign with arms)
> *T: What one's that Oliver?*
> *Oliver: Add*
> *T: Well done, Oliver—it's adding. Now, our special maths word of the week is 'take away'. It's take away this week. And we're going to be learning all about taking away. When we take away, we are finding less—everyone, show me the sign for less* (children uses arms to show minus sign).
> *T and children: Less*
> *T. We're taking away, we're finding less.* (Pointing to the number on the board). *So, if we've got 22 children here today and Yasmin goes home, we will have one less. What is one less than 22? I want to take away one from 22. What's my answer going to be?*
> *Amadou: 21*
> *T: Good boy, Amadou! Well done—what a super answer! 21.* (writing on the board) *so our answer is 21 if Yasmin goes home. Yasmin, I hope you don't go home.* (transcribed from *Lessons in Observation* 2013)

2.1.3 Commentary

Task 1 illustrates the importance of language and communication for learning, albeit in different ways depending on what is being learnt. Much more reading or talking to people is likely to be necessary in the case of learning about a travel destination than when learning to play chess or to drive a car, for example. Children might learn about bees through explanations by an adult and watching bees on flowers and making honey live or on video. Driving involves more physical coordination and use of the senses, but even in this case driving instructors give verbal guidance, and there is 'theory' to be learnt from books or video presentations.

Some of the examples raise questions about our ability to process language in instructions and other written texts. These processes are complex and may involve internalising spoken or written instructions so that they are available to us through our 'inner voice' when driving or making a chess move, for example. However, the processing of language when we are learning about bees or planning a visit is different: we may need to draw on and evaluate different sources of information in order to construct a 'picture' that makes sense and corresponds to our interests. This is an ability that we develop gradually, which means that adults and older children are generally more proficient at it than younger children.

Task 2: the transcript of part of a lesson shows how much a teacher of very young children needs to use language, as well as, for example, symbols and gestures, to get new concepts across and enable children to relate them to their existing knowledge, in this case contrasting 'taking away' with 'adding'. It underlines the fact that communication does not depend on language alone: as in this case, teachers can support learning by using body language, stress, repetition, objects, etc. to reinforce students' learning.

2.1.4 Task 3

In their different ways, depending on age and the context and focus of learning, children and adults acquire new knowledge and skills constantly throughout life.

In what ways is language important in the following types of learning that typically take place in educational settings? What other resources apart from language do people draw on in these kinds of learning:

(a) Learning multiplication tables (e.g. 6 × 3, 8 × 9)
(b) Learning about dinosaurs
(c) Learning about similes and metaphors
(d) Learning about thermodynamics

2.1.5 Task 4

Watch the first 5 minutes of the video at https://youtu.be/NA_orCahXiM

(a) What kind of language is used to help the children understand how vegetables grow?
(b) How do the children relate the new information to their existing knowledge and to their experience of eating food?
(c) Note down one or two of the questions and explanations the gardener uses to engage the children's attention and get them thinking.

2.1.6 Commentary

Task 3: while Task 1 was about learning mainly outside school, here the focus is on learning that commonly takes place in the classroom. In some of the examples more than in others, symbols and illustrations are likely to be used in support of language, for example in arithmetic and in a lesson about dinosaurs. The crucial factor in successful learning is the way in which the 'learner' relates the language to the non-linguistic support as they learn. The third example shows that some learning in school is directly or indirectly about language itself—in the case of metaphors and similes, about the ways in which language itself often depends on imagery and association.

Task 4: where feasible, schools enhance children's learning by taking them out of classrooms into the real world where they can be involved in experiences and language use that helps them more easily to understand concepts and processes. In this case, by enabling children to relate vegetables which are growing in a garden to vegetables eaten for lunch new cognitive connections can be created with children's previous experiences and knowledge ('rabbits eat carrots', says one child).

2.1.7 Summary

In the Oxford English Dictionary, cognition is defined as '*the mental action or process of acquiring knowledge and understanding through thought, experience, and the senses*' (OED). Language is an essential aid in this process, not just as part of thinking but as a stimulus to learning. Task 2 focused on an example of the way the social use of language, including body language, and thought are involved in taking a cognitive step in numeracy.

Many psychologists in the field of language and cognition have written about the relationship between language and learning. The tasks above illustrate what has come to be known as the 'constructivist' theory of learning. 'Constructivism is a learning theory which affirms that knowledge is best gained through a process of action, reflection and construction … The constructivist framework relies on the learners to be in control of their own acquisition of knowledge and encourages the instructor to serve as a facilitator' (Brau 2018). In spite of his early death, one of the best-known advocates of what has come to be known as constructivism was Lev Vygotsky (1896–1934), who looked closely at the role of language in children's thinking and learning from a very early age. Vygotsky's view was that cognitive development is essentially a social process that depends on interactions with others (Vygotsky 1978). Communication and interaction are the main means which are available to 'more capable peers' and adults, including teachers, who are trying to support learning, although, as seen in Task 2, body language, drawings, moving objects in relation to each other and so on are also valuable, especially in combination with language.

2.1.8 Questions for Reflection

(a) Think of your own experiences with children in learning situations. In which situations are non-linguistic signs, symbols, images, real objects, etc. most likely to be needed as much as (or more than) language? In which others is language more essential than anything else?
(b) In your experience of supporting the learning of older students in classrooms, in which situations have you found it especially advantageous to use reading and writing activities to support or consolidate learning?

2.2 Section 2: Context and Communication

In this section, we look at ways in which context and situation influence the decisions teachers and students make when communicating.

2.2.1 Task 5

Think of an educational context that you know well, and address these questions:

(a) In that context, what influences the ways in which students and teachers communicate?
(b) How does classroom communication in that context differ from communication in other settings?

2.2.2 Commentary

Factors influencing the way teachers and students communicate in classrooms include:

- The layout of the room, usually with a display board of some kind and a desk and chair for one person at the front, and numerous places for students facing them.
- The age of the students.
- The fact that there may be up to 30 students (or many more in some countries) in the room, being talked to, and usually controlled, by one other person, the teacher.

But your answers will of course vary according to the context(s) you have in mind.

The nature of classroom communication varies according to the teaching method being used. Very commonly, in oral communication in the classroom the proportion of time taken up by the teacher is much greater than the time available for students to communicate. In addition, the type of communication often involves set patterns, mainly questions from the teacher and answers from students, feedback on students' answers, instructions and so on. By comparison, when students are working in small groups, the nature of communication is more like communication outside the classroom, although there is much less freedom when it comes to the choice of the topic and the purpose.

2.2.3 Task 6

Below is a transcript of classroom interaction in a year 5 (age 10–11) primary classroom. What can you deduce from the interaction about each of the aspects listed below?

- The situation
- The conditions/constraints on the students and the teacher
- The topic and purpose of the interaction
- The language users themselves (students and teacher).

(a) *Teacher (T): Keighley, would you read out number nine for us?*
(b) *Keighley (K): (reads) "The moon changes shape because it is in the shadow of the earth."*
(c) *T: Right, now what does your group think about that?*
(d) *K: True*
(e) *T: What, um, why do you think that?*
(f) *K: hm, because it's when earth is dark then, hm, we're not quite sure but we think it was true*
(g) *T: Right, people with hands up (to K) who would you want to contribute?*
(h) *K: Um, Sadie?*
(i) *Sadie (S): I think it's false because when the sun moves round the earth, it shines on the moon, which projects down to the earth.*
(j) *T: (nods) do you want to choose somebody else? That sounds good.*
(k) *S: Matthew*
(l) *Matthew: Well, we weren't actually sure 'cos we were (thinking) the actual moon changes which it never does, or, if it is our point of view from earth, which it puts us in the shadow.*
(m) *T: That's a good point isn't it, it doesn't actually change, it looks as if it changes shape to us, that's a really good point. (from Dawes et al. 2010, pp. 105–106)*

2.2.4 Task 7

What are the likely reasons for the following?

(a) The differences between the nature and purpose of the teacher's questions (c), (e) and (g).
(b) The differences between the way Keighley expresses the opinion of her group and the way Sadie expresses the opinion of her group.
(c) Why the teacher does not say whether any of the answers is right or wrong.
(d) Why the teacher chose not to help the students to express themselves more clearly.

2.2.5 Commentary

The transcript in Task 6 provides examples of talk where classroom communication is less dominated by the teacher and 'freer' in nature. The teacher is in control, but in this case, she is not trying to teach the students facts or language. Instead, she is getting the students to report back on their own earlier discussions in groups, so her interventions are much shorter. In addition, although she nominates the first student, the others are chosen by the student who answered previously. However, the interaction is still subject to the constraints of the task (reacting to the statement at (b)) and the teacher's expectation that the class will have responses to offer. The teacher does not allow discussion among the students to continue.

The students' reactions to the statement about the moon that had been discussed in groups vary considerably: Keighley is not sure whether it is true, although her group thought so; Sadie thinks it is false, and Matthew says that in his group they were not sure. The teacher says 'right' to Keighley's answer and *'that sounds good'* to Sadie's response, but she only says this at the end of the interaction. It is clear that the teacher expected the students to have used their time in groups to think about the statement and to come to some kind of decision about whether it is true or false. At this stage, she is not worried about whether they have reached the 'right' answer: it is more important that they have used their existing knowledge and experience to weigh up in their groups the truth or otherwise of the statement. In such a situation it is normal that students' answers should be tentative (e.g. 'we weren't actually sure') and that the teacher should accept this uncertainty and continue to encourage them to reflect on the problem.

Task 7 was an opportunity to look more closely at the ways in which both the teacher and the students use language in their interactions, and at how the language used by both teacher and students matches their intentions as language users and as participants in classroom learning. For example, the teacher deliberately encourages student engagement by pursuing her question to Keighley to show that different opinions are possible within the same group: Keighley is apparently less sure about the answer than the rest of her group. Unlike Keighley, in (g) Sadie does not talk about her group's opinion, only her own, and she is less tentative than Keighley. The teacher deliberately avoids saying which answer is correct because she wants the thinking and the discussion to continue into another phase of the lesson (illustrated in the next section). Neither does she try to help students to express themselves more clearly, which might distract students from the topic of the discussion. Matthew formulates his response in rather confused English, but he gets his message across and receives some positive feedback on his 'good point'. In the following task, the different linguistic means available to teachers when guiding or supporting learning or simply managing a class and its interaction within smaller groups are explored further.

2.2.6 Task 8

Teachers make choices about the way they use language in teaching, and the way they use language affects how students react and respond. Table 2.1 below contains some examples of different ways of using language in common classroom situations. In each case, what different effects (if any) might the two different ways have on the way students respond and/or their attitude?

Table 2.1 Example of classroom language use

Teacher's intention	Language used
To get students to form groups for a discussion activity	a. Now, get into groups of four
	b. What size group works best for you?
To evaluate a student's answer	a. No, that's not quite right. Try again
	b. Are you sure about that? Why do you think that's right?
To introduce a new topic	a. Who has heard of Pythagoras? How do you know the name?
	b. Today we're going to be learning about Pythagoras's theorem to do with triangles.
To make sure that students understand what they need to do	a. Maria, please read out the instruction on the board
	b. Can you summarise what you have to do, Peter?

2.2.7 Commentary

This task explores in more detail some of the communicative options teachers have and the effects of different kinds of teacher intervention. In the first example about how a classroom activity should be organised, asking a question such as (b) may be more consultative and more motivating for certain students, but it may also take longer. On the other hand, it can be good for students to think about their learning preferences and to feel that these are being taken account of. The second example concerns feedback on students' responses. Again, time is a factor, but it is important on occasions for teachers to consider giving students a chance to assess their own or each other's answers, as in option b), rather than simply giving positive or negative feedback. In the third example, it may well take longer for students to think about whether they have heard Pythagoras's name somewhere and in what connection, but at least there is the possibility of linking a new topic to existing knowledge and using students' responses to get the ball rolling. On the other hand, will that demotivate or motivate students who have never heard the name 'Pythagoras' before? The last example highlights the need for teachers to ensure that students all understand instructions for exercises or activities. Option a) gives some responsibility to a student, but if the wording of the instruction is not clear, it may be more useful to check understanding as in option b). However, it may also be wise to get other students to confirm that Peter has understood correctly.

2.2.8 Task 9

Some of the language that teachers use is focused mainly on helping students to learn, while other language is aimed at organising students' work, controlling behaviour and so on.

Sort the examples below into two groups: 1) encourages learning and understanding; 2) aims to organise and control the lessons and the students.

(a) "Yasmin, could you pass round these worksheets please."
(b) "Now, what I want you to do in your groups is to read through the different points of view about the impact of Copernicus's and Galileo's work on the development of science and agree on the three most important points."
(c) James, can you tell us what your group thought was most important."
(d) "The first thing to remember about electro-magnetism is that it depends on the relationship between magnetic poles (north and south) and electrical charges (negative and positive) …"
(e) "On Monday, I told you that this week we would be working on the history of the slave trade in order to try to understand its impact on Africa, America and Europe over the last 300 years and more. Today …."
(f) "OK, we've just listened to a well-known poem by Dylan Thomas, and most of you said you liked it. In pairs, can you express in your own words what he meant by "Do not go gentle into that good night, /Old age should burn and rave at close of day;/Rage, rage against the dying of the light"."
(g) "So the man asks Marie, 'Qu'est que vous voulez boire?' You know what 'boire' means. What might Marie's answer be?"
(h) "Now everyone, you really need to pay attention. We're going to learn about two important formulae for measuring geometrical areas, and you will need them when we do the practical work in pairs afterwards."

Table 2.2 Two ways in which teachers use language in class

1. Encouraging learning and understanding	2. Organising and controlling the lesson and the students

(i) *"Silvia, you know the rules about using mobile phones in lessons. Switch it off and put it away."*
(j) *"We're going to be looking at the Vietnam war this lesson. Who can tell me anything about it, for example, when it happened, who was involved, why it happened and so on?"*
(k) *"That's a really good point that Helen's group made—just switching from petrol-driven to electric vehicles is not going to be enough by itself to limit global warming."*
(l) *"Now, to do this experiment safely, you need to put on your protective glasses and set up the equipment as shown in this little video."*
(m) *"Hello everyone. I hope you enjoyed the sunshine at the weekend."*
(n) *"OK, for the groupwork, can people in row 1, 3 and 5 turn your tables round so that you can form groups of 4 or 5 with the people behind you. But please do it quietly."*
(o) *"I'm not sure I agree with you that free speech is always a human right. What if you accuse somebody of a crime that they didn't commit, or say something hateful to someone because of their religious beliefs?"*
(p) *"Can you open the window, Leila—it's getting stuffy in here."*

2.2.9 Commentary

Leaving aside the different levels of strictness adopted by the teacher, the division between these two kinds of teaching language may sometimes not be hard and fast, for example in b. and j. However, in most cases, it is clear in which examples the teacher's aim is to support learning and in which his or her aims are organisational or related to classroom logistics. For example, b. involves communicating or clarifying the nature and intended outcome of a learning activity (group 1 in the table), while a. is aimed simply at getting a learning task into the hands of students while the teacher does something else (group 2). Item c. is also in group 2, while d. is in group 1, as are e., f. and g. Even though it is essential for students to focus on a task say, in geometry, example h. does not directly help them to understand any geometry, and i. is aimed at controlling a student's behaviour irrespective of the focus of the lesson.

2.2.10 Task 10

Look back at the transcript in Task 6 and find instances where the teacher uses language more for <u>organisational purposes</u> than to support actual learning.

2.2.11 Commentary

There are only a few 'organisational' examples in the transcript, namely.
- a. *Teacher (T): Keighley, would you read out number nine for us?*
- b. *T: Right, people with hands up (to K) who would you want to contribute?*
- j. *T: (nods) do you want to choose somebody else?*

It can be argued that even the question the teacher asks at c. ('Right, now what does your group think about that?') is supportive of learning, so it belongs in group 1 because, even if there is no explanation, it is putting the onus of thinking on the students, while 'That sounds good' in the second part of j. indicates to Sadie and others that they are on the right track, thus also supporting their learning. In real lessons like this one, the balance between organisational as opposed to learning-related language is sure to vary according to the nature of the class and the behaviour of the students.

2.2.12 Summary

The importance of context was explained as follows in the *Common European Framework for Languages*, a publication that has had an important influence on the learning and teaching of language:

> It has long been recognised that language in use varies greatly according to the requirements of the context in which it is used. In this respect, language is not a neutral instrument of thought like, say, mathematics. The need and the desire to communicate arise in a particular situation and the form as well as the content of the communication is a response to that situation. (Council of Europe 2001, p. 44)

The CEFR goes on to list various elements that constitute or affect the context of communication. These are features of educational and classroom settings as well as of other 'domains' of language use, such as personal life, work and the 'public' domain of citizenship or organisational membership. Whatever the domain, the elements affecting linguistic communication described in the CEFR include the following:

- Situations that occur within domains. These are determined by a wide range of factors, for example: different locations and times; the structure and procedures in an organisation (e.g. there are differences between primary schools and secondary schools); the people involved (e.g. the teacher, the teacher's assistant, the students, the head teacher, especially the roles they have); the objects in the environment (equipment, furniture, possessions, items for sale, etc.); the events that happen (e.g. bad behaviour in class, a late arrival or absence); the actions performed by the people involved; and the kind of language people have to deal with (printed or spoken, dialogue or monologue, formal or informal, etc.).

- Conditions and constraints, such as physical conditions that affect speech (clarity, noise in the surroundings, etc.) or writing (font size, handwriting, light, etc.); social conditions (e.g. how many people are involved, how well we know them, etc.); and time pressure.
- The language users themselves: their attention to what is going on and attention span, their personal experience and the effect of it on memory and understanding, the way they categorise language, their state of mind (tired, distracted, enthusiastic, etc.) and, of course, their hearing and/or eyesight. These factors affect the language user's attitude, expectations and engagement.
- The topics or 'themes' of communication, which depend both on the domain and on the interest, preoccupations and intentions of the language users.
- The purpose or purposes of the language users: what do they intend or hope to accomplish by communicating? (adapted from ibid., pp. 44–46)

This view of communication and context is summarised visually in Fig. 2.1 with reference to the educational domain of the school.

Broadly speaking, the same 'rules' apply within the educational domain as in a social situation outside education. Classroom teaching and learning can be broken down into numerous 'sub-situations' according to factors such as the size of the room and the group of students, the subject being taught and the stage of the lesson. Each sub-situation brings with it certain constraints and conditions which may vary considerably across different national and educational contexts and traditions. These include the nature and quality of the curriculum being followed, the teaching and learning resources provided and the amount of time available. The language users involved are usually the teacher and the students. They all contribute to the conditions and constraints in many ways: the teacher's training and previous experience, as well as, for example, her personality, mood and voice, may all have an important impact in a given lesson. Where the students are concerned, apart from the obvious factor of age, things are much more complex: even if there are only 25 or so of them in the class, each is an individual with his or her own personality,

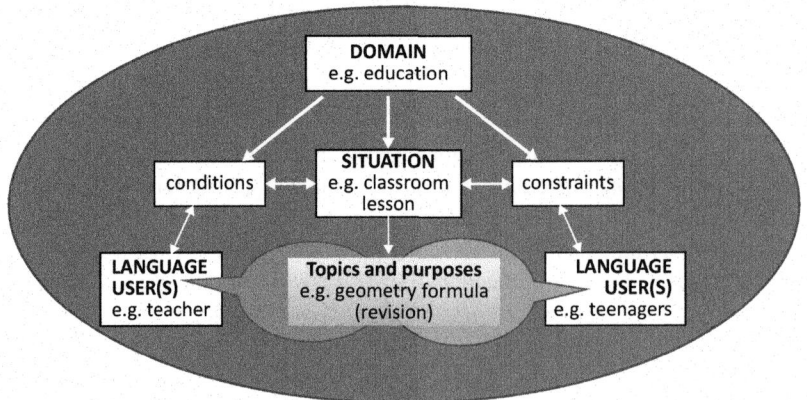

Fig. 2.1 Communication in context

background, level of motivation and state of mind. In addition, some may have learning disadvantages or advantages related to their competence in the language of schooling, hyperactivity, parental supervision and so on.

But larger issues are even more dominant among the conditions and constraints and usually impinge dramatically on the nature of the communication. These are the fact that one of the language users, the teacher, is in a position of authority, and that the students generally have little choice about participating in the lesson and will face sanctions if they refuse to do so or need formal authorisation if unable to do so. The students also generally have little say in the way the lesson is organised and progresses. In other words, due to the unequal nature of the 'power relationship' and the numbers of language users involved, the social situation in classrooms is often far more complex as an arena for linguistic communication than, for example, an everyday social encounter with a neighbour.

In spite of the complexity and logistical challenges of the classroom teaching and learning situation, the communication that takes place is usually relatively clear and comprehensible, if often one-sided. Apart from procedural matters such as those to do with behaviour and attention, the topic and purposes of the communication are usually clearly established by the teacher, underpinned by the curriculum and aided by the textbook and other resources being used. But, because there are so many didactic options in teaching and supporting learning and so many ways in which different students can learn, many types of 'talk' (and writing) are used. In the next section, we look at these in more detail.

2.2.13 Some Questions for Reflection

(a) Try to recall an instance when a teacher's way of communicating to you as a learner made a difference to your motivation and learning. What was it about her/his communication that made a difference?
(b) Write a short message to a newly qualified secondary school teacher in your system, advising her about ways of communicating that would help maintain her students' attention and motivate them to learn.

2.3 Section 3: The Uses of Language in Teaching

2.3.1 Task 11

Give three different examples in each case of the kinds of language teachers might use when they are:

(a) beginning a lesson
(b) securing and focusing students' attention

(c) introducing a new topic and key information about it
(d) setting up a learning activity
(e) supervising and monitoring learners during a learning activity
(f) ending a learning activity
(g) dealing with learners' queries, misunderstandings, etc.
(h) moving on to a new topic
(i) dealing with disruptive behaviour in the classroom.

2.3.2 Commentary

This task underlines the obvious point that teachers have many options open to them when selecting language for routine teaching and teaching-related activities. For example, to start a lesson the teacher might say: 'Good morning, everybody', or 'Sit down please' or 'How are you this morning?' or a combination of these. Their choice of language will depend partly on personal preference, habit and methodology, but also on factors in the classroom such as students' level of attention and engagement, the nature of the subject and the topic being taught or the activity being introduced, even the time of day and the day of the week. Outside the teaching situation, it is useful for teachers, however experienced they are, occasionally to think of a range of different ways of interacting in class so that they can vary their language or adapt it more readily to different classroom circumstances. Audio-recording parts of one's teaching is a good way of stimulating this kind of reflection and trying to answer the question: 'how could I have done that differently or more effectively?'

2.3.3 Task 12

Watch the first 8 minutes of this video: https://www.youtube.com/watch?v=sURBgKRGrIU. Describe the teacher's main teaching objectives. What kind of language does he use to try to achieve these objectives? List a few examples of the language he uses.

2.3.4 Commentary

It is clear from the clip that the teacher's main purpose is to find ways of making a theoretical geometric rule interesting and meaningful to his students by engaging them in problem-solving and by relating geometry to real life. The plan of the golf hole (aided by the golf club in his hand) is a means of focusing attention on his questions and remarks: 'what's the point of it [the game]?', 'If you're a good golfer you're supposed to do that hole in 5 shots', 'but is that the name of the game?', 'What am I trying to do when I'm playing this golf?', 'Perfect answer: you're trying to do it as quickly as possible with as few shots as possible' and so on. Using informal language like this (with matching body language) the teacher encourages the children to think for themselves, understand the challenge facing a golfer on a hole like this and relate it to geometry. Although it is unlikely that any of them would have played much real golf, the facial expressions of the students indicate their engagement. The teacher's approach enables him then to easily embark on other tasks focusing on the theorem.

2.3.5 Task 13

Watch the first 8 minutes of this video: https://youtu.be/LSDJ84jJ36M. What do the examples of teaching and the discussion with the consultant tell you about the difficulties this teacher faced? List some aspects of language and communication that the consultant focuses on.

2.3.6 Task 14

Compare the teaching approach and way of communicating of the teacher in Task 13 with that of the teacher in Task 12. What are the main differences? Why are they so different?

2.3.7 Commentary

Although the lesson in Task 13 is also on geometry and with students of a similar age, it offers a clear contrast to the lesson in Task 12. It demonstrates how important language, including body language, is in dealing with procedural issues such as moving from one phase of a lesson to another. The teacher is at first unable to get all the students to focus on the lesson, even with the help of her assistant, so she needs to put almost all her efforts into simply ensuring that the students pay attention rather than learning. The consultant advises her to focus on aspects of communication such as intonation and on finding a consistent way of getting attention. He suggests that she signals that she is waiting for their attention by using 'behavioural narration' ('John has put his pen down and is listening, Mary has stopped writing and is paying attention', etc.) and the teacher also uses a sound signal (tapping the glass).

Without communication strategies for managing student behaviour, unproductive procedural interaction can take over from productive teaching–learning interaction, a problem that teachers of teenagers may face quite often in some contexts. In addition, the ways in which a teacher engages and maintains the interest of students in the topic and task can make a big difference to both the learning process and the outcomes.

2.3.8 Summary

It is self-evident that the ways in which teachers use language in their teaching depends on what they are trying to do to support learning. The *Common European Framework of Reference for L*anguages includes 'mediation' among the key areas of language use described. *The CEFR Companion Volume* (Council of Europe 2020) describes mediation as follows:

> *In mediation, the user/learner acts as a social agent who creates bridges and helps to construct or convey meaning, sometimes within the same language, sometimes from one language to another [...]. The focus is on the role of language in processes like creating the space and conditions for communicating and/or learning, collaborating to construct new meaning, encouraging others to construct or understand new meaning, and passing on new information in an appropriate form. The context can be social, pedagogic, cultural, linguistic or professional.* (Council of Europe 2020, p. 90)

The reference to 'pedagogic' contexts is important. In a sense, all teaching is mediation, although mediation is much broader than just teaching. A salient feature of most teaching is that one person, the teacher, provides mediation for a group of other language users, the students, in a power relationship. This is not the case, for example, in mediation between two adults who are neighbours or workmates where one of them has knowledge or expertise, for example about gardening or using given software, that he or she is sharing with the other.

As was clear from Task 13, dealing with a group of students in a formal educational context also brings with it certain additional responsibilities beyond teaching, such as ensuring that members of the class are present, are paying attention, understand instructions, etc. The type of 'procedural' mediation involved in achieving this is different from mediation that is designed to help students to achieve the planned learning outcomes relating to knowledge, concept building or skills. Students may also intervene for procedural reasons such as explaining why they are late or have not done their homework, asking for more time or more explanation, etc. In general, however, while these types of talk may contribute to the conditions and constraints of the situation, they do not impact directly on learning, except when they disrupt learning in some way.

Mediation between the teacher and students and among students is part and parcel of the 'framework for dialogic teaching' proposed by Alexander (2018). As part of this framework the following principles are proposed. Classroom teaching and learning should be:

- *'collective (the classroom is a site of joint learning and enquiry)*
- *reciprocal (participants listen to each other, share ideas and consider alternative viewpoints)*

- *supportive (participants feel able to express ideas freely, without risk of embarrassment over 'wrong' answers, and they help each other to reach common understandings)*
- *cumulative (participants build on their own and each other's contributions and chain them into coherent lines of thinking and understanding)*
- *purposeful (classroom talk, though open and dialogic, is structured with specific learning goals in view)'* (Alexander 2018, p. 6).

Following such principles means first that students must be able to engage in a range of different kinds of 'learning talk' and that teachers must develop and use a broader repertoire of 'teaching talk' and questioning than has traditionally been the case in the 'initiation-response-feedback' style of teaching.

From the teaching point of view, 'teaching talk' that fits with the context and teacher's purpose may be a logical choice. However, in line with the principles proposed for dialogic teaching, talk that is aimed at helping learners to learn—and to learn how to learn from one another as well as through the mediation offered and the activities organised by their teacher—is of paramount importance. In many lessons or parts of lessons, especially in plenary teaching, this is often not the kind of talk that takes place. A certain amount of time is inevitably taken up with the kind of teacher talk that focuses on organisation or behaviour discussed in Task 9, and initiation (by the teacher) and response by a student, followed by feedback ('good', 'OK', 'not quite', etc.) from the teacher, often predominate. When the whole class is being taught, even if there are only 25 students in the class, there are generally few opportunities for individual students even to answer questions because allowing each student to respond individually would take too long. It is also less usual in plenary teaching for students to be able to engage in discussion with the teacher, to argue and justify their opinions, to tell their own stories, etc.

This is not to say that plenary work in the classroom is not useful for students—far from it. There are all sorts of reasons why it is necessary. These include:

- establishing learning goals
- focusing the class's attention on a new topic
- giving or eliciting information about the topic in order to set the scene
- setting up a task or activity
- checking understanding
- organising the way students should work and setting a deadline
- assessing students' learning
- bringing the class together to review and/or evaluate the results of a task
- dealing with doubts and questions that may be relevant to all
- establishing a sense of community and responsibility in a class
- focusing the class's attention on a projected image or other visual support
- and so on.

On the other hand, if a task is motivating and students' attention is focused on it, allowing them to work part of the time in smaller groups encourages other kinds of productive 'learning talk', and these will be explored in the next section. Apart from providing a change from plenary teaching and offering many more opportunities for students to talk in ways that suit them individually, such group activities provide experiences of 'dialogic learning' which contribute to and complement what happens in the plenary phases of teaching.

2.3.9 Questions for Reflection

(a) In your context, to what extent are principles like those suggested by Alexander for dialogic teaching reflected in classroom teaching and learning?
(b) In your experience, what kinds of 'teaching talk' really help students to develop their understanding of new concepts?

2.4 Section 4: Learning Talk and Context

Whatever the subject and objectives of a lesson or learning activity, the ways in which the teacher and learners use and interact in the spoken language have a considerable impact on what and how they learn. In this section, we will look at some features of learning talk and teaching talk and their roles in learning.

2.4.1 Task 15

Describe the kinds of talk used by students in the following interactions with teachers.
(a) *T: What do you think causes the temperature of the human body to rise?*
   S: Is it to help us fight infection?
(b) *T: Who can tell me how we say: 'I want a return ticket to Lyon' in French?*
   S: I think it's: "Un billet aller-retour à Lyon, s'il vous plaît"
(c) *T: What did your group think the causes of the First World War were, Susanna?*
   S: We weren't sure: some of us said it was a conflict between the different empires competing for power, others said it was mainly nationalism ...
(d) *T: You should know how to spell 'receive' by now, Luca.*
   S: Oh yes, sorry: it should be ei, not ie.
(e) *T: Explain Pythagoras's theorem*
   S: It's something to do with triangles, isn't it?

2.4 Section 4: Learning Talk and Context

2.4.2 Commentary

These examples illustrate the kinds of interactions that often take place between teacher and students in plenary teaching. Most of the students' answers are single sentences or are tentative, either in the form of a question inviting approval or correction (a) or using 'I think …' before recalling the answer from memory (b). In the case of c), the student summarises the opinion of a group she has been working with on the question. Some of them invite further advice or confirmation: (e) for example, in which the student seeks confirmation that he is on the right track before attempting an answer. Depending on the approach taken, this advice or confirmation can come either from the teacher or other students.

Taken together, these examples illustrate different ways of answering questions to indicate how confident or not students are about their responses. However, they are limited as regards advancing students' learning.

2.4.3 Task 16

Following their research work in schools in a range of countries, Alexander and colleagues proposed a list of the kinds of 'learning talk' that students need to have in their repertoires and to use in their learning. These are listed in the left-hand column of Table 2.3 (below).

Below the table there is a transcript of discussion in a small group of 10- and 11-year-olds who are talking about the way the moon is seen from earth. What different kinds of 'learning talk' can you identify in the interaction?

Table 2.3 Repertoire of learning talk (based on Alexander 2018, p. 8)

Repertoire of 'learning talk' needed by students	✓	Which of these occur in the excerpt below? Where? What language is used?
1. Narrate		At g: Gabrielle talks about going out early in the morning and still seeing the moon
2. Explain		
3. Speculate		
4. Imagine		
5. Explore		
6. Analyse		
7. Evaluate		
8. Question		
9. Justify		
10. Discuss		
11. Argue		

(a) *Viola (V): OK (reads) "The moon changes shape because it is in the shadow of the earth."*
(b) *Frannie (F): No, that's not true ... because there's the clouds that cover the moon.*
(c) *V: no it isn't ... yes ...*
(d) *Gabrielle (G): Yes*
(e) *V: Because in the day we think, oh the moon's gone, it hasn't gone, it's just the clouds that ...*
(f) *F: ... have covered it.*
(g) *G: Yes, that's why I, like, every time, well on Sunday I went out and it was like five in the morning right, and the moon was still out so that's fine 'cos it was still dark, right?*
(h) *V: Yes*
(i) *G: So when we went out it was like five, four, four o'clock, something like that, like at that time there wouldn't be the moon out would there, but I saw half the moon out and I said, I said to my Mum's friend, I said "Look Tony, there's the moon already out" and he said "Oh yes." Because in the morning when we came, there was the clouds.*
(j) *V: So what do we think?*
(k) *G: I think it's false.*
(l) *F: False.* (Adapted from Dawes et al. 2010, p. 105).

2.4.4 Commentary

This transcript provides good examples of how, through talking in a group, students can have the time and concentrated attention needed to work collaboratively on a problem. The students build on—or in some cases disagree with—one another's interventions and refer to personal experience. A completed list of examples would look like this:

Examples of kinds of learning talk in the transcript#;

Narrate: at g: Gabrielle talks about going out early in the morning and still seeing the moon
Explain: at b. Frannie: *"... because there's the clouds that cover the moon"*
Speculate: at i. Gabrielle. *". at that time there wouldn't be the moon out would there"*
Imagine: at e. Viola: *"... Because in the day we think, oh the moon's gone"*
Explore: from b to i—three students
Analyse: at e. Viola: *"... it hasn't gone, it's just the clouds that ..."*
Evaluate: at k. Gabrielle: *"I think it's false"*
Question: at j. Viola: *"So what do we think?"*
Justify: at i. Gabrielle: *"Because in the morning when we came, there was the clouds."*
Discuss: from b. to i.—three students
Argue: no clear examples

The discussion is quite informal and similar to the talk that students might engage in outside the classroom. However, it is constructive and collaborative in the sense that the students work together to reach a conclusion.

Alexander's repertoire of learning talk is complemented by some additional conditions. For their learning talk to be effective, students need to listen, think about what they hear, give others time to think and respect alternative viewpoints (Alexander 2018, p. 8). It is hard to tell from a transcript how these conditions were met, but Gabrielle was clearly given time to tell her story and speculate about what she saw while others listened. In this short extract, there is, however, little evidence of alternative viewpoints and quite a lot of agreement.

2.4.5 Task 17

What kinds of learning talk are exemplified in the following excerpt involving three girls aged 12–13 in a secondary school looking at an illustration and talking about how they think Saxon migrants settled in early England? How does the discussion help the students to move towards answering this question?

(a) *Betty (B): The Saxons used er timber, didn't they, to … Yes,to build houses?*
(b) *Teresa (T): They cleared a … Say they found a forest and you know they're probably all forests near the …*
(c) *B: Yes. They cleared it all away and then built all the little huts and brought all their animals and …*
(d) *Carol (C): All the family and that … They'd have to be pretty big huts.*
(e) *T: Yes.*
(f) *B: Why did they live in valleys?*
(g) *T: I suppose so … so they'd be sheltered*
(h) *B: Yes, for shelter … and so … there was less risk … of being attacked I should think.*
(i) *T: Yes*
(j) *C: Because they could only come from two directions* (from Barnes 1976, pp. 54–55).

2.4.6 Commentary

Douglas Barnes, one of the pioneers of exploratory talk whose work Alexander, Mercer and others have since built on, recorded this and other examples of group interaction. He provided his own commentary on these interactions, which is reproduced below in adapted form.

(a) Betty seems to be making a statement, but it turns into a hypothesis (speculation in Alexander's terms) which invites discussion.

(b) Teresa picks up the thread and suggests the need to find a site which offered building materials in the form of timber.
(c) Betty develops or explores the idea further.
(d) Carol seems to continue the topic, but switches from the animals mentioned by Betty to the families and their likely size.
(e) This is acknowledged but isn't picked up by the other two girls.
(f) Instead, Betty refers to the illustration they have and changes the subject to the likely location in a valley, and seems to try to answer her own question …
(g) …. which Teresa does.
(h) Betty accepts this answer but doesn't seem sure, as shown by her pauses and 'I should think' while she evaluates it.
(i) Teresa agrees.
(j) Carol offers or imagines another reason why valleys were probably a preferred location.

The interaction contains a mixture of explaining, speculating and imagining, questioning and justifying. What is clear is that, as in Task 16, the students stimulate and build on each other's talk about this historical topic, sometimes continuing each other's thoughts, sometimes going in new directions, and co-constructing their answer to the question.

2.4.7 Task 18

Some of the ways the teacher's repertoire of 'teaching talk' and the students' repertoires of 'learning talk' work together can be seen in the third longer excerpt below, which is also from the lesson about the view of the moon from the earth (with 10–11-year-old children). Towards the end of the lesson the teacher is following up the previous discussions in groups with an illustrated presentation of the way the orbit of the moon and the revolutions and orbit of the earth affect what we can see of the moon at a given time and location.

As discussed in the summary of section 3, much of the spoken and written language teachers use in educational settings is mediation. Look at the teacher interventions in the transcript below. To what extent and in what way does each of them support learning?

The teacher has a large photo of a half-moon on the interactive whiteboard. She also has on a table a lamp (sun) a globe (earth) and tennis ball (moon)

(a) *Teacher (T):* Can anybody describe to me why we can only see one side of the moon from earth? Gabrielle?
(b) *Gabrielle:* (inaudible; nobody else offers a response)
(c) *T:* OK, we can only see one side of the moon from earth because the moon is going round the earth, ok, and it keeps the same side of itself to the earth all the time like that. This little dot here, (indicating dot on the tennis ball) look, that's

one of those craters on the moon. If we're in the UK here, we can only see this dot here, and we can't see anything on this side at all because it doesn't turn round, it keeps that dot (orbits the moon round the earth)—we have to colour it so that we will be able to see. OK, let's see why the moon actually changes shape. It takes about a month, 27, 28 days for the earth, for the moon to go round the earth. A 'moonth', that's what a month means. Yes 27.3 [days] if we're going to be precise. OK?

(d) Child: A 'mownth'
(e) T: A 'moonth', that's why it's called a month. Here we are, somebody was saying they thought it might have ice, doesn't have any water, no atmosphere and no water. It's just rock. OK. This phrase, "the phases of the moon", we use to mean the way the moon appears to, as Matthew pointed out, change shape. The way the moon appears to change shape. You can see here we've got this half-moon effect you see here? (indicates whiteboard)
(f) All: Yes
(g) T: But there's something making a shadow on the moon here, let's look what that is. Because that's what we need to find out before we finish today. Carlie, are you with me?
(h) Keighley: I brought in a book in which it shows all the different stages of the moon.
(i) T: Right, ok, that'll be helpful. We'll look at it in a book 'cos I think to see pictures really helps, doesn't it? Ok, let's just see if we can work it out now.

(The teacher positions the ball, the "earth" and the lamp in a line, with the earth in the middle; the "moon" is however lifted up so that the lamp shines on it.)

(j) T. Here's the earth, here's the sun, here's the moon. Right. How much of the moon do you think we can see from earth?
(k) Children: Half *(which is wrong; this would be a full moon)*
(l) T: Think! The moon; this is the sun, our source of light, it's really shining off into space, we're facing the moon, here we are—we're facing the moon, how much of that moon can we see?
(m) Children: Half/ a third maybe?
(n) T: Right
(o) Walter: We can't see the sides, or the back.
(p) T: We can't see any of this (indicating the back of the "moon")
(q) Walter: So we can only see about a third (children still do not understand)
(r) T: Right look, if the sun's shining from here there is nothing between the sun and the moon, so from here on earth what we can see is a circle, a big shiny full moon. Right? That's a full moon, we can see the whole caboodle if we're here on earth and the sun is over there. However, have a look now, what happens now? If I put the moon here (between the sun and the earth) here's the sun, is there any light from the sun falling on this moon that we would be able to see from earth?
(s) Children: No
(t) T: What would we see if the moon is in that position?

(u) *Children: Nothing*
(v) *T: Yes, it would be totally dark. We get a completely black effect because we can't see it, we can only see it if there is light falling on it, and all the light is falling on this side and we're not over there, we're over here. Yes?*
(w) *[....]* (Dawes et al. 2010, pp. 106–107)

2.4.8 Commentary

Here, following discussion in groups, during which the teacher went from group to group collecting answers from each group, her teaching role is much more prominent. She starts off with a quite tricky question, which is a development of the original theme of discussion. The students are not able to answer, so the teacher uses mediation to explain why we can only see one side of the moon from earth, using her visual aids to demonstrate the reason. She then goes on to deal with the question about the moon changing shape, which was discussed in groups in the excerpts in section 1. Her mediation role includes explaining the origin of the word 'month' in English, recalling or reiterating points raised by students in the class about ice on the moon and the 'phases' of the moon, referring back to and building on what students have said in the first part of the interaction as she explains the phenomenon (with demonstration), and asking questions to check that the children are following. She also politely acknowledges Keighley's mention of the illustrated book she has brought in. This is quite like 'traditional' teaching, in which the teacher explains facts and the students listen, but the difference is that students have already thought about and discussed the question among themselves, drawing on their existing knowledge, and the teacher deliberately refers back to that discussion. This acknowledgement of individual students' contributions as part of the mediation and learning process helps maintain motivation.

Then, from intervention j. and k. onwards, the teacher uses the tennis ball, globe, light and the whiteboard to help sort out the ideas in the children's minds about the view of the moon from earth. Instead of beginning the class with this demonstration she first got the children to actively engage with the phenomenon in their own thinking, discussion and reference to deliberations in groups (e.g. Task 8 in this Section), but also elicited the children's first ideas (Task 2 in Section 1). This enables the teacher to capitalise on the children's (often mistaken) ideas during the demonstration.

This kind of collaborative teaching and learning may not be suitable for all subjects and all lessons, but it is one of a range of options open to a teacher that are important both from the point of view of 'co-constructing' learning and for maintaining and enhancing student motivation and engagement in learning.

2.4.9 Summary

While we are familiar with the various kinds of teaching talk that traditionally take place when classes are being taught 'in plenary' and with the ways in which students are likely to respond to it, the kinds of learning talk that can take place when students work in small groups are less easily explored. However, it can be seen from the transcripts in this section that, in contexts where the social dimension of learning is understood and valued and work in smaller groups in classrooms is feasible, dialogic interaction can provide plentiful opportunities for learning. This kind of talk encourages students to use one another's ideas, arguments, explanations and so on to build up their individual 'reinterpretation' and understanding. The work done in plenary can be usefully prepared for, reinforced and extended by the process of co-construction in groups, and can be further consolidated by a return to plenary teaching in which the results of the group work are reviewed and expanded on and confirmed or adjusted.

Douglas Barnes summarises the complementarity between learning talk and teaching talk well: *'Teachers teach classes, but pupils learn as individuals, each constructing slightly different versions of the meanings made available during the interchanges shared by the whole class and the teacher. Both the shared construction and the individual struggle to reinterpret are essential'* (Barnes 2008, p. 8).

Students are individuals and, although in education systems they spend a large part of their time in classes of 25 or more, each individual student has their own way of learning or further developing their knowledge, skills and awareness. The mixture of supervised group work and whole classwork exemplified in the transcripts in this section illustrates how individual can be allowed the space to build up their learning individually and socially through dialogue within groups.

Teachers can exploit group work using similar ways of building on ideas and interaction with students that is 'exploratory' rather than a means of transmitting knowledge top down. As Neil Mercer states:

'Teachers have a professional responsibility for helping their students to build new understandings upon the foundations of their previous learning, and language is the main tool available to the teaching profession for doing this' (Mercer 2000, p. 52).

It is therefore essential that teachers, whatever subject they are teaching, understand how language works in educational settings, and can use it effectively in their teaching in different ways for in different learning situations.

The ways in which mediation is used by a teacher are all part of his or her language repertoire, an area we will go on to explore further in later units.

2.4.10 Some Questions for Reflection

(a) Try to recall instances in your own experience as a teacher or student in which talk in class played an important part in your and/or your students' learning. Make notes about it and be ready to exchange the experiences with a colleague or course colleague.
(b) Note down three characteristics of good, productive teaching talk.
(c) In the educational contexts you are familiar with, how frequently do learners work in small groups, and for what purposes? Give reasons for this.

2.5 Conclusion

In this unit, we have considered in some depth the ways in which teachers use language in the educational context mainly to support students' learning and cognitive development, but also to manage the many different aspects of classroom work. We have also looked at the ways in which students use language in their learning, both in response to their teachers and also with peers in their work in smaller groups. The tasks have exemplified how use of language by students and by teachers varies widely across a range of teaching and learning situations and have shown that the ways in which teachers choose their 'talk' can have an important impact on students' motivation, learning and behaviour.

Unit 3 examines the importance in learning of students' individual 'language repertoires' and explores various styles of communication that can be used by teachers and textbook writers to enhance these repertoires and to guide and support students in their learning.

References

Alexander R. J. (2018). Developing Dialogic Teaching: Genesis, Process, Trial. *Research Papers in Education*. Retrieved June 8, 2020, from http://robinalexander.org.uk/wp-content/uploads/2019/12/RPIE-2018-Alexander-dialogic-teaching.pdf

Barnes, D. (1976). *From Communication to Curriculum*. Penguin.

Barnes, D. (2008). Exploratory talk for learning. In N. Mercer & S. Hodgkinson (Eds.), *Exploring Talk in Schools*. Sage.

Brau, B. (2018). Constructivism. In R. Kimmons (Ed.), *The Students' Guide to Learning Design and Research*. EdTech Books. Retrieved June 3, 2020 from https://edtechbooks.org/studentguide/constructivism

Council of Europe. (2001). *A Common European Framework of References for Languages*. Council of Europe. Retrieved June 3, 2022, from https://www.coe.int/en/web/portfolio/the-common-european-framework-of-reference-for-languages-learning-teaching-assessment-cefr

Council of Europe. (2020). *CEFR Companion Volume with New Descriptors*. Council of Europe. Retrieved May 23, 2022, from https://rm.coe.int/common-european-framework-of-reference-for-languages-learning-teaching/16809ea0d4

References

Dawes, L., Dore, B., Loxley, P., & Nicholls, L. (2010). A talk focus for promoting enjoyment and developing understanding in science. *English teaching: Practice and Critique, 9*(2), 99–110.

Lessons in Observation. (2013). Evaluating Teaching and Learning: Early Years Foundation Stage (EYFS) Reception Numeracy (Excerpts). Retrieved April 30, 2020, from https://www.youtube.com/watch?v=WwUCufOeOdE

Mercer, N. (2000). *Words and Mind—How we Use Language to Think Together*. Routledge.

Vygotsky, L. (1978). *Mind in Society*. Harvard University Press.

Chapter 3
Unit 3: Language and Communication in Education 2

In Unit 1, we looked in general terms at the nature, purpose and style of language in use. Then, in Unit 2, we considered the role of language in learning and in teaching, and the ways in which individual language development affects learning and achievement.

In Unit 3, we consider how language use varies according to subject and the resources used. We also examine the importance of students' individual linguistic repertoires. We then explore how questioning and other types of prompts are used in teaching and ways in which teachers can use so-called 'scaffolding' to support and advance learning.

3.1 Section 1: The Language Repertoires of Individual Students

This section focuses on the key notions of a student's language **repertoire**, i.e. the linguistic skills and competences they can mobilise at a given point in their schooling. It will also put the spotlight on the fact that, in many classrooms around the world, students bring with them competences in more than one language and may need support in developing their skills in a language of schooling, which may be relatively new to them.

3.1.1 Task 1

Use Table 3.1 below to reflect and write notes on your own language repertoire.

Table 3.1 Thinking about your language repertoire

What kinds of communicative situations outside your family or circle of friends are you most confident in?
Give examples of topics or situations in which you can understand quite a lot but could not express yourself confidently.
In your main or first language, what kinds of writing do you find easiest and most difficult?
What significant differences are there between your spoken language in informal situations (e.g. with friends) and in formal situations (e.g. dealing with people you don't know outside your home)?
When listening to people speaking your main or first language, are there accents and ways of speaking that you find difficult to understand?
Apart from your main first language, in which other languages can you: – Read instructions? – Write emails? – Watch or listen to a news item? – Have a five-minute conversation about personal information?

3.1.2 Commentary

Although we seldom think about them, our language repertoires are complicated. We often have some familiarity with one or more other languages, or at least know a few words or expressions, even if they are 'borrowed' into our own first language, and we can recognise accents. Our repertoires in our first language may also vary considerably depending on our communicative needs and habits. We may use specialised language for some areas, for example to do with our work or hobbies, but not for others; we may understand certain regional accents and expressions in our first language more easily than others because of who we work or socialise with; or we may feel much more comfortable communicating in informal language in conversation than we do when using more formal language in, for example, an interview situation. Depending on our opportunities to use languages, our repertoires in our first and in other languages evolve constantly as we gain more experience of and exposure to language(s) in different situations and being used for different purposes.

Reflecting on questions like those in Task 1 can offer insights into areas where teachers may feel they want to strengthen their own linguistic repertoires for personal and for pedagogic reasons, especially as the classes of the students they teach become more and more diverse. One of the key responsibilities of all teachers, whatever their subject, is to help students to develop their language repertoires for education and for life. This implies that all teachers also need an awareness of their own repertoire and how it has developed.

3.1.3 Task 2

Which of the following situations would present a challenge for you in your own first language? In those cases, how might you try to overcome the difficulty?

(a) Being asked personal questions by someone from a different language and/or cultural background.
(b) Having a conversation with someone whom you have never met before and who has a strong regional accent.
(c) Answering questions related to your job when the other person is unfamiliar with that kind of work.
(d) Reading a technical article about a subject you do not know about, for example a medical condition, new computer software or a philosophical concept.
(e) Having to write an email message to complain about the quality of service, for example home repairs or a holiday booked through a travel agent.
(f) Trying to calm down an angry or distressed neighbour who does not speak your language at all well.

3.1.4 Commentary

These common situations are challenging in different ways because each of us has a different language repertoire depending on our experiences of learning and using language(s). Understanding what someone is saying when their knowledge of the language is limited can be tricky. A valuable skill is to find ways of helping them by rephrasing a question or remark in simple language, for example 'Do you mean ....?'. Being genuinely sympathetic, rephrasing or checking what the problem is without being put off by a culturally different way of behaving might also be useful in situation (f). In (b) the challenge is different and may well be just a matter of pronunciation. Asking people to repeat what they have said more slowly may make it easier to understand them. (c) is more to do with register—language that is specialised in one way or another. As with case (b), this works two ways: the person answering the question may need to find ways of 'translating' the technical terms into simpler language, and the person asking the question should not be worried about asking for clarification or examples. (d) is also about register, but if there is no one around to help understand the specialised terminology, dictionaries and encyclopaedia entries, which are now available electronically, may be the only solution. In situation (e), the challenge may be more a question of lack of practice in writing this kind of message than due to lack of the right language. In complaining, as in other situations, it is important to use the right type and tone of language to ensure that the complaint is clear but also to avoid giving unnecessary offence.

3.1.5 Task 3

Watch the short video on bilingualism in education at.
https://www.youtube.com/watch?v=eYiQKw8v24M&feature=emb_imp_woyt

- According to the speaker what are the four main benefits of being able to use another language for different age groups?
- How does the speaker's input relate to the notion of a linguistic repertoire?
- If you can speak another language in addition to your first language, what have the main advantages been for you personally?
- What does the speaker mean by a 'healthy language diet'?

3.1.6 Commentary

The speaker mentions various benefits, including 'building cognitive reserves', improved ability to do cognitive tasks and even staying healthier for longer, in the sense that language learning has been shown to delay the onset of dementia by up to 5 years. She also states that children who are bilingual, in this case meaning able to use two languages (not necessarily with equal competence), are able to focus and concentrate better on tasks than other children.

The speaker is citing research evidence that is hard to dispute without analysing it and reviewing other research, but people who do speak more than one language generally think of it as an asset in their lives rather than an irrelevance. They also often find it easier to learn further languages, and to spot similarities and peculiarities in languages, and they often enjoy talking to people from different language and cultural backgrounds and finding ways of bridging 'language gaps' (this has certainly been the authors' experience). The fact that people who can only speak their first language usually envy those who also speak other languages is another signal of the perceived benefits of bilingualism.

3.1.7 Task 4

Look at the statistical information in Table 3.2 below and the sentence that follows about Austrian schools. What implications might the data have for the pre-service and in-service training of teachers in the UK and in Austria?

In Austrian state schools, between 26% and 28% of all students use more than one language during a normal day (data from the Österreichisches Sprachenkompetenz Zentrum: http://www.oesz.at/OESZNEU/main.php?page=045&ID=626).

Table 3.2 Percentage proportion of children in a selection of local authority areas in the UK whose first language is not English

Local authority	% in primary schools	% in secondary schools
Urban areas		
London Tower Hamlets	70%	63%
London Islington	50%	37%
Bradford	39%	32%
More rural areas		
Hampshire	8%	5%
Antrim and Newtownabbey (Northern Ireland)	6%	1%
Cumbria	4%	3%
Renfrewshire (Scotland)	4%	2%

Source: https://dataguide.migrationobservatory.ox.ac.uk/population-trends/how-many-children-of-migrants-are-there-in-the-uk/(The Migration Observatory)

3.1.8 Task 5

Read and comment on these two short quotations from remarks by a teacher of English in an Austrian vocational school.

> *In my own practice I saw that it is also very useful for us as teachers to try out the first languages of our pupils (and we have a lot of different languages in our school). This doesn't only help to create relationship (...), but increases also our awareness for difficulties our learners may have.*
>
> *When I ask my learners how this or that works in their first language, they very often say that they don't know. I think that there are two possible explanations for this. First, that they don't know enough in or about their first language. This is the common explanation which might be true when they are born in Austria and use their first languages only as a spoken language at home within their families. Second, I think that this might be because of the two different ways of learning the first and a second or third language. You learn a first language by imitating your parents when you are a baby and later on by using it in different contexts, but you do rarely think about how your language is formed even when you are educated in school. So this is than natural and it is up to us as teachers to increase their interest in these differences and/or similarities. What we do in our school, is that we focus less on grammar and more on different chunks which can be used in a given situation.*
> (Gerda Piribauer, private communication, used with permission)

3.1.9 Commentary

Task 4: pre-service teacher education in the UK currently takes little or no account of differences between the urban and rural contexts in which schools are located, but it is clear that serving teachers in urban schools are likely to need provision in INSET programmes for ways of responding to the multilingual and multicultural classes they are confronted with on a day-to-day basis. In the Austrian context, it is clear that trainees and teachers need guidance on how to take account of linguistic and cultural diversity in state school classrooms.

The Austrian teacher's comments in Task 5, based directly on her own experience, provide an insight into her own coping strategies, which are rooted in empathy and understanding for the migrant children she works with, but the second quote also hints at an agreed institution-wide response which may well have been worked out in an in-house staff development session. In addition, she points out, interestingly, that a student's first language repertoire may be different in origin, function and extent from the one s/he needs to develop in the course of schooling. Students who are recent migrants are likely to need this new language for both instrumental and integrative purposes while retaining their first language for use in the home and with compatriots. The next task looks at some of these issues from the perspective of migrant children themselves.

3.1.10 Task 6

The following quotes are all from a study in the UK on the ways in which schools integrate migrants. What do they tell you about the impact on children's developing language repertoire of the experience of migration and the need to start afresh?

1. A Year 10 pupil from Lithuania reflected: *'I was panicking because I didn't understand anything and some teachers, they really wanted us to do the work but I didn't know what the work was, and what to do or how to do it because it's like different rules and a different culture. Things are done a bit differently here and it was hard to get used to it.'* (p. 56)
2. A pupil in a London secondary school: *'I remember when I came here five years ago, we had morning breakfast for students who were not fluent yet in English. And that really helped me because then I was able to bond with people like me and bond together and learned together. And that was really helpful because I thought that was the whole learning, the whole thing of adapting to a new school and stuff.'* (p. 57)
3. A pupil at a secondary school in the South of England: *'[my first day] was scary, but I found Miss X because she can speak Italian, so I was very comfortable with her. The people they helped me so much and Miss X she helped me. It was good.'* (p. 58)
4. A pupil in Year 10 described [...] reading books in her native Russian language in the school library as: *'... a comforting thing to do. When you move countries, you leave your home and your friends behind but your language is something you can keep hold of'*. Conversely, some pupils in other schools expressed worry that their first language had deteriorated since they had started school in Britain. (p. 59) (from Manzoni and Rolfe 2019)

3.1 Section 1: The Language Repertoires of Individual Students

3.1.11 *Commentary*

The Lithuanian pupil's comment brings home the emotional and cultural as well as the linguistic challenges that migrants face when they are 'transplanted' into a new context. She was clearly in need of support based on a teacher's understanding of the impact on her of being deprived of her mother tongue as a means of understanding and also of asking for help. The second comment also focuses on the very low base from which such pupils have to start, and the crucial importance of acceptance by others and socialisation as a way of beginning to adjust to new realities. The third quote highlights the emotional impact of this kind of requirement to adjust, and it is a nice counterpoint to the Austrian teacher's strategy of showing empathy by taking an interest in her students' native languages. The importance of acknowledging and valuing student's own first language (also stressed by the speaker in the video in Task 3) is echoed in the Russian student's pleasure at being able to maintain contact with her language through reading. In all these cases, we can see how migrant pupils are confronted with the need to adapt to the language of their new classrooms and to rebuild their individual language repertoires from scratch if they are to succeed in their new educational environment. Manzoni and Rolfe sum it up in their study:

> *Pupils recognised the importance of becoming proficient in English in order to fit in and progress with learning. It was clear that many valued the support of a particular member of staff who helped with English either on a one to one or group basis. Pupils also appreciated having contact with a teacher who could speak their home language, though not necessarily for practical reasons.* (2019, p. 60)

Here, Manzoni and Rolfe are clearly alluding to the emotional and identity-related importance of maintaining the mother tongue as a part of a migrant student's language repertoire. They go on to emphasise just how much is at stake for migrants who arrive later in their school careers:

> *Students who arrive in the later years of compulsory education face particular challenges acquiring English to the level necessary to pass public examinations. This has implications for their progression to post-16 academic or vocational study.* (ibid., p. 63)

3.1.12 *Task 7*

Earlier in the report on the same study, one teacher is quoted as saying:

> *There isn't a big gulf because actually the language acquisition of a lot of our [monolingual] British children, is probably worse, because what we found is that if a child is proficient in one [other] language, actually they pick English up very quickly, whereas the children who haven't got much language at all, which [is the case for] some of our very poor ... British, who come in with speech and language problems, are the kind of ones that it's really difficult to move.* (Manzoni and Rolfe 2019, p. 19)

(a) In your opinion and experience, what are the most common language problems at school for children aged 8–10 from disadvantaged backgrounds who know only the language of the country where they are living?
(b) By comparison, what language challenges at school might be faced by recently arrived migrant students of the same age who know one or more other languages but are not yet proficient in the language of the country where they are now going to school?

Use Table 3.3 below to make notes.

Table 3.3 Possible difficulties with language at school

	Monolingual children from disadvantaged backgrounds in the country where they go to school	Children recently arrived from abroad who speak one or more other languages but are not yet proficient in the language used at school
Understanding teachers' instructions		
Giving clear answers to questions		
Working in a group with other children		
Following instructions in a textbook or test		
Writing short paragraphs about their home or country		
Reading and understanding stories		
Making friends		
Asking teachers for help		
Other difficulties: which?		

3.1.13 Commentary

A common situation in classrooms, especially in Europe, is that different students have radically different language profiles. A dozen or more languages and cultures may be represented in their class of 30. Those with languages of origin and home languages which are different from the language of education may, at least initially, have difficulties in all the areas listed in the table, even when asking the teacher to help or trying to make friends However, it is also quite often the case that those for whom the language of schooling is a second or additional language, especially those in their primary years, quickly learn to cope with it as well as many of their monolingual classmates do, partly because they do not want to be seen as 'different' from their peers. As suggested by the speaker in Task 3, perhaps this ability to learn to use the language is because their linguistic repertoire and experience of learning and using one or more other languages makes them more adaptable than monolingual students.

Monolingual pupils, especially those from disadvantaged backgrounds, may also have language problems of their own. Again, all the situations mentioned except making friends may present challenges because doing those sorts of things is not part of their normal language repertoire. Both monolingual and bilingual or plurilingual learners may also suffer from disorders such as dyslexia or simply lack experience in using language for such a wide variety of purposes due to shyness, lack of opportunity to interact with others at home, weak reading skills and so on. It is therefore crucial for teachers to be aware of the diverse language profiles of individual students and the difficulties that some of them are likely to face in working with the kinds of language in which learning and teaching take place. There is no escaping the fact that, irrespective of the subject being taught, all teachers are also language teachers, with a duty to support their students in developing the language skills needed in their education, which are different from those needed for everyday life outside the classroom.

3.1.14 Task 8

Imagine you are a primary school teacher working with 8–9-year-old children. You know that in your class there are eight children who speak languages that are different from the one spoken in the country where you are working. Three of these languages have different writing systems from the language of the country where the school is. You yourself do not know much about these languages.

You decide that you wish to take advantage of this multilingualism for two main reasons:

(a) In order to acknowledge the different language profiles of these pupils and thus add to their self-esteem and confidence.
(b) As a means of raising the children's, especially the monolingual children's, awareness of other languages and of arousing their general interest in languages, writing systems and cultures.

Possible ways of doing this might include:

- Setting aside a lesson each week to focus on other home languages represented in the class.
- Enabling students with other languages to 'teach' some words and expressions to their peers.
- Asking students to 'interview' each other about their home languages and cultures.

Choose one of these options, or another that you think of, and write notes on how the activity would be introduced and managed.

3.1.15 Commentary

There are several ways that can be and have been used to give pupils opportunities to demonstrate and think about the languages in their classroom. If well handled, all of them can stimulate and raise children's awareness. As suggested above, one way is to programme a 'languages day' or a 'languages lesson' each week for a period of time. As part of the day or lesson, one or two children with home languages and knowledge of languages that are different from the language of the school environment can be given the chance to 'teach' other children words or phrases in their language and can also show how these are written. If careful guidance and help with, for example, visual aids is given by the teacher, even 5 or 10 minutes can lead to a sense of achievement and recognition for the individuals doing the 'teaching', as well as raising the awareness of other students in the class. If they wish, students with other home languages could add something about their home culture, for example about food or music. Another option, especially in classes with many children with other language backgrounds, would be for children to prepare questions in order to 'interview' each other in pairs or groups about the languages they know, what they feel about them and what it is like to be bilingual or multilingual.

Several other ideas can be found in *Using Multilingual Approaches: Moving from Theory to Practice* (Heugh et al. 2019), which is a resource book intended for teachers in India and Africa, but which contains detailed plans of activities that may be relevant in many other contexts.

3.1.16 Task 9

When working on language points with individual students and with the whole group, it is useful to be aware of the differences in their language repertoires and language background.

- What means could you use to find out more about students' language repertoires in a lower secondary class including monolingual and plurilingual students?
- How might information about students' language repertoires be useful to you as a teacher and to teachers of other subjects?

3.1.17 Commentary

A good way of making students, as well as teachers, aware of their language competences and repertoires is through self-assessment. Even if they only know a few words in another language, students can be asked to assess their own skills in different languages on a scale from 'elementary' to 'good' or 'very good'. Depending on their age, more detail can be asked about their ability to speak, understand the spoken language and read and write in the languages concerned. Learners can also ask each other questions about the languages they know, how they learnt them and how well they know them, as well as reasons why they may want to acquire more competences. Simple home-made self-assessment tasks and materials can be developed to match the age and needs of students.

This information about the language repertoires of individual students can be an invaluable way of getting to know a class better and of being in a position to acknowledge their linguistic and cultural background. Where necessary, it is also useful when taking account of students' individual needs when they are using and developing their skills in the language of schooling. A class list that includes information about the linguistic repertoires of individual students is essential for teachers of all subjects if developing linguistic ability and responding to language needs are to be focused on across the curriculum. Some students are likely to need more support in certain areas, especially when dealing with 'academic' language in their reading and writing, and individualised help may be needed.

3.1.18 Summary

All users of a languages have an individual language 'repertoire', an ability to communicate in one or more languages and/or varieties of a language. A whole range of 'portfolio' solutions have been developed under the auspices of the Council of Europe to assist students and teachers with the assessment of linguistic ability across languages. Various education authorities, schools and other bodies have developed the portfolio concept to match the needs of their learners. More information about the European Language Portfolio scheme can be found at https://www.coe.int/en/web/portfolio. This kind of portfolio is relevant to learners whatever their level of competence in the languages they have some knowledge of. They are often used and updated by individual learners working autonomously and under teacher guidance for reflection and awareness raising. However, the 'language biography' section of the portfolio, which traditionally includes a summary of the user's 'plurilingual profile', a goal-setting section about what learners hope in the future to be able to do in the language and a section on intercultural awareness and experience, can also be usefully worked on in pairs or small groups.

A person's language repertoire is determined by various factors:

- Linguistic background, for example which language or languages are used in the home during childhood, and what variety of the language(s)
- The range of experience with the spoken and written language(s)
- The current level of literacy and oracy, as well as personality factors such as shyness.

The concept of 'repertoire' can also be applied to a person's first language. In this case, the breadth and depth of the repertoire determines how well the individual can manage in environments where speakers are using different regional or national varieties of the language (e.g. Scottish English, Indian English), where different levels of formality are needed (talking to elderly people, young people, presenting to work colleagues, interviews, etc.), and when different types of reading and writing are necessary (academic language, specialised instructions, formal letters, etc.).

One of the objectives of education, and one that concerns all teachers, not only teachers of language, is to broaden students' repertoire so that they are able to use language effectively in their general educational development and their learning in specific subject areas. This implies understanding the differences between 'informal' or 'conversational' language and 'academic' language. Little (2010) made the following distinctions:

> *First, from a cognitive point of view the distinction is not absolute and boundaries are often blurred. For example, social chat among friends is cognitively undemanding, but if in the course of such chat you try to persuade others of your point of view, the task may quickly become cognitively demanding. Conversely, classroom talk often includes passages of conversational as well as academic language. Secondly, the distinction does not refer to speaking on the one hand and writing on the other: some writing tasks use conversational language (e.g., e-mail, text-messaging), while academic language is a characteristic of much of the spoken communication that occurs in classrooms and other academic contexts.*
> (Little 2010, p. 19)

Certain characteristics mark out academic language as different from informal conversational language. These will be explored in more detail in Unit 4, but they include in particular the special vocabulary associated with different subject specialisms, differing discourse patterns (e.g. passive voice as in 'the liquid was heated' as opposed to 'we heated up the liquid'), and a range of verbs and expressions that can be used widely for academic purposes but are less common in informal language use, such as 'indicate', 'prove', 'is evidence that', 'contradicts' and 'seems that'.

The view of a language repertoire we have developed in this section goes beyond the numerous definitions such as the one quoted on page 57, which refer only or mainly to bilingualism or multilingualism, and is much closer to a sociolinguistic view, like the one proposed by Blommaert and Backus:

> *In early definitions, repertoires [were] seen as a triad of language resources, knowledge of language ('competence') and a community. Due to developments in the study of language competence and in the study of social organization, this triad can no longer remain intact. In a super-diversity context, mobile subjects engage with a broad variety of groups, networks and communities, and their language resources are consequently learned through a wide variety of trajectories, tactics and technologies, ranging from fully formal language*

learning to entirely informal 'encounters' with language. These different learning modes lead to very different degrees of knowledge of language, from very elaborate structural and pragmatic knowledge to elementary 'recognizing' languages, whereby all of these resources in a repertoire are functionally distributed in a patchwork of competences and skills [...].
(Blommaert & Backus 2011, p. 2)

This definition takes full account of the complexity involved in the development of a language repertoire in learners and teachers alike. At one end of the spectrum is the code-switching which migrant children have to cope with on a daily basis and at the other end is the need for learners to enter and master a whole range of increasingly specialised linguistic registers, subject by subject, at secondary level and in higher education. We have looked at how teachers can support and facilitate this process, and what that means in methodological terms. Teachers also need to be on the lookout for feedback from their learners, which may come in a variety of ways, to help them to develop their own repertoires in ways that better support learning.

We have seen that many students have also developed a 'plurilingual repertoire'—a range of competences in more than one language. This repertoire and the differences between their ability to use one of the languages as compared to others may depend on whether they were brought up in a different country, whether the language(s) spoken at home are different from the language of schooling, the purposes for which the different languages are used and so on. For example, a given student may be more proficient in reading and writing the language used in school but more confident in speaking in the language he or she has grown up with. The extent of teacher support given to the development of this plurilingual repertoire is certainly also a significant contributory factor.

3.1.19 *Questions for Reflection*

(a) What have you learned about your own language repertoire by completing Tasks 1 and 2?
(b) Many teachers have to contend with multilingual and multicultural classes, and it can be challenging. Based on your own experience, and also on what you learned from the tasks in this section, what opportunities and advantages can you see in working in such a context?
(c) What support (if any) is available to teachers in the same context to help them to diagnose and cater to the language needs of migrant students?

3.2 Section 2: Language and Subjects

This section looks at the challenges to students who are involved in developing their language repertoires in the various subjects in the school curriculum, especially as regards the understanding and use of different kinds of academic language.

3.2.1 Task 10

Read through the page below (Fig. 3.1) from a science textbook for secondary school students aged 11–14. How do the curriculum subject (science) and the specific topics (energy storage and transfer) influence the ways in which the language is used?

3.2.1 Energy adds up

Learning objectives

After this section you will be able to:
- use a model of energy transfer between stores to describe how jobs get done
- describe how the energy of an object depends on its speed, temperature, height, or whether it is stretched or compressed
- show how energy is transferred between energy stores in a range of real-life examples.

◀ Energy is a bit like money.

Do you have some money in your pocket? If you know how much you left home with and you didn't spend any on the way, then you know how much you have now.

Conservation of energy

Energy cannot just disappear, and you cannot end up with more than you had at the start. Energy cannot be created or destroyed, only transferred. This is the **law of conservation of energy**.

A State the law of conservation of energy.

Energy stores

There is energy associated with food and fuels (and oxygen). You can think of that energy as being in a **chemical energy store**. Energy is transferred from the store when you burn the fuel or respire. There are other types of energy store:

Energy to do with...	Type of energy store
food, fuels, batteries	chemical energy store
hot objects	thermal energy store
moving objects	kinetic energy store
position in a gravitational field	gravitational potential energy store
changing shape, stretching, or squashing	elastic energy store

Before and after

A camping stove burns gas, which is a fuel.

▲ Camping gas is a chemical store.

	Before:	After:
What we have	unburnt fuel, more oxygen	less fuel, more carbon dioxide and water
	cold soup	hot soup (and slightly hotter air)
Thinking about energy	more energy in the chemical energy store	less energy in the chemical energy store
	less energy in the thermal energy store	more energy in the thermal energy store

If you could measure the energy in the chemical and thermal energy stores you would see that:

total energy before = total energy after

B Name five types of energy store.

48

Fig. 3.1 Page from a UK science textbook (from Gardom Hulme et al. 2017, p.48)

In terms of vocabulary, grammar, tone, etc., how different is the language in the textbook from the oral language a teacher might use when teaching about the same topics?

3.2.2 Commentary

This extract from a science textbook illustrates some ways in which the characteristics of the language selected for learning activities in a textbook—instructions, informative texts, etc.—relate to the subject in question. In the science textbook, the page begins with the kind of question a teacher might ask (about money in the students' pockets), but the short explanations of energy conservation and energy stores are more technical in nature. Words like 'conservation', 'transfer', 'associated' and 'respire' (instead of 'breathe') are more 'academic' and challenging for many students, and the same is true of the distinctions between 'thermal', 'kinetic', 'gravitational' and elastic' in the tables. For this page in the book to be really useful as part of learning, a teacher would probably need first to introduce the topics and concepts, and then elicit and explore examples, and generally 'lift the information off the page'. The connection between energy and money in the pocket and the example of the camping stove give the teacher and students useful ideas to work with and build on. However, such a textbook page is likely to be most valuable as a complement to and extension of a teacher's work, for example when students go through it in group discussion or read it later.

3.2.3 Task 11

Figure 3.2 is a page from a history textbook for students of the same age. Compare it with the extract from the science textbook in Task 3.10. What differences and similarities do you notice in the nature of the language and the way it is used to communicate information? Which of these differences are due to the subjects in question (science and history), and which might be related to other factors such as the author's approach? What other factors might be involved?

Fig. 3.2 Page of a history textbook (from Wilkes 2014, p. 23)

3.2.4 Commentary

This sample shows that, as in spoken language used in the classroom, in written language there are opportunities to use radically different approaches. In this sample, labels such as 'FACT!', 'Hungry for more?' and 'Wise-up words' are used for information boxes, and labels are introduced into cartoon-like images. These devices and the dramatic language may help to motivate students and keep their attention focused on what might otherwise be rather dull information. The language used under the heading 'Poorly boy' is typical of a less academic written genre, albeit with gruesome detail that might appeal to youngsters of this age. Again, especially where the 'work' is concerned, the teacher's involvement in bringing alive the information on the page and interaction between students in pairs and groups would enhance learning. The 'obituary' task is a good example. Here students are asked to write something in what for them will be a new genre. The teacher may well want to show an example and point out some features of obituaries before asking students to start work on their own versions for Edward VI. It is also possible that doing the 'design' part of the task in pairs would provide opportunities for collaboration.

3.2.5 Task 12

How might teachers using these textbooks best introduce and build on the activities in their oral communication with the students? Choose one of the two samples and write some brief notes on:

- What the teacher might say, ask or discuss with students <u>before</u> asking them to open their books.
- What the teacher could do <u>after</u> their students have finished the textbook activities in order to consolidate or further students' learning.

3.2.6 Commentary

A caricature of unimaginative teaching might feature a teacher who greets the class and then says 'Open your books at page 42. You have 15 minutes to do exercises 3 and 4.' This is problematic in at least two ways. First, there is no effort to 'warm' students to the topic and to the learning objectives being focused on. Such warming up may well be crucial if they have just returned from a break or have recently finished a lesson on a completely different subject. Secondly, however well-illustrated and engagingly written, for some students printed words on the page or on a screen are more challenging to process than spoken language, so going straight to the textbook without any prior oral interaction about the objectives or the topic may be a disadvantage and even undermine learning.

Various ways can be used to help students ease into a new textbook unit or page. These include asking them to refer to and share their existing knowledge (about energy sources and storage in the one case, and Tudor England in the other), or introducing the topic by reference to a previous lesson, and/or explaining briefly what the unit contains and what students will be expected to do. Additionally, when the students first look at the unit there are opportunities to point out key elements, check their understanding of instructions or deal with difficult vocabulary and so on.

After doing one or a series of textbook activities, or while checking responses, it is important that students are invited to show what they have learned by giving additional examples and expanding on what they have read. They can also be given opportunities to ask questions, seek clarification and give feedback on how interesting, difficult, etc. the activity was, which may help the teacher to plan future lessons.

3.2.7 Task 13

The transcript below is of group discussion among 14- and 15-year-old students preparing a science experiment in the form of a game about electricity using light and sound. They are discussing how to write instructions and 'teach' the concept of the electrical circuit to younger students aged 9–10 (in a later session). Read through the transcript and note down the following:

(a) Some specific features of the language that relate to the subject they are talking about and the activity they are preparing.
(b) Some examples of where, judging by the language they are using, you think students are 'learning' from each other, or learning collaboratively with each other.
(c) *Mark (M): We have to say something about this wire stuff.*
(d) *Peter (P): Yeah ... it's bent to make it harder ...*
(e) *Joanna (J): No, it's about circuits. We need to tell them to watch out for the buzzer ....*
(f) *Susie (S): We can show them ... what to do ...*
(g) *P: I can do it really well ... look (he performs the game)*
(h) *J: Stop mucking about ... if you do it right all the time, they won't know about the buzzer ...*
(i) *P: Bzzz*
(j) *M: if we show them once then break the circuit, we can show them what the battery does ... how it makes it ...*
(k) *P: ... makes it buzz. The circuit makes it buzz*
(l) *S: it's not just the circuit—it's the electricity in the circuit. It's really important that they know that. And the way the source of electricity is conducted ... but I think they'll know that batteries are the source of electricity ...*
(m) *J: the two work together ... they give a flow of energy and power which illuminate the light bulb. You pass the flow of charge through the wire ...*
(n) *P: Yeah ... I've got it ... it's the flow of energy.* (from Nicholson 1999, p. 30)

3.2.8 Commentary

Here the focus is on the language used by a group of four students preparing for a science project, and specifically on the ways in which students collaborate to develop or confirm their understanding and to reach conclusions. It highlights some differences between textbook language and students' free use of spoken language during discussion in a small group, and also between group discussion and the usually much more restricted spoken language used by students during 'plenary' teaching of a whole class. In the transcript, there are clear examples of students using specialised language such as *'buzzer'*, *'break the circuit'*, *'flow of energy and power'*, and there are also instances where they react to one another's ideas, for example: *'P: "… makes it buzz. The circuit makes it buzz." S: " It's not just the circuit—it's the electricity in the circuit"'* is a good example of a student picking up and building on another students' remark.

3.2.9 Summary

Teaching language and learning language are not always oral: textbooks, worksheets, online or projected learning materials and tests and examinations play a considerable role in the learning and assessment of students. It is extremely important that the language used in instructions, tasks and other content in these materials and in the worksheets prepared by teachers is written in such a way as to facilitate learning—and to reduce the need to teachers to give lengthy supplementary explanations. As writers of textbooks and digital materials for any subject and the teachers who use them know very well, it is not a simple matter to ensure that all instructions, tasks and exercises are clear and easy to understand and can be used as efficient and effective means of supporting learning, Clarity is also especially important in examinations and tests, where poorly written instructions and the way tasks are worded can discriminate against certain kinds of students.

The implication for teachers of all subjects and others involved in selecting and creating learning materials in schools is that each publication, especially those that are being considered for future adoption, should be carefully reviewed not just for its attractiveness and coverage of curriculum objectives but also for the clarity and simplicity of the language used in instructions, guidance and learning activities. During the selection process, the language repertoires of the students and the potential role of the materials in enhancing these repertoires need to be borne in mind. In addition, the skill of preparing 'home-made' handouts, other digital materials and tests for the classroom with clear and easy-to-follow instructions is one that all teachers need to acquire. Having an internal system of 'quality control' for such resources and reflecting after each lesson on the effectiveness or otherwise of such instructions and tasks are ways of helping to develop this skill.

Whatever written resources are used, an essential part of teaching is the ability to engage students' attention by leading into and introducing the resource in a way that highlights its relevance to what is being learned and helps students to understand instructions, layout and unfamiliar terms. Equally important are the ways in which the teacher can build on what is in the written resource, relate it to students' experience and prior learning and encourage students to take their learning beyond what is 'in the book'.

3.2.10 Questions for Reflection

(a) Think of some really effective textbook or teacher-produced material that you have used in class as a teacher or student. What main features of the language, layout and other content made it a useful aid to teaching and learning?
(b) In your experience, what are the best ways of handling new terms or difficult vocabulary related to a subject, such as science, geography or language itself that comes up in a lesson? How can a teacher try to ensure that all students understand the new term?

3.3 Section 3: Scaffolding

3.3.1 Task 14

In building and building repairs, scaffolding is often used to enable builders to reach the upper storeys and roof of a house or other construction, thus supporting the building or repairs process. Read this explanation of the term 'scaffolding' as used in teaching and supporting learning.

> *The metaphor of scaffolding has been widely used in recent years to argue that, in the same way that builders provide essential but temporary support, teachers need to provide temporary supporting structures that will assist learners to develop new understandings, new concepts, and new abilities. As the learner develops control of these, so teachers need to withdraw that support, [and] only to provide further support for extended or new tasks, understandings and concepts.* (Hammond and Gibbons 2001, pp. 1-2)

Look at Table 3.4, which lists some learning situations in which 'scaffolding' would commonly be provided. What linguistic and non-linguistic forms might the scaffolding take?

Table 3.4 Situations where scaffolding may be useful

Situation	Scaffolding that might be provided
1. Learning to ride a bicycle	
2. Learning to write the letters of the alphabet	
3. Learning to work out the area of a circle	
4. Understanding the relationship between magnetism and electricity	
5. Understanding the causes of the French revolution	
6. Learning how to write an essay about the arguments for and against prisons	

3.3.2 Commentary

Each situation may call for quite different types of support. In the first, apart from encouragement and advice about balance and use of brakes, there may well be physical support to begin with in the form of stabilising wheels or a hand on the saddle. In the second case, demonstration or stencils of the letters of the alphabet that can be used for tracing are likely to be more useful than words, and in both cases feedback in the form of encouragement and further guidance will be important. In the third and fourth examples involving children at a later age, prior learning could be drawn on through questioning, and visual demonstration is more or less essential. In 3, a step-by-step approach is needed since an understanding of terms like 'circumference', 'radius' and 'diameter' is necessary, as well as an introduction of the new concept of 'pi' to describe the ratio of circumference to diameter. Together with spoken language and prompts, using and drawing visuals, and getting students themselves to use visuals, is essential. In 4, depending on their age, students will know something about electricity and magnetism as separate phenomena, but interest will need to be stimulated in the relationship between the two, which some students may have ideas about. Live or video demonstrations can provide means of eliciting ideas from students about the relationship between electricity and magnetism and stimulating further suggested experiments or examples. In both, teachers are likely to use textbooks as a means of clarifying concepts and to provide back-up, and as we saw in the previous section, textbooks themselves often provide forms of scaffolding. In case 5, by contrast, scaffolding is most likely to focus on developing an understanding of social conditions and the class system in eighteenth-century France through use of documents and images, and of how a mass movement could be set in train through political action, even without the aid of mass media. Scaffolding might involve comparison between the likely causes of the French Revolution and those underlying the later Mexican or Russian revolutions. Again, a well-designed textbook and suggested reading may be useful, especially as these can extend learning into autonomous homework for preparatory or follow-up purposes. In the last case, the focus of scaffolding is most likely to be on the style and organisation of the specific genre of the 'for and against' essay. Here, getting students to identify and explain the features of some sample essays on other topics may well be advantageous, as would an oral discussion of the advantages and disadvantages of prisons in the form of a short debate. More complex learning situations such as this are more and more likely to require scaffolding through language rather than by visual or other non-verbal means.

In an early work on scaffolding several elements were identified:

- getting the learner interested in the task and topic
- simplifying or 'reducing' the scope of the task
- keeping the learners focused on the task so they are not distracted
- highlighting the most important points or steps
- limiting learners' frustration, especially when they are having difficulty

- if necessary, demonstrating or modelling what needs to be done so that learners can imitate it. (adapted from Woods et al. 1976, p. 98).

3.3.3 Task 15

Look at the following exchanges. How is the adult or teacher using language to help the child or student progress in their learning? What are the main differences between the kinds of scaffolding used in each?

(a) (A young child is trying to put different shaped pieces through the right holes in the top of a box)
   Parent: *Does the yellow one fit in that hole, Ellie? Which hole is like a star?*
   Young child: (looks at the shape and the holes and points): *Star—yellow ...*
   Parent: *Yes, that hole is like a star, isn't it? Good girl! Pop it in. And the green one? ...*

(b) Teacher: *What's a good word for someone who refuses to change their mind or their behaviour?*
   Student: *Pig-headed? My mum calls me that.*
   Teacher: *It's quite a good expression, but I wouldn't use it in history homework. Who can think of another word beginning with 'o', 'ob'?*
   Students (together) *Obstinate!*
   Teacher: *Yes, 'obstinate'. How do you spell it, Jordi?*

(c) Teacher: *Look at the pictures on the screen. Do frogs and snakes belong to the same family of animals? What do you think, Nell?*
   Nell: *I'm not sure. Frogs like being in the water and some snakes do too.*
   Teacher: *OK, what do we call animals that can live in water and also out of the water?*
   Mikey: *Amphibans? I think frogs are amphibans.*
   Teacher: *'Yes, amphibians'* (emphasising the pronunciation and writing it on the board)—*what do you think, Nell?*
   Nell: *Yes, frogs are amphibians, like toads?*
   Teacher: *Yes, toads are similar, aren't they. What about snakes or lizards, or crocodiles? Crocodiles can stay in the water a long time too. In the close-up pictures can you see any differences between the skin of the crocodile or snake and the skin of the frog and the toad?*
   Alice: *The snake and crocodile have like scaly skin, but the frog doesn't?*
   Teacher: *Yes, reptiles have scales on their bodies, but amphibians don't. How would you describe the skin of amphibians like frogs?*

(d) Teacher: (looking at jars of crystals on a shelf) *OK, well done. The experiment you did last week to grow crystals worked very well. Some of them look beautiful! And in your groups, you've discussed how you did it. Now we need to write up the experiment in more formal scientific language. Can anyone give me some words or expressions you could use in the report?*

Amy: *'Solution? Saline solution'?*
Teacher: *What do you mean by 'saline'?* (she writes 'saline' on the board).
Amy: *Mixed with salt?*
Teacher: *OK. You said, "we poured lots of salt into warm water". How would you express that in a more formal written description of the experiment? What would you need to change?*
Ricardo: *Get rid of 'we' to make it more impersonal? and maybe 'lots'?*
Teacher: *But how can you get rid of 'we'?*
Isabel: *We could write: "A large quantity of salt was poured into warm water"?*
Teacher: *What do others think?*
Jake: *Yes, that's good, and we could add some more detail: "half a litre of water was heated and put into a glass container"—something like that?*
Teacher: *Wow, that's pretty good, Jake. Do you know the grammatical name for that kind of sentence?*
Chloe: *I think it's 'passive', whereas 'we poured ...' is 'active'?*
Teacher: *That's right, we call it 'passive voice'. In pairs, can you give me some more examples of sentences in the passive that could go in this written description of your experiment.*

3.3.4 Commentary

These exchanges exemplify the kinds of language that is used to help a child or students with a task, but usually language is combined with other scaffolding support that refers back to existing previous knowledge. The small child in a) knows at least some colour words and shapes, and in b), the teacher uses a sound to prompt students to come up with the less familiar word 'obstinate'. In c), pictures are used to elicit a contrast between reptiles and amphibians, but the students were first prompted to name some examples. Mikey at least almost knows the word 'amphibian', and Nell can offer a couple of examples. This shows how students themselves participate in the scaffolding process for their peers. The more complex scaffolding in d) shows how, by gently guiding students to identify and exemplify differences between informal spoken language and more formal written language, a teacher can encourage students, led by one or two more adventurous ones, to gradually come to their own conclusions about how a written report on an experiment might differ from an oral description.

Vygotsky's well-known concept of the 'zone of proximal development' (ZPD—Vygotsky 1978) encapsulates an important aspect of his views on learning. Paraphrasing Vygotsky's own words, the 'zone of proximal development' is the 'distance' between the current actual cognitive developmental level of a person as shown by the way they might solve a problem, such as the difference between shapes or between amphibians and reptiles, on their own, and the level of cognitive development that they can potentially achieve when an adult or a capable peer guides them in solving a problem through some means of scaffolding. The interactions in Task 15 offer simple examples of the role of scaffolding. Scaffolding by parents, teachers and peers supports the theory of social and educational constructivism which derives from the work of educational psychologists like Vygotsky of the mid-twentieth century. This scaffolding helps children or students to bridge the gap between their current level of cognitive development and the next step and to 'construct' their new learning. It is, however, important to note that in a class of 25 or 30 students, the current level of development may vary considerably from student to student. For example, one or two may know the term 'passive voice' or 'amphibian' and be able to provide examples, but others may not. Unlike a parent working or playing with one child, the challenge for teachers is to be able to adjust the level of scaffolding and the complexity of language according to individual as well as collective needs and to find various means of bridging the gaps that may exist.

3.3.5 Task 16

In the following transcript, a teacher was working with 8–9-year-old children. They have been reading the poem in Fig. 3.3.

Which interventions by the teacher can be described as 'scaffolding' in that they help the children to understand the description of the eagle and the metaphors the poem contains? (Note: S refers to different unnamed students.)

1. *T: what was the poem about?*
2. *S: an eagle*
3. *T: OK, and what kind of animal is an eagle? Big, small …?*
4. *S2: it's a bird—quite big. I've seen one in the zoo.*
5. *T: and where is this eagle? What kind of place is a 'crag'?*
6. *S3: part of a mountain?*
7. *T: yes, but this one is next to the sea, so ….*
8. *S3: like a cliff?*
9. *T: Yes, like that. Do we know if it's a high or low crag?*
10. *S4: I think it's quite high because it's close to the sun.*
11. *T: what do you think Jenny? What does 'ringed with the azure world' mean?*

Fig. 3.3 The Eagle by Alfred Lord Tennyson (1809–1892)

The Eagle

He clasps the crag with crooked hands;
Close to the sun in lonely lands,
Ringed with the azure world, he stands.

The wrinkled sea beneath him crawls;
He watches from his mountain walls,
And like a thunderbolt he falls.

12. S5: *Yes, high: 'ringed'—like he can see all around him. What's 'azure'?*
13. T: *What kind of word is it? Noun, adjective ....?*
14. S5: *must be an adjective describing the world? Like a colour?*
15. S6: *'azul' in Spanish is blue.*
16. T: *I didn't know that, Jaime, but you're right. 'Azure' is a poetic word for blue. Is there anything in the poem that makes the eagle sound a bit human?*
17. S1: *yes, 'he' and 'him'... and 'stands'*
18. S3: *why couldn't it be 'she' and 'her'?*
19. T: *good question Rosie—it could be. But 'stands'? Does that make the eagle sound human? Any other words that make him or her sound human?*
20. S7: *I think lots of birds and animals stand if they have legs and feet. But 'hands'—birds don't have hands, they have claws.*
21. T: *do you agree with Nell? What about 'stands' and 'hands'?*
22. S6: *yes, lots of animal stand. But birds don't have 'hands', but they can hold onto a branch or a rock like we can*
23. T: *the poet doesn't say 'hold on' though—he says ....*
24. S6: *'clasp'*
25. T: *Yes. Listen again: 'He clasps the crag with crooked hands'. What do you notice about that line?*
26. S8: *lots of words with 'c'.*
27. T: *Yes, we talked about that last week. Do you remember?*
28. S5: *'alliteration'?*
29. T: *well done, Jenny.*

3.3.6 Commentary

This longer transcript provides a good example of how the scaffolding provided during the lesson gently moves students, who have almost certainly not actually seen an eagle on a rock, from their unclear view of the bird to a clearer idea of the poet's description and to some understanding of how certain poetry works. The teacher brings up one aspect—the human-like characteristics of the eagle—to stimulate students' thinking, but one response is not quite on the right track: 'he stands ...'. The teacher's response isn't a flat rejection but instead a question to make the children think. She then responds to students' contributions by guiding them further. For example, in a follow-up to 'hold', the teacher asks what other less common word the poet uses, and then goes on to the question of poetic language and the term 'alliteration'.

Even at this simple level, providing scaffolding can be a gradual and quite lengthy process, and it also needs to be followed up in some way so that students consolidate the learning they have achieved. For example, it may be useful to come back to this poem in a later lesson and to ask students again the meaning of certain new words, like 'crag' and 'clasp', or to ask them to rewrite it in more modern language, to give more examples of alliteration, etc., and eventually to write a short poem of their own about an animal or bird.

3.3.7 Task 17

Scaffolding can be constructed <u>before</u> the building of a house starts, but as in Task 16, it can also be added piece by piece as the building grows and new elements are added (or old elements, like the roof, are repaired). Imagine that a different teacher using the same poem decides to plan scaffolding work before introducing it to the children. What activities, tasks, visual aids or other resources might she use?

3.3.8 Commentary

In Task 16, the teacher provided scaffolding as the children needed it, or at moments when she believed it was necessary. Instead of doing this, or in addition to doing this, she could have prepared some materials and tasks for the children to do beforehand. The most obvious aid to understanding might be a photo or picture of an eagle standing on a high rock. The children might be asked, for example, first to work in groups to describe the picture focusing on questions like:

– What kind of bird is it? Do you know any other birds of this kind?
– What food do birds like this eat?
– Why is it standing on that rock?
– How big is it compared to garden birds?
– Describe its feet, its beak, its feathers. And so on.

A similar rather more demanding task might be the preparation of small group project to produce a poster about a birds-of-prey in which children share the knowledge they have, do a little research and find or draw pictures of eagles.

Another possibility is a vocabulary-building activity. The children in pairs or small groups could be asked to think of or find words that describe different ways of holding, such as 'hang onto', 'grip' and 'grasp'. They may also find 'clasp', but if not, it can be added to the list and demonstrated with body language. A similar activity could be done with words that describe different kinds of rock such as 'cliff', 'boulder', 'granite' and eventually 'crag'. The reason for doing this before the children read or listen to the poem is to make it easier for them to understand. There is, however, an argument for doing the vocabulary exercise without introducing 'clasp' in one case or 'crag' in the other: students could be asked to guess the meaning of words they don't know, or they could be asked to find yet another word for 'hold' (or 'cliff') in the poem. In this case, the vocabulary building will potentially have provided hints for working out the meaning of a new word from the content of the poem.

Another part of preliminary scaffolding might focus on the form of the poem. The children have probably already done some work on rhymes and could be asked to find words that rhyme with 'land' or 'wall'. The idea of alliteration might be introduced with reference to another poem, and they could be asked to invent some examples of alliteration in pairs.

Such activities are ways of building or designing scaffolding into learning before the main focus of learning is introduced to ease comprehension. This does not exclude also providing scaffolding as it is needed during a task or the reading of a text. The decision as to whether scaffolding should be designed in beforehand or provided 'at point of need' during an activity, or both, will depend on the level of unfamiliarity of the text and task in relation to what the teacher knows about the students' language and literacy repertoires.

3.4 Task 18

In the lesson extract below, the teacher working with 12- and 13-year-old students is helping them to understand how historical enquiry works by comparing the role of a historian with that of a detective searching for clues after a serious incident, in this case a fatal car crash.

Sharpe (2001) cites a distinction made between three different types of scaffolding used at 'points of need':

(a) <u>Repetition</u> of what a student says (example: 'educated guesses' at 2)
(b) Acknowledging a student's remark <u>and then modifying it</u> so that it is more technically appropriate (e.g. 'computer reconstruction' at 6)
(c) <u>Transforming the information</u> offered by the students: the teacher takes up the idea behind the student's remark and 'offers it back' in a more contextually appropriate way. (e.g. 'scene of the crime' at 5)

Identify some other examples of these three kinds of scaffolding by placing a), b) or c) after the teacher's words where appropriate.

1. *TEACHER (T): So let's think about how the police might deal with a serious or fatal road accident like the one described in the newspaper article and compare that with how a historian works on events that happened many years or even centuries ago.*
   A STUDENT (S): Um, they try to work out what happened; they could have, like, educated guesses.
2. *T: Educated guesses. How do they make educated guesses? What do they do?*
   S. Maybe they make a note of the names of people who saw it and try to work things out, like ...
3. *T: OK. They talk to witnesses or read their statements and they look for what they call collaborative evidence. What else do they use other than collaborative evidence?*

S: ... look in the car, at the skid marks or anything it hit.
4. T: They look at objects.
   S: They examine ...
5. T: They examine, let's call it, the scene of the crime. OK. How do they do that? they look at the car. So why are they looking at the car? What do they use?
   S: Um, computers.
6. T: Yeah, they could make a computer reconstruction from what witnesses say to work out what happened, how fast the car was going, who ....
   S: How it happened
7. T: What else? Who does this kind of work?
   S: Police scientists
8. T: Police scientists, yes, or forensic experts
   S: They hypothesise
9. T: They hypothesise, yes. and what other evidence might they use?
   S: They could check CCTVs [recordings from video cameras on roads]
10. T: Yes, they could look at CCTV footage. What other forensic evidence ... what else?
    S: Fingerprints? Blood samples? (examples of scaffolding are adapted from Sharpe 2001)

3.4.1 Commentary

This more complex example shows some of the linguistic means, apart from questions and prompts, that teachers can use when offering scaffolding. Other instances of the three types of scaffolding:

- Repeating: 'examine' at 5; 'hypothesise' at 9
- Modifying: 'objects' at 4; 'forensic scientist, forensic experts' at 8
- Transforming: '... they look for what they call collaborative evidence' at 3; 'look at CCTV footage' and 'forensic evidence' at 10.

3.4.2 Task 19

As we saw in Tasks 10 and 11, scaffolding is also often 'designed into' textbooks and is also a feature of many teachers' self-made materials as well as of Internet help pages. The scaffolding provides a means of helping people to process written texts containing new or less familiar concepts and to carry out tasks and activities related to them. Look at the following section of an article from wikiHow (Fig. 3.4). List three examples of scaffolding which is provided to help readers to focus on specific points.

3.4 Task 18

HOW TO SEARCH THE INTERNET
part 1: starting your web-search

1. <u>Go to a search engine</u>. A search engine is a website that collects and organizes information on the internet and makes it available for searching. Search engines use algorithms to display the most relevant search results based on trends, your location, and sometimes even your web activity. Many search engines have their own mobile apps that make searching easier on your phone or tablet. [...]

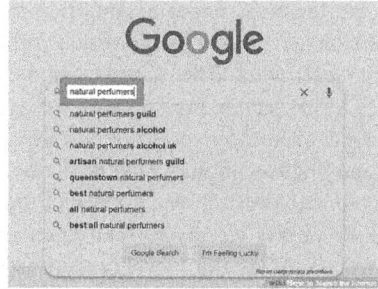

2. <u>Type what you're looking for into the search bar</u>. You'll find the search bar at the top of most search engines. You can enter a single word, a sentence, a phrase, some numbers, or anything else you wish.
   • If you're searching for a multi-word phrase, surround it in quotation marks so the search engine knows to keep those words together. For example, "natural perfumers", "Trader Joe's dried mangos".
   • Sometimes it's helpful to phrase your search like a question, such as What is Cardi B's real name?, What was James Baldwin's last book?, or Is there a vegan Chinese restaurant in Portland?

3. <u>Press the ↵ Enter or ⏎ Return key to run your search</u>. This displays your search results in a list. If you're using a smartphone or tablet, you may have to tap Search or Go instead.

4. <u>click or tap a result to view it</u>. If you've found a website that looks like what you want, click or tap it to open in your browser. To go back to the search results, click or tap your browser's back button.

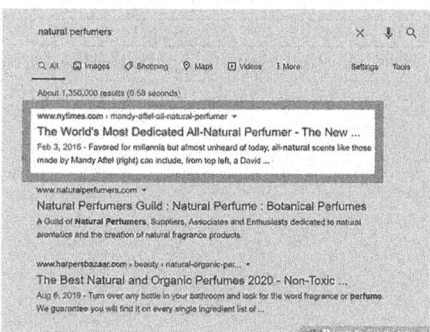

The results display differently depending on what you're looking for. For example, if you searched for the word "weather" in Google or Bing, you'll see a weather chart with the local conditions at the top of your results. If you scroll down a little, you'll probably see some news articles about the weather, as well as links to popular weather websites. If you search for an address or location, you'll usually see a map and/or information about the business or landmark.
If you scroll down through the first page and don't find what you're looking for, click or tap the next page number or Next at the bottom to view the next set of results.
The best results are often on the first page, but sometimes you'll need to dig a little deeper to find that magic result.

Fig. 3.4 How to search the Internet (from an article by Nicky Levine MFA provided by wikiHow) (a wiki building the world's largest, highest quality how-to manual. Please edit this article and find author credits at wikiHow.com. Content on wikiHow can be shared under a Creative Commons License)

3.4.3 Commentary

It is likely that the first thing readers will notice on this page is the images. These are designed mainly to clarify what Google pages look like for people who are not used to searching the Internet, such as students starting to use a computer and elderly people who may be just beginning their Internet journey. The images are perhaps more familiar and less engaging than the textbook pages exemplified in Section 2. They do, however, support the structure and content of the guidance with its four subsections which are, almost literally, scaffolded. The subsections are clearly numbered, and the first introduces the key term 'search engine', which may already be known to readers but not fully understood, and readers may not be aware, for example, of how search engines use trends and your location. At the next step, the process of starting a search is exemplified, again with illustrations, not just of the search engine but also of a keyboard or keypad. Examples are given of alternative ways of searching that may lead to more useful results. At the third level readers are given examples of the kinds of results that the search engine may offer, and then, lastly, information about how search results may differ depending on what you are searching for, and advice about how to find the most useful result for your purposes. These illustrations, clearly labelled steps and examples, all offer support to the reader, as well as some encouragement to start experimenting with searching the Internet.

3.4.4 Task 20

Read the paragraph from Charles Darwin's *On the Origin of Species* (Fig. 3.5). Imagine that, at the beginning of a series of biology lessons for 13- and 14-year-old students, you wish to introduce them to Darwin's ground-breaking work. What steps could you take <u>before</u> asking students to read these paragraphs to make the text easier for them to read and understand? What other steps might be useful during or after a first reading?

3.4 Task 18

> "To sum up the circumstances favourable and unfavourable to natural selection, as far as the extreme intricacy of the subject permits: I conclude, looking to the future, that for terrestrial productions a large continental area, which will probably undergo many oscillations of level, and which consequently will exist for long periods in a broken condition, will be the most favourable for the production of many new forms of life, likely to endure long and to spread widely. For the area will first have existed as a continent, and the inhabitants, at this period numerous in individuals and kinds, will have been subjected to very severe competition. When converted by subsidence into large separate islands, there will still exist many individuals of the same species on each island: intercrossing on the confines of the range of each species will thus be checked: after physical changes of any kind, immigration will be prevented, so that new places in the polity of each island will have to be filled up by modifications of the old inhabitants; and time will be allowed for the varieties in each to become well modified and perfected. When, by renewed elevation, the islands shall be re-converted into a continental area, there will again be severe competition: the most favoured or improved varieties will be enabled to spread: there will be much extinction of the less improved forms, and the relative proportional numbers of the various inhabitants of the renewed continent will again be changed; and again there will be a fair field for natural selection to improve still further the inhabitants, and thus produce new species.
>
> From *On the Origin of Species by Means of Natural Selection*, chapter 4, by Charles Darwin (first published in 1859)

Fig. 3.5 A challenging text

3.4.5 *Commentary*

Scientific texts in general, whether written recently or many years ago, can be a challenge for young students. There are, however, good reasons why they should be asked to read and try to make sense of them, whether to gain a better understanding of a key concept, such as natural selection in this case, or to increase their awareness of how scientific breakthroughs and discoveries are made, or to improve their own sensitivity to different kinds of language.

For students with differing language and literacy repertoires, a text like this can be made easier to read and understand through preparatory 'designed-in' scaffolding. This need not—should not—involve explaining the concept being focused on but rather should focus on easing students into the text. Some options include:

(a) Tapping into prior knowledge: students are likely to have heard Darwin's name, and they may know about his voyage in the ship called 'the Beagle' to collect fossils of different species. They could be asked to find out more or to mention at least one of his theories.
(b) Pre-teaching certain vocabulary that may be unfamiliar to students: this can usefully involve students in groups trying to work out for themselves the meanings of terms and their relationship to one another, their connotations, etc. Here words like 'species' (a key biological term), 'intricacy', 'oscillations', 'terrestrial', 'renewed elevation' and several others call for some preparatory work.
(c) Headings: you could divide up the text into more paragraphs and introduce headings to help student orientate themselves. The text is near the end of this

section of the book, but it still falls into progressive topic areas, such as 'evolution in a large continental area', 'the effects of geological change on evolution' and 'competition of species'.
(d) Getting student to identify and highlight topic sentences or main clauses while they read may also be helpful. Examples include *'I conclude ... that for terrestrial productions a large continental area ...., will be the most favourable for the production of many new forms of life, likely to endure long and to spread widely'* and *'the inhabitants, at this period numerous in individuals and kinds, will have been subjected to very severe competition'*. This may be tricky, given the number of subordinate clauses in some sentences, so another useful exercise might involve asking students to break up long sentences into shorter ones without so many subordinate clauses.
(e) With a text written many years ago, it may be worthwhile and necessary to discuss how the language—in this case, the written language—has changed. Students are probably already familiar with the way science textbooks present information. After a first reading, they could be asked to discuss why, in this extract, sentences are so long, and the first person is sometimes used, or to pick out words and usage that they consider 'old-fashioned', such as 'polity', 'many will exclaim' and 'the islands shall be reconverted'.

This kind of scaffolding is sometimes called 'easification'. This is a way of making a text more accessible to students so that they can derive more insights and learning from it, and so that it can be used more effectively as a springboard for further learning.

3.4.6 Summary

The examples offered in these tasks illustrate the importance of scaffolding as part of the mediation work which teachers do in classroom interaction, although it shouldn't be forgotten that when working in small groups and pairs, students can also provide scaffolding for their peers, as was seen in some of the tasks in Unit 2 and in Task 13 in this unit. As is clear from Task 19, scaffolding is also often used by people writing self-help guidance, for example on the Internet, and by textbook writers as a means of smoothing students' progress through the material contained in textbooks, especially when students are working autonomously for example on homework tasks.

As Sharpe (2001, p. 32), among others, pointed out, a distinction can be made between scaffolding that is 'designed in' as part of planning a lesson or a teaching module or material, and 'point of need' scaffolding used by teachers in an adaptive way as part of their teaching or follow-up to a learning task. In both cases, depending on the subject and the learning aims, a wide variety of linguistic and non-linguistic means of providing scaffolding is available to teachers. However, whether designed in or provided at point of need, effective use of scaffolding depends on the ability to select the most appropriate means of responding to the needs of the students, including individual students, at a given time, and following up the scaffolded learning task with an intervention or further work which confirms the progress in learning achieved with teacher support.

3.4.7 *Questions for Reflection*

(a) Thinking of your own practice as a teacher and your own subject area, or your experiences as a student, what scaffolding techniques have you found most effective?
(b) What guidance would you offer to a novice teacher about how and when to use scaffolding, and how to follow it up?

3.5 Section 4: The Impact of 'Teaching' Language and Questions on Learning and Language Development

As we saw in Unit 2, some teaching language is focused mainly on encouraging learning, while some is intended mainly to organise and control events in the lesson. In this section, the focus is on questions and other forms of teacher communication that aim to help students learn.

3.5.1 *Task 21*

Read the brief transcript below from the beginning of a biology class for 11- and 12-year-olds. The teacher is standing beside a large diagram of human head and chest.

T: *Do you remember what we were discussing last lesson? Julian?*
S: *Breathing*
T: *yes, what parts of the body are involved in breathing, Sally?*
S. *The nose and mouth*
T: *OK Anything else? Habib?*
S: *the lungs?*
T: *Yes, the lungs. Cathy, how does air get to the lungs from the nose or mouth? What do we call these tubes?*
S: *the bronchii?*
T: *Yes, or the bronchial tubes. And why do we need to breathe?*
SS. *To stay alive (laughter)*
T: *OK, you need to breathe in order to live. Why? What happens in the lungs?*

- How does the teacher use questions in this first part of the lesson?
- How effective do you think her questions are in helping students to remember?

3.5.2 Commentary

This task examines one way in which teachers' questions typically work as mediation in classroom teaching. In this transcript, the teacher is checking whether her students know from their previous lesson how human breathing works and which organs are involved. These are not the kinds of questions normally used in social interaction because she knows the answers, but this is probably the most frequent use of questions by teachers and is also a kind often used by parents with their children. The teacher also evaluates the answers because she wants to encourage the students.

The process is efficient—the teacher asks and gets answers to about six questions in a short time—and there is variation between the different questions, but from an outside perspective the procedure might be seen as rushed, and there is little other interaction apart from questions and answers. However, the rationale for asking this kind of question in this rapid-fire way is first to focus students' attention on the topic of the lesson and, second, to remind them of what they already know/have learned. Within the short period the teacher nevertheless manages to nominate at least four students, vary her questions and ask a rather more challenging follow-up question.

3.5.3 Task 22

A comparison is often drawn between 'closed' questions, for which there is a clear and short answer, and 'open questions', which require thinking about, often as preparation for a more complex answer that can stimulate learning. In education, there is a contrast between questions which the teacher knows the answer to and which are asked to check learning (category 1), and those that are 'genuine' questions that ask students for information or opinions that the teacher does not yet know about (category 2).

Which of the following questions are in which category?

(a) Which planet is nearest to the sun?
(b) Why are you more interested in Mars than in Venus, Hugo?
(c) Can you work out which planet is shown in this photo?
(d) Why do you think some people believe that there is life in other parts of the galaxy?
(e) What is a 'light year'? Can you give me an example of how it is used as a measurement?
(f) What did we learn yesterday about black holes in galaxies?
(g) When was Neptune discovered?
(h) Why do you think it took so long for scientists to realise that the earth orbits the sun, and not the other way around?
(i) How did you come to be interested in astrology, Marianne?
(j) What did you use to watch the eclipse of the sun?

3.5.4 Commentary

This task draws the distinction between the kind of question asked in Task 21, 'closed' questions to which the answer is already known (at least by the teacher), and other questions used by teachers, as well as in normal interaction outside educational settings, where the questioner wants to obtain information or an opinion. The questions at b, d, h, i and j are clearly in this category, even though in one or two cases the teacher may have a certain kind of answer in mind, as in d and h. One or two other examples are not so clear. For example, in c, does the teacher know which planet is depicted in the photo, or is it a completely open question which students (and the teacher) may need to research?

3.5.5 Task 23

Questioning is a very widely used and important part of any teacher's repertoire since questions can serve such a wide range of purposes in education. In their book *Teaching, Questioning and Learning*, Morgan and Saxton identified three main functions of teacher questions:

(a) Questions *'which elicit information ... which draw out what is already known ... and establish appropriate procedures for the conduct of the work.'*
(b) Questions *'which shape understanding ... that help teachers and students fill in what lies between the facts and sort out ... how they are thinking about the material.'*
(c) Questions *'which press for reflection ... which demand intellectual and emotional commitment by challenging [the student] to think critically and creatively'*. (Morgan and Saxton 1991:41)

Look at the following questions and categorise them as a, b or c.

1. "There is a big difference between 'vegetarian', which we discussed yesterday, and 'vegan', which, as we just saw, is also often mentioned in restaurant menus. Who can tell me what the difference is, and why a person would choose to be a vegan rather than a vegetarian?"
2. "What did we learn about the nature of tectonic plates last week? George, can you remind us?"
3. "Do you remember how to calculate the area of a right-angled triangle?"
4. "Some people believe religious education should be banned in state schools, while others believe it is an important part of the curriculum. What do you think? Can you discuss the question in pairs for 10 minutes."
5. "Imagine this scenario: you are walking down a street and suddenly you hear some youngsters racially abusing a Muslim woman who is wearing a burqa, a complete veil. Would you walk on, or would you intervene in some way? Explain why."

6. *"We worked quite a bit on impressionist art last term, and we talked about the style of painting of various famous impressionists. This week we have been looking at and discussion the meaning of some well know expressionist paintings. What are the main differences between expressionism and impressionism?"*
7. *"OK, what are the main things we need to remember when writing a CV for a job application? Claire, can you start."*
8. *"Some people call themselves 'citizens of the world' rather than mentioning their nationality or cultural background. What do you think they mean by such a phrase? Do you see yourselves as a citizen of the world?"*
9. *"If you had to choose one book or film or piece of music to take with to a desert island, which would you choose and why?"*
10. *"Having now looked in detail at the main characteristics of a tropical climate, what are the main differences between the tropical climate and the temperate climate, which you are more familiar with?"*

3.5.6 Commentary

The differences between these three kinds of questions are usually quite clear, but are dependent on the context of learning, including the needs of students.

- Questions 2, 3 and 7 are in category a because they refer to previous knowledge or leaning.
- Questions 1, 6 and 10 are in category b because they link more recent learning with previously acquired knowledge.
- Questions 4, 5, 8 and 9 are in category c since answering them involves reflection and critical thinking, as well as some kind of personal commitment.

All three kinds of questions help move learning forward in different ways depending on the subject and the learning situation.

3.5.7 Task 24

For over half a century, Bloom's *Taxonomy of Educational Objectives* has been an important point of reference in education in many contexts. It characterised what were seen as the main cognitive stages in any kind of formal education, especially at primary and secondary level. More recently, the Taxonomy has been revised and amended as *A Taxonomy for Teaching, Learning, and Assessment* (Anderson et al., 2001).

Look at the list below of headings from the Revised Taxonomy—cognitive process dimension

1. **Remember** (e.g. recognising)
2. **Understand**—determining the meaning of messages, including oral, written and graphic communication (e.g. classifying, explaining)
3. **Apply**—carrying out or using a procedure in a given situation (e.g. implementing)
4. **Analyse**—breaking material into its constituent parts and detecting how the parts relate to one another and to an overall structure or purpose (e.g. differentiating, organising)
5. **Evaluate**—making judgements based on criteria and standards (e.g. checking, giving a critique)
6. **Create**—putting elements together to form a novel, coherent whole or make something original (e.g. producing, planning) (categories adapted from Krathwohl 2002, pp. 214–215)

Now indicate which questions or instructions from art lessons relate to which of the six levels of the *Revised Taxonomy* above by putting the relevant number beside each question.

3.5.8 An Art Teacher Might Say …

(a) *What did we learn about impressionism last week?*
(b) *How would you describe the main characteristics of impressionist paintings as compared to abstract paintings?*
(c) *Can you give me an example of an early impressionist painter?*
(d) *What are the differences between the styles of Monet, Cezanne and Pissarro?*
(e) *Where have you heard the phrase 'déjeuner sur l'herbe' before?*
(f) *Prepare a brief illustrated presentation to explain why you particularly like the work of one of the artists we've discussed.*
(g) *Can you use what you have learned in the last week to write a brief description of the main features common to the work of impressionist painters?*
(h) *What do you think the painter is trying to express in this painting?*
(i) *Which movement in art came first, cubism or surrealism?*
(j) *Who can summarise the main points in the video about Salvador Dali's work that you just watched?*
(k) *Can you work out who the speaker believes was the best impressionist artist?*
(l) *Which of the two painters was not French, Pissarro or Van Gogh?*
(m) *Thinking of what we've learnt over the last two months, I want you each to produce a painting in an impressionist or an expressionist style of a person or a view that you know.*
(n) *Who can explain the technique of pointillism?*
(o) *Use your knowledge of nineteenth and twentieth century movements in art to categorise the five paintings on pages 10 and 11.*
(p) *Which of these paintings do you think best captures the atmosphere of Paris in the early twentieth century?*

(q) *Read this description of Picasso's 'Guernica'. Then, using the same approach, write a description of Chagall's 'Paris through the window'.*
(r) *Which of these painters were impressionists and which were not?*
(s) *Use your knowledge of the styles of the five painters listed to decide which of them produced each of the paintings I'm going to show you.*
(t) *In your groups, please work out a plan for an exhibition of works of art by students that combines twentieth century and twenty-first century styles.*

3.5.9 Commentary

This task introduces elements of the revised version of Bloom's *Taxonomy*. The original version (1956) provided a hierarchical framework for classifying curricular objectives. The revised version, published in 2001, was intended to offer a tool for broader use. It offers a two-dimensional table relating different types of 'knowledge' to levels of cognition, ranging from 'lower order' to 'higher order' thinking skills. The table allows objectives, learning activities and assessment procedures to be worked on before teaching and reflected on afterwards. The authors of these taxonomies and many users recognised the ways in which the language, including questions, used by teachers and also written instructions in textbooks and tests, can be matched to the dimensions in the taxonomies (various lists of verbs relating to each of the cognitive dimensions have been published to help teachers, e.g. University of the Highlands and Islands 2016, pp. 8–10).

In this task, the focus is on how the kinds of questions asked or instruction given by teachers, or in written exercises and tests, vary according to the cognitive aims being focused on in learning. The list of cognitive dimensions in task 24 and below, ranges from 'lower order' or less challenging at the top to 'higher order' or more challenging at the bottom. The suggested correlation of the questions with the different 'levels' of cognitive process is as follows:

- Remember: a, e, i, l
- Understand: c, j, r (b?)
- Apply: g, q, s (m?)
- Analyse: b, k, o (r?)
- Evaluate: h, p, (f, s?)
- Create: f, m, t (q?)

This was not a straightforward task, and as can be seen from the items in brackets in this list, some of the questions/instructions seem to involve more than one type of cognitive process. In other words, this categorisation of cognitive processing, and any other, needs to be handled with care rather than be used in a rigid manner. It is important to remember that the six categories of the taxonomy are not discrete: a task or a question in class may relate to more than one of them. Equally importantly, over a period of learning classroom discourse needs to embrace all six categories at different times and for different purposes.

3.5 Section 4: The Impact of 'Teaching' Language and Questions on Learning... 95

One implication of this task is that it is important and helpful for teachers, whether they use Bloom's *Taxonomy* as a point of reference or not, to think about the cognitive level of what they are expecting of their students when formulating questions and instructions. Is the question or instruction appropriate given where students are in their learning and the cognitive aims of the activity or task, and are students equipped to be able to respond in the way expected?

3.5.10 Task 25

Questions are one way of prompting students to provide evidence of previous learning, or their opinion, or other information. Apart from asking questions, what other kinds of language can teachers use to elicit such evidence, opinions or information?

Read the following transcript and identify other ways in which the teacher does this.

(a) *Teacher (T): OK, let's have a discussion about that: Anna just said: "governments are much too slow to tackle the problem of climate change". Now get into pairs and talk about that for 3 minutes.*
(b) *T: (4 minutes later): right, you two were having quite an argument (pointing to Ruben and Leticia). Let's hear what you thought about it.*
(c) *Ruben: I don't know much about other governments but ours is moving quite quickly: diesel cars are banned from next year, there are more and more wind farms being built, and ...*
(d) *Leticia: Yes, but we are still importing coal, and the tax on petrol hasn't gone up much to generate more tax for green projects ...*
(e) *T: wait a minute, I didn't understand the logic of that. What do you mean?*
(f) *L: if you tax petrol and diesel more there could be more money for helping people to insulate their homes properly and it would encourage people to buy electric cars.*
(g) *T: OK. Sara, you look as though you disagree ...*
(h) *Sara: Well, I agree up to a point, but people living in the country can't manage without their cars because of bad public transport. It would be unfair to punish them ...*
(i) *T: I see. Give me another word that might be better than 'punish' in this context.*
(j) *Winnie: erm ... 'penalise'?*
(k) *T: OK, yes 'penalise' is better, I think. Think about why. We'll come back to that later. Jonas, you're desperate to say something ... Let's keep to the point though: "governments are too slow to tackle climate change".*
(l) *Jonas: It seems as if politicians aren't too worried, and they take ages to get anything done. But for people our age, it's really urgent. What's going to happen to us in 30–40 years' time?*
(m) *T: Right, so it's an age issue, is it? Tell us what you would do if you were the government.*

(n) *Luca: Zoe and I thought it should be a national emergency, like the Covid pandemic or a war: lots more effort should be devoted to tackling the problem ...*
(o) *T: give us some concrete examples of what they could or should do in the near future, then ...*
(p) *T: we haven't got all day for this: we're going on to the project planning task soon.*

3.5.11 Commentary

This transcript demonstrates various other ways in which teachers can elicit responses or action from students. In this case, she uses hardly any questions to stimulate discussion and thinking. There is a mixture of communicative techniques, all of which can be used as alternatives to questions, especially where interaction among students is being stimulated.

The sequence begins with inviting reactions to a statement. A version of this is commonly used in tests or quizzes: *'Mercury is closer to the sun than Venus—true or false?'* In a debate or discussion, stating a firm opinion, whether genuine or not, is a good way of provoking a reaction. The teacher also uses *'Let's ...'* twice as a less directive way of getting a response, and she uses *'I didn't understand ...'* to seek clarification or elicit an explanation. Then rather than saying *'What do you think, Sarah?'*, she says *'you look as though you disagree ...'*. This highlights that, depending on the circumstances, facial expression, body language and simple repetition of a word can elicit responses, as can statements indicating impatience like *'we haven't got all day ...'* or, in other circumstances, positive feedback such as *'I like the way you phrased that, but ...'*. However, imperatives or instructions such as *'tell us what you think ...'* or *'give us some concrete examples ...'* are almost as common as questions in teaching and need to be framed just as carefully as questions. It is worth bearing in mind that, in oral communication in the classroom, tone of voice, body language, facial expression and eye contact can affect the way students react to what teachers say just as much as—or even more than—the words actually spoken.

3.5.12 Summary

It is important that the teacher's own language awareness and language repertoire are well enough developed to help their students to gradually expand their individual language repertoires to cope with academic language alongside informal and other uses of language that are common outside school, and to provide models of the kinds of language needed. As discussed in Unit 2, a key part of a teacher's work is to 'mediate' concepts and knowledge, and to demonstrate to students how this can be done in other situations. This is just as important in less 'verbal' subjects such as maths and physics as it is in language, science, geography and history.

Task 23 focuses on the purposes of questions. Unpacking questions in the ways suggested by Morgan and Saxton (and others) makes the options available to teachers clearer and relates questions to the cognitive processes and the aims being addressed during teaching and learning. It enables teachers to carefully plan what questions to ask for what purposes, and also to help students themselves to plan the questions they might ask the teacher and one another.

Thinking about how to formulate questions, instructions and other means of introducing and setting up learning activities in relation to the cognitive demands of the given learning activity is essential. Task 24 in this section invited you to relate examples of question and instructions to the categories of the revised version of Bloom's *Taxonomy*. Whether teachers, materials writers and those devising tests refer to the cognitive processes in this *Taxonomy* or not, it is important that they consider which thinking skill(s) their planned questions, instructions and tasks are designed to stimulate as part of their students' learning.

3.5.13 *Questions for Reflection*

(a) Think back to your own educational experience and identify instances where a teacher's or a lecturer's mediation skills might have made learning easier for you.
(b) Were less demanding or more demanding cognitive challenges made easier for you as a student? Did the level of cognitive challenge increase as you got older? And was it greater in some school subjects than in others?

3.6 Conclusion

In this unit, we first considered the notions of the 'language repertoire' of students from the point of view of the increasingly common phenomenon of multilingualism in schools and students whose first languages are different from the language of their schooling, and the special challenges and opportunities this presents to teachers. We then looked at the use of written and spoken language in the teaching and learning of specific subjects. This led to an exploration of the use of language and other types of communication in scaffolding students' learning as they move through the so-called zone of proximal development described by Vygotsky. Finally, we looked at a range of means of questioning and elicitation that teachers need to have available in their own repertoires as a means of stimulating students' thinking and scaffolding cognitive development.

In Unit 4, these aspects of language in education will be explored in more depth in combination with a focus on the development of students' literacy and oracy.

References

Anderson, L. W., Krathwohl, D. R., Airasian, P. W., Cruikshank, K. A., Mayer, R. E., Pintrich, R., Raths, J., & Wittrock, M. C. (Eds.). (2001). *A Taxonomy for Learning, Teaching, and Assessing: A revision of Bloom's Taxonomy of Educational Objectives*. Longman.

Blommaert J., & Backus, A. (2011). Repertoires Revisited: "Knowing Language" in Superdiversity in Tilburg Papers in Culture Studies 24

Bloom, B. S. (Ed.). (1956). *Taxonomy of Educational Objectives—The Classification of Educational Goals*. McKay.

Feilke, H. (2012). Bildungssprachliche Kompetenzen – fördern und entwickeln. *Praxis Deutsch, 233*, 4–13.

Gardom Hulme, P., Locke, J., & Reynolds, H. (2017). *AQA Activate for KS3: Student Book 1*. Oxford University Press.

Hammond J., & Gibbons, P. (2001). What Is Scaffolding? In J. Hammond (Ed.), *Scaffolding: Teaching and Learning in Language and Literacy Education* (pp. 1–14). Primary English Teaching Association. Retrieved August, 2021, from https://files.eric.ed.gov/fulltext/ED456447.pdf

Heugh, J, French, M, Armitage, J, Taylor-Leech, K, Billinghurst, N, & Ollerhead, S (2019). *Using Multilingual Approaches: Moving from Theory to Practice—A Resource Book of Strategies, Activities and Projects for the Classroom*. British Council. https://www.teachingenglish.org.uk/article/using-multilingual-approaches-moving-theory-practice

Krathwohl, D. R. (2002). A revision of Bloom's Taxonomy: an overview. *Theory into Practice, 41*(4), 212–218.

Levine, N. How to search the internet. wikiHow, ("a wiki building the world's largest, highest quality how-to manual. Please edit this article and find author credits at wikiHow.com. Content on wikiHow can be shared under a Creative Commons License"). Available at https://www.wikihow.com/Search-the-Internet. Accessed 28 August 2022.

Little, D. (2010). The-linguistic-and-educational-integration-of-children-and-adolescents. Strasbourg: Council of Europe. https://rm.coe.int/the-linguistic-and-educational-integration-of-children-and-adolescents/16805a0d1b (accessed October 2021)

Manzoni, C., & Rolfe, H. (2019). *How Schools are Integrating New Migrant Pupils and their Families*. National Institute of Economic and Social Research.

Morgan, N., & Saxton, J. (1991). *Teaching, Questioning and Learning*. Routledge.

Nicholson, H. (1999). Talking in Class—Spoken Language and Effective Learning. In E. Bearne (Ed.), *Use of Language Across the Secondary Curriculum* (pp. 26–37). Routledge.

Oleschko, S. (ed) (2017). *Sprachsensibles Unterrichten fördern*. Arnsberg: Landesweite Koordinierungsstelle Kommunale Integrationszentren (LaKI) Nordrhein Westfalen. Available at: https://sprachsensibles-unterrichten.de/wp-content/uploads/2017/12/Buch_Sprachsensibles-Unterrichten-foerdern.pdf. Accessed 26 January 2022.

Sharpe, T. (2001). Scaffolding in Action—Snapshots from the Classroom. In J. Hammond (Ed.), *Scaffolding: Teaching and Learning in Language and Literacy Education* (pp. 1–14). Primary English Teaching Association. Retrieved August, 2021, from https://files.eric.ed.gov/fulltext/ED456447.pdf

Vygotsky, L. (1978). *Mind in Society*. Harvard University Press.

Wilkes, A. (2014). *Key Stage 3 History: Renaissance,Revolution and Reformation: Britain 1509-1745*, Student's Book. Oxford University Press.

Woods, D., Bruner, J. S., & Ross, G. (1976). The Role of Tutoring in Problem Solving. *Journal of Child Psychology and Psychiatry, 17*(1976), 89–100.

Chapter 4
Unit 4 Language and Communication in Education 3

In Unit 3, we looked at the important role of language across subject boundaries in teaching and learning at all levels of education and introduced the concepts of a language repertoire. In this unit, we further explore the notion of a language repertoire as it applies to both learners and teachers and consider ways in which it can be developed and enriched. We also look in more depth at literacy and oracy, and the part they play in the development of a language repertoire. We go on to discuss the range of different genres which learners may be exposed to and/or expected to master during formal education.

4.1 Section 1: The Impact of Schooling on the Development of a Student's Language Repertoire

4.1.1 Task 1

Read this short extract from a tea-time conversation between a parent and a primary school child. What strikes you about the exchange?

> Ellie: *Mum, what's an adjective?*
> Mother: *Why do you want to know?*
> Ellie: *Miss Barclay wrote it on the board today, but I don't remember what it means.*
> Mother: *It's a word that describes something else, like tasty. These cakes are tasty.*
> Ellie: *Or yummy!*
> Mother: *That's right, yes. Now eat up and go and play!*

4.1.2 Task 2

Now read this extract from a conversation between a parent and a teenage son. How does it differ from the previous sample?

> Alex: Dad, can you check this maths problem for me? I'm not sure I'm right.
> Father: OK, I'll take a look. Can I see the textbook too?
> Alex: Sure—there you go.
> Father: Wow, this reminds me that it's a long time since I did maths. What's a coefficient?
> Alex: It's a number used to multiply a variable.
> Father: I think you might have lost me, Alex. I do vaguely remember something like that in algebra, but.., ...
> Alex: OK, never mind, Dad. I'll give Ethan a ring. He's a maths nerd.

4.1.3 Commentary

These two extracts, recreated from our own lived family experience, show in microcosm how a child's language repertoire begins and continues to develop through schooling. Ellie shows a first sign of engaging with the metalanguage of grammar after a classroom experience, and her mother is able to help her to make sense of it. This is typical of the way in which a child's language repertoire is expanded through exposure to new terms, in this case to ways of describing language which she already uses. The second extract illustrates how subject specialist terms begin to be important in a secondary school context, also showing how a parent's command of such terms is reduced because they are no longer needed. This father's experience is far from unusual! However, children do respond to formal schooling and its linguistic trappings in different ways, and some are alienated by the academic language that they need to master in order to do well.

Both these extracts were concerned with definitions of terms, an area of academic language which remains important throughout schooling and on into adult life, depending on the academic and career choices a student makes. However, the development of a broad and deep language repertoire is crucial to both cognitive and emotional development as the next tasks illustrate.

4.1.4 Task 3

Read through this classroom discussion during a history lesson. How does the teacher's questioning open up ways of seeing things for these teenage learners?

> Teacher: How many of you saw the news about the statue in Bristol last week?
> (Several students say 'I did'. One or two say 'What statue?')
> Teacher: Whose statue was it?
> Marcus: I think his name was Colston, sir.

> Teacher: Yes, you're right. Edward Colston. Who knows why he has a statue in Bristol?
> Amy: Maybe he was Lord Mayor or something like that.
> Teacher: You're quite warm, Amy. He was certainly well known in Bristol. He was an MP. And he was a rich man. But why was his statue thrown in the harbour? Does anybody know?
> (silence)
> Teacher: Let me jog your memories. We talked about the rise of ports in Britain last month. Bristol became rich and prosperous in the 17th and 18th centuries. How did that happen?
> Martha: It was because of all the new trade with America.
> Teacher: Well remembered, Martha. What kind of trade was that?
> Jeff: Well, I think it was bananas and tobacco.
> Teacher: Right, Jeff. That was harmless enough. But was there any other kind of trade? Maybe something a bit less acceptable?
> Anna: I know, sir. It was people from Africa—slaves for the plantations.
> Teacher: You've got it—but why were they brought to Bristol? ………
> Marcus: To be sold, sir.
> Teacher: And what's the connection with Colston and his statue?
> Emily: He was a slave trader. That's how he got rich. And now slave trade is not allowed. That's why he was thrown in the harbour.
> Teacher: Absolutely right, Emily. Now what do we think about that action? Was it the right thing to do?

4.1.5 Commentary

In this extract, children's collective knowledge is brought to the surface and shared through talk, and specifically by the teacher's questions. These questions are exploratory in nature, rather than being aimed simply at checking what the learners know. He uses a piece of recent news to get the class to reach back into history and to make the connection between Colston and the slave trade. Learners are encouraged to express themselves and to take part actively in this exploratory talk, which culminates in an opportunity for them to consider the rights and wrongs of the action taken by protestors in Bristol based on what they know about history. In this way, their thinking is engaged, and their oracy skills are developed. The teacher addresses them in an appreciative and respectful way and also scaffolds their contributions through prompts, and this encourages them to contribute. There is no need for specialist terms in this discussion, but it does open up ideas that the children are encouraged to put into words. Typical follow-up activity might include research into the slave trade, a report on Colston's life and work or a debate about the rights and wrongs of public activism like the incident in Bristol, any of which would help to enrich learners' language repertoire by enhancing their levels of literacy and/or oracy.

4.1.6 Task 4

In this classroom extract, the teacher uses innovative ways to introduce young students to the notions of alliteration and onomatopoeia in poetry. How effective do you think her methods are and how does it contribute to students' understanding of how language works (Fig. 4.1)?

> Teacher: OK, everyone. Listen to me for a moment.
> (Teacher makes a soft, prolonged hissing sound)
> Teacher: sssssssssss! What animal makes a sound like that?
> Michael: A snake, miss!
> Teacher: That's right. Now can you all join me and we'll make the sound together, but very softly, please.
> Teacher and class together: sssssssssss!
> Teacher: Why did I ask you to make the sound softly?
> Ruth: Maybe because snakes a very quiet when they hiss.
> Teacher: Spot on, Ruth, and you said it—we call the sound 'hissing'. What do you notice about that word? Yes, Rachel?
> Rachel: It sounds like a snake's voice!
> Teacher: Absolutely, and there are lots of words like that, lots. Some are connected with the sounds animals make. Do you know any more?
> Various students shout out examples: moo! oink! miaow! woof! etc
> Teacher: Thanks, that's enough. Does anyone know what we call words like that?
> (silence)
> Teacher (writes on the board as she speaks): We call it 'onomatopoeia'. We'll look for some examples in poems later this term. Now though, another question about that hissing sound. If you want to attract your friend's attention during class and you don't want me to hear, what sound do you make?
> Wayne: I'd just go 'pssst!'—you know—very quietly.
> Teacher: Good, Wayne. Can you all do that now? Just make that 'pssst' sound, and emphasise the hissing part.
> Class: Lots of 'pssst' sounds.
> Teacher: OK, quiet now. And after you've got your friend's attention, will you talk in a normal voice?
> Rachel: No, miss. I'd whisper.
> Teacher: Right! Because you don't want anyone else to hear. What do you notice about the word 'whisssper'? (she stresses the 's' sound)
> Mark: It's like hissing, miss.
> Teacher: Yes, you noticed it. Can you listen now while I read a short poem to you and tell me what you notice?
> (teacher reads this Hardy poem aloud, stressing the 's' sounds in each line Fig. 4.1)

Fig. 4.1 'In a Whispering Garden' by Thomas Hardy

> That whisper takes the voice
> Of a Spirit, speaking to me,
> Close, but invisible,
> And throws me under a spell
> At the kindling vision it brings;
> And for a moment I rejoice,
> And believe in transcendent things
> That would make of this muddy earth
> A spot for the splendid birth
> Of everlasting lives.

Teacher: Well?
  Several students together: The 'sss' sounds.
  Teacher: Exactly. This is a trick some poets use to create an atmosphere in a poem—just repeating a sound over and over again. It's almost like playing with language to create an effect. We call it 'alliteration'—another long word. (writes the word on the board) Now it's your turn. In your pairs, just look at the poem on your handout and read it, stressing that 's' sound as you do.
  (Students read to each other in pairs).
  Teacher (later): OK, for your homework, first I want you to find a short poem on the internet with either alliteration or onomatopoeia, save it, and to be ready to present it in our next lesson on Friday. Then try to write a very short poem of your own using one or the other of these devices.

4.1.7 Commentary

This teacher has found a way of inviting her teenage students into terms which belong to the discourse of literature. She starts by eliciting ideas from them, focusing on this 's' sound and its associations and impact. Students can easily relate to the sound of a snake and to the notion of whispering in class. She then gives them an opportunity to 'play' a bit by imitating the snake and by making a whispering noise, before leading them through the poem with a noticing task as she reads it aloud. Importantly, she then gives them the chance to experience the same poem as readers themselves, thereby reminding them that poetry is there to be listened to as well as read. In each case, she arrives at the literary terms of onomatopoeia and alliteration through interaction with her students and by drawing on constructs they already have available and can therefore relate to. The homework task gives students some freedom of choice and is exploratory in nature, but it is aimed at reinforcing their understanding of the two terms and developing their subject-based literacy and language repertoire.

4.1.8 Task 5

Read this brief extract from the introduction to a secondary school biology textbook. What does it tell you about the way specialisms develop and consequently how specific discourse communities might be established?

> *Biology is the science that studies life, but what exactly is life? This may sound like a silly question with an obvious response, but it is not always easy to define life. For example, a branch of biology called virology studies viruses, which exhibit some of the characteristics of living entities but lack others. Although viruses can attack living organisms, cause diseases, and even reproduce, they do not meet the criteria that biologists use to define life. Consequently, virologists are not biologists, strictly speaking. Similarly, some biologists study the early molecular evolution that gave rise to life. Since the events that preceded life are not biological events, these scientists are also excluded from biology in the strict sense of the term.*

https://openstax.org/books/biology-2e/pages/1-2-themes-and-concepts-of-biology#0

Access for free at: https://openstax.org/books/biology-2e/pages/1-introduction

4.1.9 Commentary

This brief extract gives us an insight into the way that a subject discipline defines itself. It does this in two ways, firstly by a positive statement about the nature of biology, but secondly by establishing boundaries between biology and two other scientific disciplines. Many other subject areas identify themselves in this kind of way, and in doing so they help to establish a discourse community which is identifiable and which students can be admitted to during their lessons. This can be challenging for students at early secondary level, but they will need to get used to expressing themselves in 'scientific' terms both in speech and in writing. That discourse community will be further identified for students through the scientific methods and the terminology it uses as the next task begins to illustrate.

4.1.10 Task 6

Look at and comment on this exchange between teacher and pupils during a biology field trip:

> Teacher: What can you see down there?
> Student 1: Worms and beetles. Yuck! Disgusting!
> Student 2: And ants, they're very active.
> Teacher: I'm glad you noticed that. So, let's start thinking like biologists! What good do you think worms do?
> Student 1: Well, I know that birds eat them.
> Student 2: And they must live underground so we can't see what they're doing there all the time. Sir, why do they live underground?
> Teacher: Right, it's good that you are thinking about that. It's to do with what worms eat. Look at the ground around these two. What do you see?
> Student 2: Mostly dead leaves and bits of bark, and just lumps of soil.
> Student 1: Do they really eat that stuff?
> Teacher: They do, and it makes a difference. Earthworms are sometimes called eco-engineers, and we're going to find out why.

4.1.11 Commentary

These young students are being introduced to a particular topic in the biology syllabus through a field trip. They initially react to the worms, ants and beetles as any youngsters might, but the teacher immediately engages them on a different level when he urges them to start thinking beyond their initial affective reaction. Through the questions and answers that follow, and thanks to the immediacy of the situation, the students start to develop more understanding of the importance of earthworms, and this will eventually lead to an assignment in which they write or speak about what they have found out and learned. Thus, oracy and literacy are developed alongside subject know-how, and the role of the teacher here is facilitative and learning-oriented rather than teacher-centred.

4.1.12 Summary

The extracts and tasks in this section show how teachers can contribute to the developing language repertoires of their learners, starting very early when pupils arrive at primary school with little more than the language of home and family at their disposal. The tasks also highlight the importance for learners of acquiring the terminology they need in each school subject. Teachers need to build gradually from this base, always being aware of the difficulties that learners face with the language needed to explain and understand new concepts and new processes associated with learning. Starting where learners are is a good basic principle in the teaching of any subject, but it applies particularly to recognising the extent and limits of learners' language repertoires and to a teacher's skill in adjusting inputs and managing interactions in ways that gradually expand and develop their repertoires and keep their learners involved. The gentle approach taken by the biology teacher reminds us about the value of this strategy as a way of beginning to lead learners slowly towards the discourse they will need in order to access and consolidate their subject knowledge. It is not easy for some subject teachers to make this kind of shift, or indeed to develop their own linguistic repertoires in ways that allow them both to teach their specialist subject and to keep up to date in it through reading specialist literature and taking part in in-service training. It is, however, very important that teachers of all subjects develop the awareness and skills necessary to support their students as they gradually acquire the language they need to progress in the subject.

4.1.13 Some Questions for Reflection

(a) Take a moment to recall an instance from any stage in your own education when you struggled to understand something a teacher was saying or explaining to the class. Jot down a few notes about the incident and your feelings at the time. Were you the only one who didn't understand or were there others in the class with the same difficulty? Mention how it was resolved, either for you individually or for the whole class. If you can't recall such an instance, you might refer to a class you have observed or taught in which a similar problem arose.
(b) How can you, as a teacher, tell that there is a gap between the language you use when you are teaching and your learners' understanding of it? What signals might a class give you and what strategies might you use to bridge the gap?

4.2 Section 2: Aspects of Literacy and Oracy

Literacy has long been a fundamental concept in education and in life after education. Oracy is a much newer term but is regarded as equally important to success in schooling and in a career. In this section, we probe more deeply into both these concepts and into their relevance to the development of a language repertoire.

4.2.1 Task 7

Consider the following definitions of literacy. In your opinion and based on your experience, which of them best describes the 'literacy' among pupils and students at school and among adults?

(a) *'Literacy is the ability to identify, understand, interpret, create, communicate and compute, using printed and written materials associated with varying contexts'* (Montoya 2018, p. 1)
(b) *'The issue of what literacy is all about becomes more and more complex. It is not just about how pupils become successful readers and writers, but also about the kinds of texts they read and write and the value placed on those texts [...]. Literacy is not innocent, nor can it ever be neutral; questions about literacy are bound up with questions about the diversity of cultural contexts in which texts are produced.'* (Bearne 1999, pp. 11–12).
(c) *'Literacy is not an all-or-none skill but a continuum of gradually increasing levels and domains of ability. At least five factors are involved:*

   – *Learning to read texts of increasing formal difficulty ... with understanding*
   – *Learning to read texts from an increasingly wide range of everyday contexts (e.g. road sign, newspapers, medical labels etc.) with understanding*
   – *Learning to write (or type) with increasing fluency*
   – *Learning to write in response to an increasingly wide range of demands (e.g. letters, forms ...)*
   – *Learning to spell [correctly].'* (from Crystal 1995, p. 427)

4.2.2 Commentary

Quotation a) offers perhaps the clearest definition, while in definition c) Crystal unpacks what acquiring the ability to read, understand and create written texts actually involves. In the second quotation, Bearne underlines the point that literacy is not simply a set of technical skills: it is the ability to understand and communicate intended meanings and messages effectively in written form, whether interactively (e.g. in correspondence with somebody via email or social media), or in 'one-way communication' (e.g. reading a book or writing an article for publication). It is not 'innocent' or 'neutral' in the sense that each writer has a personal reason for expressing in writing what he or she wishes to say in a certain way, and each reader has their own way of interpreting and reacting to what they read. A key advantage of written communication is that the reader or writer has time to reflect on, explore or revise a text several times, which is generally much more difficult to do in spoken communication.

Literacy as represented by the combination of the quotations offered is such an important part of children's education that teachers of all subjects at all levels need to focus on it in a coordinated way so that by the end of schooling youngsters have a sound foundation to continue building on. As adults we do not stop enhancing our literacy: the learning processes described by Crystal and Bearne are potentially lifelong.

4.2.3 Task 8

Now consider this definition, taken from an official document rather than from the work of individual experts. What extra dimensions does it offer to your understanding of the concept?

> Literacy is defined as understanding, evaluating, using and engaging with written texts to participate in society, to achieve one's goals, and to develop one's knowledge and potential. (https://www.oecd.org/skills/ESonline-assessment/skillsassessed/ The Organisation for Economic Co-operation and Development)

4.2.4 *Commentary*

Your responses to this task may vary according to your context. However, a number of insights may emerge, among them:

- The definition characterises literacy as an important transferable life skill which goes beyond the language skills of reading and writing; curriculum documents often recognise this but this doesn't always translate into action at classroom level.
- In many teaching and learning situations, a teacher is likely to check *understanding* of a written text but less likely to ask learners to *evaluate* it or to *engage* with it critically.
- For the definition to be widely applicable, the notion of 'text' has to be a broad one, including diagrams, photographs, infographics, spoken inputs and other sources which learners may be exposed to in subjects across the curriculum.
- Underlying the definition is the role of literacy in preparing learners for citizenship and for fulfilling their individual potential; in many subject-based classes, this important perspective on literacy may be overlooked if the focus is on bare subject knowledge and accuracy in written language rather than on its wider relevance and applications beyond the classroom.

- The definition seems to emphasise the reading and processing of written texts and to be only marginally concerned with writing (suggested by the verb 'use'). Being able to write coherently is certainly a goal of any education system, but not all teachers expect their learners to write about their subject, maybe because the development of writing is largely seen as the responsibility of the teacher of the language of schooling. Fully understanding the scope of literacy is crucial if teachers are to play a part in expanding their students' language repertoire.

4.2.5 Task 9

In one further definition which narrows down the concept of literacy, McConachie and Petrosky state that 'disciplinary literacy' *'involves the use of reading, reasoning, investigating, speaking and writing required to learn and form complex content knowledge appropriate to a particular discipline'* (2010, p. 16).

What does this add to the definitions in Tasks 7 and 8? What are the implications of this definition (a) for a language teacher and (b) for a specialist subject teacher?

4.2.6 Commentary

Whereas a relatively simple view of literacy may suffice at lower levels of schooling, it is clear from this definition that it takes on more complexity as students reach deeper levels of subject knowledge. The addition of 'reasoning' and 'investigating' takes it beyond language skills and into the area of transferable or transversal skills which will need to be more finely tuned from discipline to discipline. This probably implies a need for language and subject teachers to work together to ensure that all these aspects of literacy are included in students' learning experience. An example of this might be in the framing of a hypothesis to investigate a scientific phenomenon, which would require students to be able to express hypothetical meaning, using the grammatical conventions needed to express conditions (the business of a language teacher), alongside an ability to think and reason clearly enough to formulate the hypothesis in terms appropriate to the investigation (the responsibility of the subject teacher).

4.2.7 Task 10

Read the following brief discussion of oracy. From your own experience and thinking of your own context, what are the most important advantages of a good and broad level of competence in oral communication?

> *[…] Poor communication in workplace teams is common, and this can inhibit creative problem solving and lead to poor decision-making. The same applies to communication*

between staff and customers, carers and their clients, teachers and students, and many other occupational relationships.

Why is poor communication so common? The reason is that the ability to use spoken language effectively (oracy) has to be learned; and even highly intelligent people may not have learned how best to use talk to get things done.

It is also important, in a participatory democracy, that all people—not just those from privileged backgrounds—develop the ability to speak confidently in public, to present effective and persuasive arguments through speech, and to examine critically but constructively the arguments presented by others.

So it is very unfortunate that, unlike literacy and numeracy, oracy is rarely taught in schools [...]. (Prof Neil Mercer, on the Oracy Cambridge website: https://oracycambridge.org/ used with permission)

4.2.8 Task 11

In parallel to literacy, oracy is defined as *'the ability to articulate ideas, develop understanding and engage with others through spoken language'* (Voice 21 2019, p. 3). In the explanation of oracy in Task 9, the writer states that oracy is rarely taught in schools. Does this match your own experience? What aspects of oracy could and should, in your opinion, be taught to school-age students?

4.2.9 Commentary

Tasks 9 and 10: oracy may be a term that is less familiar to teachers and parents. For some students, it comes more easily than literacy, but it is important that teachers should also see the development of their students'—and their own—oracy skills as an integral part of education. This is especially true in secondary education, where because of the nature of timetables and the prevalence of plenary teaching, there may be fewer obvious opportunities for students to develop the oracy skills they will need for the workplace and to be active participants in democratic society later in life. By contrast, in primary education in many contexts, shared exploratory talk does play a significant part in classroom life.

4.2.10 Task 12

How important do you consider literacy or/and oracy to be in the following childhood and adult activities?

Use the right-hand column of Table 4.1 to indicate what literacy or oracy skills you consider to be most essential in the following situations:

Table 4.1 Literacy and Oracy Activities

Context	Activity	Most essential literacy or oracy skills
1. Primary school	Taking part in a 'show and tell' activity in which children take turns to talk to the class about an object or picture they have brought in and explain why they like it	
2. Primary school	Finding similes and metaphors when reading a short story with a friend	
3. Lower secondary school	Writing a short essay on the causes of the French revolution	
4. Lower secondary school	Preparing for and speaking in favour of a motion in a school debate (e.g. on climate change)	
5. Upper secondary school	Writing a report on a chemical experiment	
6. Upper secondary school	Writing an application for a place at college or university	
7. Upper secondary school	Asking a teacher about the poor grade she has given you for an end of semester test	
8. Higher education	Taking notes in a lecture	
9. Adult life	Being interviewed by a potential employer	
10. Adult life	Talking to a doctor you don't know about a worrying condition	
11. Adult life	Chairing a community meeting about fund-raising	
12. Adult life	Writing an email to complain about rubbish collection	
13. Adult life	Informing oneself before deciding how to vote in the next national election (e.g. for member of parliament, president)	

4.2.11 Commentary

Task 11 offers an opportunity to reflect on the literacy and/or oracy demands of several routine activities that take place in school and beyond. This reminds us that each such activity assumes a certain kind and amount of prior learning, which, in most cases, could be aided by teaching. For example, in the first scenario, in primary school, a teacher will establish ground rules for a 'show and tell' activity which will help young learners to know what and how much to say when their turn comes around. In the third scenario, at lower secondary level, the history teacher will need to have prepared for the task by establishing conventions for essay writing, including layout, length, ways of connecting causes and effects, etc.

By now, it should be clear that literacy and oracy are complex notions, multilayered in nature. If their development is to be prioritised and pursued consistently during schooling, it follows that there must be means of assessing progress in both areas. Tasks 13 and 14 address this issue.

4.2.12 Task 13

What does this statement by a professional body in the USA tell you about (a) their view of assessment and (b) where the responsibility for assessing literacy lies?

> *The National Council of Teachers of English believes that literacy assessment is an integral part of literacy teaching and learning; that literacy assessment contributes to the conditions for literacy teaching and learning; and that professional knowledge about literacy assessment is a critical component of a literacy teacher's development and practice.* https://ncte.org/statement/assessmentframingst/

4.2.13 Task 14

Look at these three samples of tools for assessing aspects of literacy. Which do you find easiest for a teacher to work with? How do they differ in terms of underlying principles and beliefs (Table 4.2; Figs. 4.2 and 4.3)?

Table 4.2 Sample A (to assess writing at different levels) (freely adapted and simplified from an Internet source)

	Level 1	Level 2	Level 3
Structure and organisation	Invents own stories but writing may not be coherent	Uses basic conventions of narrative writing	Links and sequences ideas and events
Awareness of reader	Focus on telling the story without awareness of reader	Adds some detail to arouse reader interest	Story engages the reader
Use of language and language effects	Tells story as if speaking	Makes good vocabulary choices	Uses adverbs and adjectives to add colour and interest
Syntax	Uses simple sentences with punctuation	Uses compound sentences with connectives	Longer and more complex sentences properly punctuated
Spelling	Spells most common words correctly	Spells some longer words correctly using phonetic clues	Spells most words correctly despite mismatches between pronunciation and spelling

\multicolumn{3}{l}{**"Listen Fors" are key words or phrases that a teacher uses to frame observations of students engaged in learning**}
GOALS	'LISTEN FORS'	USING OBSERVATION TO INFORM TEACHING
Students engage in exploration of **themes** represented in the text	• Students connect character **conflict** and character **change** with broad themes • Students discuss their ideas about what they think **the author wanted them to learn**	If I hear these things, I know students are learning about theme If I don't hear these things, I know that we need to spend more time understanding theme and how to determine theme
Students use collaborative tasks to learn	• Students connect their ideas to the **prior comments** made by members of the group • Students **agree** or **disagree** with specific parts of what others have said and explain their thinking • Students **'think out loud'**, often revising their ideas as they speak, or even contradicting themselves	If I hear these, I know students are using talk to learn or are engaging on what Barnes calls 'exploratory talk' (1976/1992) If I don't here these things, I know we need more practice and debriefing on strategies for small group talk.
Students use literary terms (mood or tone) to describe text.	• Students comment on the author's **choice of words** • Students speculate about the author's **attitude** toward the event or topic of the texts • Students describe **how they felt** while reading a particular section pf text and indicate how the author's words evoked that response	If I hear students use specific references to the text to illustrate tone and mood, I know that they're beginning to understand these literary terms If I don't hear these things, I know we need to spend more time sorting out how powerful words can evoke our responses and, provide into the tone the author wants to create.

Fig. 4.2 Sample B a literacy assessment tool recommended by the National Council of Teachers of English in the USA. (Source: Kathryn Mitchell Pierce. 'Listening In on Student Learning.' Blog post on behalf of the NCTE Standing Committee on Literacy Assessment. October 4, 2019)

> Put these words in the right order to make a full sentence in each case. The first one has been done as an example.
>
> 1. lost / passport/ I / my / have > I have lost my passport.
> 2. husband / doesn't / job / My / have / a >
> 3. day / finishes / 3.45pm / The / at / school >
> 4. card / shop / payment / This / accepts / by >
> 5. can't / car / You / your / here / park >
> 6. two / for / I / eggs / recipe / need / this >
> 7. 7 o'clock / closes / doctors' / at / surgery / The >
> 8. younger / called / My / is / Leila / daughter >
> 9. in / Fresh / is / fruit / expensive / England / very >
> 10. to / remember / Please / off / lights / switch / the >

Fig. 4.3 A typical task for assessing basic adult literacy (freely adapted from an Internet source)

4.2.14 Commentary

The quotation in Task 13 is in the form of a credo advanced by the association, emphasising an English language teacher's responsibility to integrate the assessment of literacy holistically into the teaching of literacy, and reminding teachers of their need to keep working on the development of their own literacy.

The three samples in Task 14 illustrate just some of the complexities and different aspects involved in the assessment of literacy. The first sample offers a set of level-related criteria for the assessment of children's writing, broken down into categories which suggest that a teacher has to take account of each of them separately to piece together a composite assessment and possibly a profile of each child's attainment in narrative writing. The second sample suggests what a teacher can do to carry out an informal and impressionistic assessment of the ways in which learners engage with a text. The assumption here is that learners are given a discussion-based task to carry out in groups, and that the teacher will move from group to group, listening in and taking notes using the guidelines in the third column. Interestingly, the second set of criteria refer to oracy and talk rather than directly to literacy, which is evidence in itself of the strong links between the two. This video shows what this kind of observation can yield in assessment terms, particularly in the early stages of literacy development: 'Effective Literacy Practices—Assessing Through Close Observation' https://www.youtube.com/watch?v=Vq9_HOv2W2g.

The third sample is adapted from a battery of tests, each with a slightly different reading or writing focus, which is used to diagnose literacy levels in adults. This type of test is easy enough to administer and mark, but it only provides a snapshot of aspects of literacy rather than a more consolidated and integrated overview.

In both of these tasks, the underlying assumption is that the assessment of literacy is a matter for the teacher of the language of schooling rather than for teachers of other subjects. In Unit 5, we will look at ways in which teachers across the curriculum can be made aware of ways in which they can contribute to their students' literacy development in their specialist subjects.

4.2.15 Task 15

Look at the *Oracy Framework* in Table 4.3 below. Which of the skills listed in the framework might be developed (a) in a primary classroom and (b) by subject specialist teachers in a secondary classroom? How might the framework be used as a basis for assessing learners' oracy?

Table 4.3 Oracy Framework © Voice 21, 2022. Developed in partnership with Oracy Cambridge, University of Cambridge

PHYSICAL 1. Voice 2. Body language	1. (a) Fluency and pace of speech; (b) tonal variation; (c) clarity of pronunciation; (d) voice projection 2. (a) Gesture and posture; (b) facial expression and eye contact
LINGUISTIC 3. Vocabulary 4. Language variation 5. Structure 6. Rhetorical techniques	3. Appropriate vocabulary choice 4. (a) Register; (b) grammar 5. Structure and organisation of talk 6. Rhetorical techniques, such as metaphor, humour, irony and mimicry
COGNITIVE 7. Content 8. Clarifying and summarising 9. Self-regulation 10. Reasoning 11. Audience awareness	7. (a) Choice of content to convey meaning and intention; (b) building on the views of others 8. (a) Seeking information and clarification through questions; (b) summarising 9. (a) Maintaining focus on task; (b) time management 10. (a) Giving reasons to support views; (b) critically examining ideas and views expressed 11. Taking account of level of understanding of the audience
SOCIAL and EMOTIONAL 12. Working with others 13. Listening and responding 14. Confidence in speaking	12. (a) Guiding or managing the interactions; (b) turn-taking 13. Listening actively and responding appropriately 14. (a) Self-assurance; (b) liveliness and flair

4.2.16 Commentary

There is good reason to see the development of oracy, like that of literacy, as a process starting at primary level and continuing right through to the end of secondary education and beyond. While the teacher of the language of schooling may assume main responsibility for assessing the development of oracy, every single teacher who comes into contact with a group of learners has something to contribute to the process. The primary teacher who coaxes a nervous six-year-old to speak loudly and clearly to the class is doing early work on voice, whereas a physics teacher may praise a student for the content of an oral report on an experiment but might remind her that the talk might have been better structured and organised.

Interestingly, the framework focuses almost exclusively on spoken production rather than on listening, which is usually seen as the first building block of oracy. The value of learning to listen actively is important for healthy classroom dynamics as well as the learning opportunity it offers in terms of language development. Thus, the bias towards speaking in the framework restricts its usefulness as an assessment tool for teachers who hold on to a more rounded view of oracy.

4.2.17 Summary

The tasks in this section serve to remind us that acquiring literacy is not a speedy or simple matter. As Crystal's definition in Task 7 indicates, it is a continuum: indeed, it can be seen as a lifelong process. Less obvious, perhaps, is that the acquisition of the competences that comprise oracy is also a lengthy and potentially complex continuing process, and thus also should be seen as a key aim of education.

As demonstrated in Tasks 7 and 8, settling on a definition of literacy is not simple. Dictionary definitions normally define literacy simply as the ability to read and write. The term also doesn't translate easily into other languages. German 'Alphabetisierung' and French 'alphabétisation' seem too restricted in their connotations, and this may make international discussion of related issues that much more difficult. The same applies to oracy, which is usually rendered by a circumlocution in other languages, for example 'mündliche Kommunikation' in German.

UNESCO has a clear position regarding the importance of literacy in the wider world:

> *[UNESCO] views acquiring and improving literacy skills throughout life as an intrinsic part of the right to education. The "multiplier effect" of literacy empowers people, enables them to participate fully in society and contributes to improve livelihoods.*
>
> *Literacy is also a driver for sustainable development in that it enables greater participation in the labour market; improved child and family health and nutrition; reduces poverty and expands life opportunities.* https://en.unesco.org/themes/literacy

As Crystal pointed out in his description of literacy, '*literacy is not an all or none skill but a continuum of gradually increasing levels and domains of ability*' (Crystal 1995, p. 427). While this is true of many linguistic (and other) competences, it is especially evident with literacy due to the time it takes for a person to progress through the 'continuum' as far as their schooling and circumstances allow them to. Learning how to read and write can therefore be viewed as the first steps in a lengthy process. How literacy is handled across the curriculum in the controlled environment of the school between the ages of 5 or 6 and 16 or beyond is therefore a crucial consideration for teachers of all subjects.

A term that has been used to describe what is seen as the (minimum) level of literacy needed to handle tasks involving reading and writing in everyday life is 'functional literacy', but, as is clear from the quotation above, UNESCO takes the view that everyone should have the right, and by implication the opportunity, to improve their literacy beyond this purely functional level throughout their life. Clearly, for students to reach their true potential at the end of their schooling, functional literacy is insufficient: it is necessary for them to develop their literacy further.

Another form of literacy that can be considered crucial is 'critical literacy', linked to the broader terms, critical thinking and critical awareness. In critical literacy, the focus is not simply on reading a range of different kinds of text and writing for different purposes, but on being able to identify and respond (at least mentally) to texts that are, for example, ideologically loaded, factually untrue and designed to mislead or to persuade people to follow a given course of action. Some examples of such texts were discussed in Unit 1. In the twenty-first century, it is essential that students are enabled to acquire this kind of literacy, which is alluded to in the quotation by Bearne in Task 7, because it has become far easier to disseminate such texts as the use of the Internet and social media platforms has mushroomed, including among pre-adolescent students.

During their schooling, students will need to learn to understand and work with written language in the many forms in which it now surrounds us and impacts on our knowledge, thinking and values. They also need to be critically aware of the implications of these forms of written language, and to produce appropriate writing themselves. Arguably, in the broader sense of the concept of literacy as defined by Crystal, each curriculum subject, from the early grades to the end of secondary education, has its own specific type of literacy, its own types of reading texts and terminology and its own 'norms' when it comes to writing. This brings us to a discussion of genres, which we will pursue in the next section.

Oracy is a much less familiar term than literacy. It was coined in the 1960s to bridge the important gap in discussions of school education, which focused—and still focuses—so much less on speaking and listening than on reading and writing (Wilkinson 1965). A recent definition in a UK publication, *The Oracy Benchmarks*, is as follows: '*Oracy is the ability to articulate ideas, develop understanding and engage with others through spoken language*' (Voice 21, 2019, p. 3). This publication is also explicit about what the experts concerned see as the importance of oracy in education:

> *In school, oracy is a powerful tool for learning; by teaching students to become more effective speakers and listeners we empower them to better understand themselves, each other and the world around them. Through high quality oracy education students learn through talk and to talk. This is when they develop and deepen their subject knowledge and understanding through talk in the classroom which has been planned, designed, modelled, scaffolded and structured to enable them to learn the skills needed to talk effectively. (ibid., p. 3)*

This overlap between learning to talk effectively and learning through talk is a key point, and one which makes oracy and literacy parallel in importance and sometimes overlapping in nature, a point which is illustrated in Sample B in Task 14. Both literacy and oracy are crucial life skills, not just for participation in social, business or workplace settings, but in order to continue learning, whether on a small or on a larger scale.

The *Oracy Benchmarks* set out proposed standards for the attention to oracy paid by teachers and school leaders, such as:

> *The teacher establishes and models ambitious and challenging norms for talk, ensuring that students understand the expectations for talk in their classroom. Opportunities for oracy are regular, purposeful, appropriately pitched and thoughtfully planned to ensure that students are well prepared to meet expectations.* (ibid., p. 9)

The 'norms of talk' referred to here were nicely exemplified in the clip of teaching (Pythagoras) focused on in Unit 2. The *Oracy Benchmarks* are also underpinned by an *Oracy Framework* developed in collaboration with the University of Cambridge and introduced in Task 16 above. The implication of such a framework is that the same rigorous attention needs to be paid to oracy in school education as to literacy.

Wilkinson made the point in the 1960s that primary education is far more conducive to enabling children to develop oracy than secondary education:

> *… on three main counts: first that relationships, child and adult, are usually less authoritarian and distant; second that the method of group working gives opportunities for talk which a classroom arranged in rows does not; and further the development of oracy is easily seen as a process which goes on irrespective of the subject matter, in contrast to the secondary school where 'speech' is often left to the English teacher* [i.e. the teacher of the language of schooling]. (Wilkinson 1965, p. 747)

Times have changed, and in many contexts, group work and oracy is much more a feature of secondary school education in all subjects than it was. But the fact remains, as noted above, that students in normal secondary classrooms have few opportunities to develop their oracy along the kind of continuum that Crystal attributes to the gradual acquisition of literacy.

4.2.18 Some Questions for Reflection

(a) Refer to a teaching context that you are familiar with. To what extent are literacy and oracy promoted or neglected in everyday classroom practice?
(b) What do you think is meant by 'the multiplier effect of literacy' in the UNESCO definition quoted above? How might it apply to your context?
(c) If you are a speaker of a language other than English, how would you translate these two terms, and how would you explain them to others who are not familiar with them?

4.3 Section 3: The Range of Genres which Children should be able to Understand and Reproduce in Different Subject Areas

> We use language to achieve a range of social purposes, for example, telling a story, retelling what we did on our holidays, or persuading an audience of a particular point of view about a topic such as whether students should do homework. The texts we create to achieve these social purposes can be referred to as genres or text types. (Derewianka & Jones, 2016, p. 7)

As children grow and as they progress through their schooling, they are confronted with a range of spoken and written genres which they have to understand, interpret and sometimes produce themselves. In many cases, they will need a teacher's support with this aspect of their literacy and oracy development.

4.3.1 Task 16

Below is a sample list of genres which primary or lower secondary school pupils might encounter in and out of the school environment. Which do pupils simply need to understand and which are they often asked to produce? Which are most likely to require critical thinking as a means of interpretation?

- In language and literature classes: dialogues, stories, cartoons, poems, diary entries, biographies
- In science and technology classes: instructions, reports, infographics, explanations, presentations
- In social science classes: explanations, information texts (e.g. Wikipedia), narrative accounts of events, reports
- Outside school: advertisements, blogs, text messages, news reports

4.3.2 Task 17

Consider this curriculum statement from Northern Ireland in which teachers are encouraged to develop a range of communication skills. Which genres might stimulate responses in each of the five numbered instances? What differences would there be between these 'input' genres and those which students are asked to produce?

> Teachers of any subject can encourage pupils to become effective communicators by using a range of techniques, forms and media to convey information and ideas creatively and appropriately.
> Teachers should enable pupils to develop skills in:
> 1. communicating meaning, feelings and viewpoints in a logical and coherent manner;
> 2. making oral and written summaries, reports and presentations, taking account of audience and purpose;
> 3. participating in discussions, debates and interviews;
> 4. interpreting, analysing and presenting information in oral, written and ICT formats;
> 5. exploring and responding, both imaginatively and critically, to a variety of texts.
>
> It is likely that most schools will address their key statutory obligations for Communication by providing qualifications in English (and Gaeilge in Irish-Medium settings). However, there are opportunities to develop communication across all qualifications; these are outlined in our specifications. https://ccea.org.uk/key-stage-4/curriculum/communication (numbering inserted by authors)

4.3.3 Commentary

Opinions may differ and different teachers may see the challenges across genres differently. However, in learning-centred classrooms, it is increasingly likely that learners will be asked to produce as well as understand an ever-widening range of genres. In a creative language class, learners may be asked to write as well as read stories and poems. Science subjects are often seen as 'less verbal than arts or social science subjects and yet modern science textbooks include all the written genres mentioned in the second bullet point in Task 16, and the teacher may use presentations and demonstrations with commentary as a mode of input. Learners are also often asked to make presentations and to write reports. History textbooks contain accounts of events and documentary evidence from a range of sources which learners may be asked to compare and read critically. They may be asked to review and report on their findings orally or in writing. Each of these genres has its own conventions, and teachers need to help their pupils to become familiar with them.

Beyond school, and partly thanks to the ready availability of access to the Internet, learners will need to be ever more thoroughly able to read blogs, news items and advertisements with a critical eye, learning all the time how to distinguish fact from fantasy and genuine news from fake news. All this is a challenge which teachers need to take up as they prepare pupils for citizenship as well as for examinations.

This four-stage model explains how a teacher of any subject may address this challenge (Fig. 4.4):

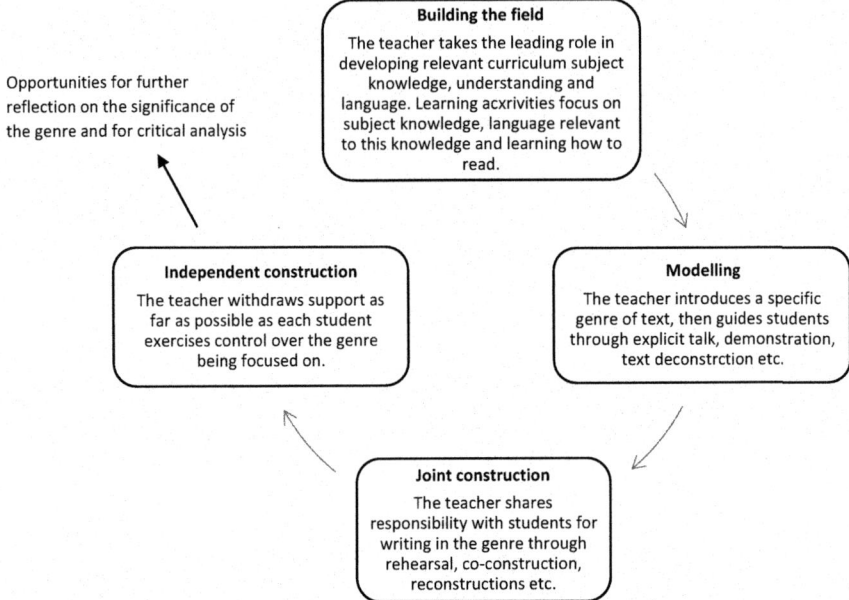

Fig. 4.4 Genre-based curriculum cycle (Hammond 2001, p. 28, cited in Beacco et al. 2016)

'Building the field' at the initial stage is, in many classrooms, a teacher-led phase of a lesson or lessons. Depending on the subject discipline, the teacher may use visuals, verbal explanations, diagrams, dramatic techniques or other kinds of scaffolding to introduce a concept and to pave the way for exposure to a particular genre.

The second stage, 'Modelling' refers to talk, demonstration and text deconstruction. This requires a teacher to be thoroughly familiar with the conventions used in the dominant genres in her subject discipline and to be able to explain these to students. For example, she may point out to students that first-person pronouns are not usually used in experimental reports, or that hypotheses are usually expressed in an 'if' sentence. At the third stage, as the level of scaffolding is reduced, teacher and class may build up an experimental report on the board or on a computer screen, to be referred to as a model when students reach the fourth stage of 'Independent construction'. Yet few teacher education courses seem to prepare subject specialist teachers to work with language in this kind of way. It requires an ability to analyse discourse patterns, which is generally assumed to be the business of linguists.

4.3.4 Summary

Our consideration of genres in Tasks 15 and 16 focuses attention on another facet of 'repertoire', this time at the level of whole texts and the range of text types that learners and teachers encounter during schooling and beyond. Genres can be oral or written and are therefore also integral to the development of literacy and oracy. The variety and complexity of written and spoken texts that students are confronted with increase as they progress through schooling, and they are bound to need support with this challenge. Similarly, the text types that students are asked to produce in assignments and presentations will be more and more aligned with the norms of each subject discipline. The further they progress in these areas of subject-specific literacy and oracy, the better prepared they will be to face the challenges of final examinations and, eventually, higher academic studies. However, we recognise that it is far from easy for a teacher without a linguistic grounding to deconstruct texts in their own specialism as a means of helping learners to cope with these challenges. Teachers of subjects other than the language of schooling may not be familiar with terms such as 'deconstruction' and 'co-construction', and they are not likely to have been exposed to the kind of methodology suggested in the genre-based curriculum cycle. However, it seems to us that teacher education courses urgently need to address the ways in which teachers can support their students in the development of a functioning language repertoire and we will return to this and other aspects of teacher education and training in Unit 5.

4.3.5 *Some Questions for Reflection*

(a) Why is it that different subject areas work with different genres? Try to jot down a few examples of genres which are common to more than one subject area.
(b) Which school subjects are sometimes classed as 'highly verbal' and which as 'less verbal'? How does this distinction relate to genres?

4.4 Section 4: A Teacher's Language Repertoire and its Impact on the Development of Learners' Literacy and Oracy

4.4.1 *Task 18*

Below is a random list of comments and responses by secondary level students. It should be easy for you to place each comment into a possible context. In each case, state what the comment reveals about the teacher's use of language?

(a) *(speaking to parent)* "Dad, I can't understand what we have to do for homework. Miss Adams didn't really explain it to us."
(b) *(to a classmate)* "Old Jonesy loses the plot when he starts going on about Wordsworth. He's in a world of his own."

(c) *(in class)* "Sir, I don't really understand your question."
(d) *(to a classmate)* "I always get low marks for my essays but he never tells me why, or how I can do better."
(e) *(to a classmate, at the end of a class)* "After all that, I still haven't got a clue what pragmatism means so how can I write a paragraph about it?"

4.4.2 Commentary

(a) Without more context, it's difficult to be sure about the cause of this student's problem. However, in secondary schools, homework tasks are often given in a hurry at the end of a lesson, when teacher and students are already in disbanding mode. The teacher probably didn't check whether the students had understood the requirements of the homework task. The language-related teaching skills needed here are giving clear instructions, checking understanding and, if necessary, paraphrasing an instruction to make it clearer.
(b) Teachers who love their subject often forget that students don't necessarily share that intimate relationship, and the result is a kind of estrangement between students and the subject caused mainly by the teacher's use of language and concepts which are far from students' interests and reality. Teachers need to be able to modify their language and particularly the conceptual frameworks they use in order to meet students more than half-way, instead of requiring students to understand everything in specialist terms which they don't have available.
(c) Questioning as we have seen previously in classroom extracts is an essential element of interaction in any lesson, and it is very important that teachers prepare and use questions which are accessible to learners, and which require different levels of thinking from students in formulating an answer. This student is giving the teacher a chance to rephrase the question to make it possible for her to answer it. Rephrasing is an essential teaching skill requiring clear thinking and a good command of language.
(d) This student is finding it difficult to make progress in essay writing in the absence of clear and specific feedback from the teacher. Formulating feedback, whether orally or in writing, is a key skill that teachers need to master in terms of the language choices they make and hence the clarity of the message, and it is also important for students to be allowed to engage with and respond to feedback in a positive way.
(e) Abstract terms are particularly difficult for teenage students to understand, and they become more common as students progress through the secondary curriculum. A key skill for teachers whose subjects rely on understanding such terms is the ability to define them clearly and to relate them to students' experience of the world, perhaps through analogies and illustrative examples.

4.4.3 Task 19

What do these teacher–student exchanges tell you about the teacher's impact on the students' language repertoire?

a) (in a geography class)
Teacher: *Who can tell me about tectonic plates?*
Marcus: *Miss, they are sort of under the earth. We can't see them.*
Teacher: *In a way, you're right, Marcus. But they **are** part of the surface structure of the Earth. Can anyone tell me what they are made of?*
Emma: *They're made of stone.*
Teacher: *Yes, or better solid rock! And how about their size? Yes, Sarah.*
Sarah: *They're huge, Miss, and they kind of move around.*
Teacher: *That's right, they float in fact. Anything else you can tell me?*
Simon: *Well, when two tectonic plates bump into each other, they can cause an earthquake.*
Teacher: *That sounds a bit like a collision, Simon. Is that how you see it?*
Simon: *Well in a kind of way, but it's not that kind of collision. It's not like a car crash. It's sort of slow and gradual.*
Teacher: *Great, we're getting somewhere.*

b) (in an English language class)
Teacher: *OK, let's all think about what we did at the weekend. Gilles, you first.*
Gilles: *We have taken an excursion.*
Teacher: *Verb tense?*
Gilles: *Oh yes. Simple past. We took an excursion.*
Teacher: *Someone else?*
Marianna: *I was shopping in the city.*
Teacher: *'went', Marianna.*
Marianna: *I went to shop in the city.*
Teacher: *No, you can say 'went shopping'. Clara?*
Clara: *We visited our friends.*
Teacher: *Correct!*

4.4.4 Commentary

In extract (a) the teacher teases out her students' understanding of 'tectonic plates', using questions, students' existing knowledge and encouragement. She also allows students to use their own words and turns of phrase rather than insisting on technical terms but gets Simon to think about his use of 'bump into each other'. This open-mindedness allows Simon to restate his understanding with a fresh analogy. This kind of lesson is likely to enhance students' ability to identify and explain phenomena as well as just to use specialist terminology appropriately. It represents part of a much longer process of initiation into subject discourse but with the teacher's sensitivity allowing this to happen on their terms as well on hers. It is an example of a social-constructivist approach in action.

In extract (b), the teacher is single-mindedly focused on her objective of achieving a degree of accuracy in her learners' English, and she communicates this in no uncertain terms through the language she uses to respond to their contributions. She shows no interest in *what* the students tell her because she is entirely focused on *how* they say it. Indeed, her listening is directed exclusively to the errors the students might make, and other content is simply filtered out. The students featured in the extract are clearly conscious of the teacher's priorities, and this is probably why they adopt a minimalist approach in their replies—the less they say, the fewer the mistakes! This kind of approach by the teacher may pay off in terms of accuracy in the short term, but its effect on her students' motivation to communicate in English is unlikely to be positive in the long term. It tells students what she sees as important in a language lesson rather than in real-world uses of the language, and they seem ready to go along with that.

In both these instances, students are sure to pick up on the teacher's use of language and on where her priorities lie. Students are usually attentive to this kind of thing as it is in their interests—especially when it comes to assessments—to understand what kind of responses the teacher is looking for.

4.4.5 Summary

A teacher's language repertoire has to encompass both the receptive and productive dimensions of language. Teaching is as much about listening as about speaking, and a language-aware teacher will pick up linguistic as well as non-linguistic signs from learners about how they are receiving the teaching. There is clearly a cognitive side to this, but focusing on the way learners express their ideas, on how they make connections between different building blocks in the subject, and areas in which they feel more or less verbally confident is an important touchstone for the teacher to refer to when addressing the class. Even the correct pronunciation of a new specialist term like 'archipelago' or 'photosynthesis' can be a stumbling block for learners as they may be worried that mispronunciation may provoke laughter or ridicule from classmates. Awareness raising in this area is a potentially crucial element of teacher education courses. The language that learners use in their assignments also offers useful evidence for a teacher to draw on when planning from lesson to lesson. If learners avoid using specialist terms, it may be a signal that they are not yet confident enough to deploy them actively and they may need more. Teachers of all subjects will help their learners if they give clear feedback on the language that learners use as well as on the subject content in written assignments. Empathy, essential though it is, will take teachers only so far in all these instances, but good levels of language awareness and mastery of language support strategies are equally important.

Dialogic teaching and learning present a slightly different kind of challenge for teachers and learners, mainly because it is by definition largely spontaneous in nature. Teachers need the linguistic means to intervene in so many different ways in a talk-centred class: they may need to slow things down to allow everyone to catch up, to speed things up to prevent boredom or disengagement, to demonstrate how to formulate a good question and to rephrase an idea to make it more available, but also to push learners gently into new uses of language to describe new phenomena—the list goes on. In all of this, the teacher is modelling good practice and learners will probably latch on to it and imitate it when the moment is right. The benefits to the development of oracy are self-evident but also confirmed by the findings of Alexander (2013), Mercer and Dawes (2018) and others.

4.4.6 Some Questions for Reflection

(a) Why do you think some teachers shy away from dialogic teaching of the type illustrated in the geography class extract in Task 19a?
(b) Why do some teachers prefer to focus on the achievement of short-term, measurable objectives like the teacher in the extract in Task 19b?

4.5 Conclusion

This unit has brought us, through considering examples from classroom practice as well as some of the underlying theoretical issues, to an understanding of the complex relationship between a language repertoire in learners and teachers and the basic concepts of literacy and oracy. These three concepts complement each other and to some extent overlap with each other, but each also has its own place in our understanding of the role of language in education. While literacy is primarily concerned with reading and writing, and oracy with listening and speaking, a person's language repertoire refers to the multiple uses and purposes of their command of at least one language.

In Unit 5, we will look at how the issues we have introduced and discussed in Units 1–4 might be addressed in teacher education and training programmes.

References

Alexander, R. J. (2013). Improving Oracy and Classroom Talk: achievements and challenges. *Primary First*, 22–29.
Beacco J.C., Fleming M., Goullier F., Thürmann E., Vollmer H (2016). *A Handbook for Curriculum Development and Teacher Training - the Language Dimension in all Subjects.* Strasbourg: Council of Europe. https://rm.coe.int/a-handbook-for-curriculum-development-and-teacher-training-the-languag/16806af387 (accessed 21.01.2022).
Bearne, E. (Ed.). (1999). *Use of Language across the Secondary Curriculum.* Routledge.
Crystal, D. (1995). *The Cambridge Encyclopaedia of the English Language.* Cambridge University Press.
Derewianka, B., & Jones, P. (2016). *Teaching Language in Context* (2nd ed.). Oxford University Press.

Hammond, J. (2001). Scaffolding and Language. In J. Hammond (Ed.), *Scaffolding: Teaching and Learning in Language and Literacy Education* (pp. 15–30). NSW: Primary English Teachers' Association. Cited in Beacco et al. 2016. https://files.eric.ed.gov/fulltext/ED456447.pdf

McConachie, S. M., & Petrovsky, A. R. (2010). *Content Matters: a disciplinary literacy approach to improving student learning Hoboken*. Jossey Bass.

Mercer, N., & Dawes, L. (2018). The Development of Oracy Skills in School-Aged Learners. Part of the *Cambridge Papers in ELT series*. Cambridge University Press. https://languageresearch.cambridge.org/images/CambridgePapersInELT_Oracy_2018_ONLINE.pdf

Montoya, S (2018). *Defining Literacy*. Presentation at 5th GAML (Global Alliance to Monitor Learning) Meeting. UNESCO. Retrieved May 29, 2020, from http://gaml.uis.unesco.org/wp-content/uploads/sites/2/2018/12/4.6.1_07_4.6-defining-literacy.pdf

Voice 21. (2019) *The Oracy Benchmarks*. *Voice 21*. Retrieved May 22, 2022, from https://voice21.org/wp-content/uploads/2020/06/Benchmarks-report-FINAL.pdf

Wilkinson, A. (1965). *The Concept of Oracy*. Retrieved July 28, 2021, from https://doi.org/10.1111/j.1754-8845.1965.tb01326.x

Chapter 5
Unit 5: Building Language Sensitivity into Teacher Education and Training

5.1 Introduction

In this unit, we turn our attention to language studies in teacher education. The argument for a language component in initial teacher education curricula or in-service programmes for teachers of all subjects has been made in different countries and contexts over many years, and we believe that we have added weight to it in Units 1 to 4 of this book. This fifth unit is primarily targeted at those involved in teacher education and training, including those on the front line as trainers or lecturers but also policy-makers and curriculum designers. However, we hope that the material in this unit will also strike a chord with practising and aspiring teachers who may wish to enhance their understanding of some of the issues we broach. In Section 1 of the unit, we look briefly at the current situation in teacher education and training, highlighting the lack of attention given to language and literacy issues. We then go on to offer a draft 'core syllabus' which we see as a basis for designing language modules or courses in pre-service or in-service programmes in any subject specialism and explore ways of incorporating elements of it in teacher education. Section 2 invites readers to take a critical look at some task types which might be used in the implementation of a training or teacher education programme in the area of language-sensitive teaching. In Section 3, we draw on examples of existing good practice in the field from three European countries. Section 4 then explores ways of building language-sensitive teaching and learning systematically into all teacher education.

5.2 Section 1: Improving the Current Situation in Teacher Education and Training

In most countries across the world, pre-service teacher education is in the hands of higher education institutions. In some contexts, decisions about what to include in the curriculum are taken centrally, at ministry level, while in others, universities and training colleges operate with a high degree of autonomy in all matters of curriculum design and implementation. The possible consequences of these two approaches can be seen in the two extracts which now follow.

5.2.1 Task 1

The Teachers' Standards for England, updated in 2021, include the following statement under Standard 3 (of eight), which requires teachers to 'demonstrate good subject and curriculum knowledge':

> *Teachers must demonstrate an understanding of and take responsibility for promoting high standards of literacy, articulacy and the correct use of standard English, whatever the teacher's specialist subject.* https://assets.publishing.service.gov.uk/government/uploads/system/uploads/attachment_data/file/1007716/Teachers__Standards_2021_update.pdf accessed 8 September 2021

Comment briefly on this statement in the light of everything we have discussed in the first four units of this book, bearing in mind that initial teacher trainees have to be assessed according to the standards.

5.2.2 Task 2

Consider this statement taken from the website of the University of Oldenburg in Germany:

> *…. it is essential to embed the topic of language into teacher training. (……………) While language-related modules have long been mandatory for student teachers in Berlin and North Rhine-Westphalia, other federal states have been slow to catch up. "The regulations governing Master's degrees in Lower Saxony stipulate that the language issue must be addressed. But there are no education-policy rules specifying that this must be integrated into teacher-training modules. This has to change.* Source: University of Oldenburg, Centre for Teacher Education. https://uol.de/en/news/article/language-sensitive-teaching-and-learning-3806

What does it have in common with the situation in England referred to in Task 1, and how is it similar to, or different from, the situation in the context you are most familiar with?

5.2.3 Commentary

Both the UK and Germany devolve responsibility for education to their regions. This makes it very difficult to establish common standards and requirements for both schools and higher education institutions. The standards set in England should provide a basis for curriculum design in initial teacher education and for assessment of trainee teachers, but in practice these matters are left to individual teacher education institutions. Also, you will have noticed the mention of 'articulacy' and 'standard English' in the first statement, and they may have raised questions in your mind. Given the amount of interest in and research into oracy, some of which we have referred to in this book, why is it not used here alongside literacy, which is still a much more established term? And in the modern context of English as an International Language, and with all its varieties worldwide, one might be tempted to ask whether the notion of 'standard English' is at all relevant, even if it were possible to describe it adequately!

The complaint about lack of standardisation in German initial teacher education might resonate in many different countries and contexts, especially where the principle of academic freedom makes it difficult for central government to impose curriculum content on institutions. It is also particularly striking that, while many school curricula across the world stress the importance of literacy for educational success, this is not consistently reflected in teacher education curricula.

While these are examples from just two contexts, wherever we have looked we have found at best just a few examples of attention to language-sensitive teaching in initial teacher education for all school subject areas. In the rest of this unit, we look at some ways in which this situation might be improved.

5.2.4 Task 3

In in-service training and professional development for practising teachers there is even less standardisation of requirements. In some countries, the responsibility remains with higher education institutions. In some others there are specialist institutes charged with running courses for practising teachers. In others still, the onus is on schools themselves to identify training needs and to offer training in-house. There are advantages and disadvantages to each of these models, but they do have some things in common, most notably that they prioritise their programmes according to evolving needs (e.g. the proliferation of courses on aspects of working with ICT or on online teaching and learning) or in response to a deficit view of teaching (e.g. addressing poor examination results or problems with underachievement). It is really difficult for a topic like language-sensitive teaching to push its way up an in-service training agenda.

Imagine that you and one or two colleagues at the same institution have worked your way through some of the tasks provided in this book and have decided to make a case for a six-hour in-service course on the issues it has raised for you and for teachers of all subjects across the school curriculum. Put together an outline course proposal to submit to your school principal when asking for approval and funding. In tackling the task, you may find it useful to draw on insights and topic areas from Units 1–4. Use the following framework:

Title of Course and Duration
Participation: who will be invited to attend and why.
Rationale: why the course is needed.
Proposed content: a bullet point list of content areas and topics.
Possible follow-up and evaluation: a way of assessing the impact of the course on teaching and learning across the school.

5.2.5 Commentary

Clearly, responses to this task will vary, but it is intended to help users of our book to find ways of talking with professional colleagues about some of the issues we have raised and of assessing the situation in their own context. Just a few ideas:

- a catchy title might arouse interest among teachers of different subjects.
- you might want a broad-based course aimed at teachers of any subject, especially in a primary school, or alternatively a narrower focus on a subject group like natural sciences or social sciences.
- it would be good to state the basis for your rationale: what needs have been identified? What are the objectives?
- It would be good to think about the implementation of the course: input plus workshop mode? Task-based? Classroom-focused? Attention to theory?
- Maybe aim at creating a community of practice within the school with mutual support, peer observation, etc.

The examples of in-service provision we have identified are very disparate in nature, but we have seen evidence of trainers making valuable connections between teacher talk and the development of learners' language repertoires, and between the language choices a teacher makes and their impact on learners' responses and levels of motivation. This alone should mean language-sensitive teaching is a priority for training programmes, the more so because teachers are not always aware of the way they use the language of schooling in their classes or of the impact on learners and learning of the language habits they adopt and often maintain through their teaching careers.

We hope that this task has stimulated some thought about what the content and nature of a short course for practising teachers might look like. In Table 5.1 below we offer an outline 'core syllabus' containing language and communication topics relevant to language-sensitive teaching and learning. This can be used as a menu when planning either modules for teacher education degrees or opportunities for the

5.2 Section 1: Improving the Current Situation in Teacher Education and Training

in-service training and professional learning of practising teachers. The core syllabus is drawn mainly from issues covered in Units 1–4 as well as from our exploration of work being done in some universities, pedagogical institutes and government institutions, notably in Germany, Austria, the Netherlands and Switzerland. The syllabus is not intended to be exhaustive or prescriptive, and the topics are not rigidly sequenced. Instead, the list should also be seen as open-ended, in the sense that it can be adapted, added to and reorganised to suit the needs of specific groups of student teachers and teachers. For this reason, you may find it helpful to work on the tasks which follow the syllabus with someone else (Table 5.1).

Table 5.1

Language-sensitive teaching and learning: a suggested core syllabus for teacher educators and those supporting teachers' professional learning

GENERAL LANGUAGE AWARENESS
1. How language and communication work: Developing further awareness of how languages are organised and the factors that determine how they are spoken and written
a. The miracle of human language
b. The elements and systems of spoken, written and signed language
c. Spoken language: stress, intonation, body language, etc.
d. Written language: writing systems, punctuation, comparison with spoken language,
e. Text types and genres
f. Non-linguistic communication
2. Language as a social phenomenon: how language is used to communicate and interact in different social settings and contexts
a. Roles and purposes of language users as social agents
b. The functions and uses of language
c. Miscommunication and misunderstandings
3. Language choice and language use 1: how languages and their use vary according to contextual factors
a. Adaptation and variation of language due to roles and relationships
b. Context as a factor in selecting oral and/or written language
c. Accent, national and regional varieties, dialects
d. Special forms of language, e.g. in social media, SMS
e. Levels of formality
f. Language registers
4. Language choice and language use 2: how language use may vary depending on language users:
a. Language repertoires developed in early life
b. Gender and language
c. Cultural background and language
d. Social background, lifestyle and language
e. Language and the sense of identity

(continued)

Table 5.1 (continued)

5. Critical awareness of the reasons for language choice and language use: the importance of understanding how language choice and use vary according to contexts and users' purposes
a. Language used in everyday transactions
b. Language to establish and maintain interpersonal relationships
c. The uses of language in mediation and information sharing
d. Language and communication in persuasion and influencing opinion, e.g. in political, commercial and legal contexts
e. Language use in positions of authority (teacher, parent, employer, etc.)
f. Literary uses of language
g. Discriminatory language, hate speech, bullying, etc.
LANGUAGE AND COMMUNICATION IN EDUCATION
6. Language, communication and learning: the way language is used in the learning and teaching of concepts, knowledge and skills
a. Language, thought, concepts and non-school learning situations
b. Ways in which teachers can support learning: reference to existing knowledge, body language and visual aids, etc.
c. Mediation in teaching and learning; types of 'learning talk' and 'teaching talk': 'initiation-response-feedback' vs. exploratory or 'dialogic' teaching
d. Informal language and 'academic' language: basic interpersonal communicative skills (BICS) and cognitive academic language proficiency (CALP) (Cummins, 1979)
e. Language and communication in classroom management
7. Teacher–student interactions in lessons: how students and teachers use language and communication in face-to-face and online learning
a. The impact of learning context and educational culture on language and communication
b. The impact of lesson topics and intended learning outcomes on teachers' and learners' language and communication
c. Instructions—spoken, written and signed (e.g. in textbooks, tests)
d. Selecting and using questions: categories, purposes, level of challenge
e. Other forms of elicitation
f. Scaffolding: ways and means of helping students to learn new concepts and information
g. Collaborative learning and student–student interaction
h. Handling feedback on learners' work
i. Dealing with students' doubts, lack of comprehension and misunderstandings
8. Developing students' literacy and oracy: the importance of helping students to fully develop their ability to read and write different kinds of text, and to use and understand different kinds of spoken language.
a. The characteristics of students' individual linguistic and cultural repertoires
b. What is literacy? How does it develop?
c. Written texts and genres in teaching and learning
d. How can literacy be assessed?
e. What is oracy? How does it develop?
f. Oral discourse and genres in teaching and learning
g. The role of dialogue and interaction in developing oracy
h. How can oracy be assessed?
i. The development of students' language repertoires

(continued)

Table 5.1 (continued)

9. Subjects, language and communication: the ways in which language and language use vary across the curriculum from subject to subject
a. Specialist language and defining terms
b. The impact of subjects on teaching and learning language and communication
c. The impact of subjects on written genres and language forms
d. Features of subject-specific language that may be challenging for learners
10. The multilingual classroom: the importance of taking into account the different first and home or community languages and cultures represented in a class
a. Drawing on a diversity of language and cultural profiles in the classroom
b. Differing levels of competence in the language of schooling: supporting access and developing students' competence
c. Making space for other languages in learning
d. Using diversity to build linguistic and cultural awareness

5.2.6 Task 4

Assume you are preparing a new module lasting 36 course hours (plus another 54 hours of independent study) as part of a B.Ed. teacher education course. This module will be obligatory for student teachers intending to teach any subject(s) at lower secondary level. Choose some priority areas for this module from the two parts of the 'core syllabus' and suggest the order in which they should be addressed. Which of the factors in Table 5.2, and which others, do you need to take into account in your context?

Table 5.2 Factors to consider when designing a teacher education module on language sensitivity

Some factors for consideration	Importance 1=high, 4=low
1. How familiar students already are with some of the topics in the 'General Language Awareness' part of the syllabus, and the extent to which you can build on students' existing knowledge and awareness	
2. The other obligatory modules in the course curriculum, such as psychology and sociology, where there may be overlap with language and communication topics	
3. The teacher education resources that are already available or can be developed, such as topical extracts from the media, recordings of teaching etc.	
4. The additional reading and study materials available to students for use during assignments, for example in libraries and online	
5. The language repertoires and cultural backgrounds of students on your course	
6. Other: what?	

5.2.7 Task 5

Now assume you are planning a 12-hour in-service course for experienced teachers of science and technology. The course will be run over 8 weeks and will be complemented by some lesson observation. Choose priority content areas from the core syllabus, especially part B, and suggest in what order you would address them. Which of the factors in Table 5.3, below and which others, do you need to take into account in your context?

Table 5.3 Some factors to consider when designing an in-service training course on language sensitivity

Some factors for consideration	Importance 1=high, 4=low
1. The nature of the science and technology syllabus and the space for working on students' language repertoires, e.g. terminology, oral explanation, report writing	
2. Whether the course is voluntary or obligatory, and how motivated the teachers are, timing of sessions	
3. Your own knowledge and experience of teaching science and technology and/or of working with and observing science and technology teachers	
4. How willing teachers are to explore and reflect on areas beyond the limits of their own subject that are relevant across the school curriculum	
5. Whether assignments can be given between sessions that ask the teachers attending the course to try out different ways of using language in their own teaching, for example different approaches to asking questions, different ways of preparing students for writing tasks, etc., and to report back on these experiences	
6. The language repertoires and cultural backgrounds of teachers in the group	
7. Other: what?	

5.2.8 Commentary

The aim of these tasks is to enable you to familiarise yourself with the 'core syllabus' and to think about which areas are priorities in your working context. Your decisions will depend on various factors which are likely to be specific to the context in each case.

5.2.9 Task 6

An important issue in both pre-service and in-service teacher education is how to persuade students or teachers that effective use of language and communication is an integral part of effective teaching, and therefore needs to be focused on. Think about ways in which you could convince course participants of the need to give careful attention to language and communication in subject teaching. What kinds of preparatory reading, input and activities might be useful for this purpose?

5.2.10 Commentary

When choosing areas of awareness and competence to focus on in teacher education it is important to consider how these teacher competences mirror and support the language-related competences that students need to develop throughout the stages of their education. In some contexts, national or regional curricula specify language-related learning objectives for pupils and students at primary, lower secondary and upper secondary levels. These should, of course, be taken into account when choosing topics for attention in teacher education and professional development.

Whatever curricula say about developing students' language-related skills, most subject teachers will be well aware that there are diverse levels of competence in oracy and literacy in their classes due to social and linguistic background, migration or, in some cases, learning difficulties such as dyslexia. Awareness of this diversity among students' language and communicative competences can be aided by sharing among all teachers a regularly updated register of information about the language repertoires of each student. Subject teachers also understand that it is not feasible for the teachers of the language of schooling alone to ensure that students are able to meet the special demands of subject-related terminology, the variety of written texts and of writing prevalent in each subject or the kinds of oral explanation and discussion that subject teachers may draw on in their lessons. One of the reasons we advocate greater collaboration among all teachers across the curriculum on issues relating to language as well as students' general well-being is to encourage exchange, cooperation and professional learning in these areas.

5.2.11 Task 7

Read the excerpt below adapted from the Northern Ireland curriculum for lower secondary school students (ages 11–14). Note the phrase in the introduction 'at a level appropriate to their ability', which implies that not all students are expected to reach a given standard in the various areas.

Try to identify areas of the above core syllabus for teacher education that would be helpful in preparing student teachers to meet these requirements in their teaching.

Across the curriculum, at a level appropriate to their ability, pupils should be enabled to develop skills in three modes of communication.

(a) *In Talking and Listening, pupils should be enabled to:*

1. *listen to and take part in discussions, explanations, role-plays and presentations*

2. *contribute comments, ask questions and respond to others' points of view*
3. *communicate information, ideas, opinions, feelings and imaginings, using an expanding vocabulary*
4. *structure talk so that ideas can be understood by others*
5. *speak clearly and adapt ways of speaking to audience and situation; and*
6. *use non-verbal methods to express ideas and engage with the listener.*

(b) In <u>Reading</u>, pupils should be enabled to:

1. *read a range of texts for information, ideas and enjoyment*
2. *use a range of strategies to read with increasing independence*
3. *find, select and use information from a range of sources*
4. *understand and explore ideas, events and features in texts, and*
5. *use evidence from texts to explain opinions.*

(c) In <u>Writing</u>, pupils should be enabled to:

1. *talk about, plan and edit work*
2. *communicate information, meaning, feelings, imaginings and ideas in a clear and organised way*
3. *develop, express and present ideas in a variety of forms and formats, using traditional and digital resources, for different audiences and purposes and*
4. *write with increasing accuracy and proficiency.* https://ccea.org.uk/key-stage-3/curriculum/communication

5.2.12 Commentary

The aim of pre-service teacher education is to enable future teachers to have a degree of confidence in their ability to teach their chosen subject(s) effectively. Depending on what the subject is, the ways in which students can be helped to progress towards the communicative competences listed in this sample curriculum will vary. Here are some suggestions as to areas of attention to language and communication in Table 5.1 that might help prepare future teachers for these challenges.

As regards <u>talking and listening</u>, 1 b, e and f; 2 a and b; 3 c, e and f; 5 c and d; 6 d and e; 7 a, b, c and h; 8 e, f, g, h, i; 9 b; 10 a, b and maybe c.

As regards <u>reading</u>, 1 c and d; 2 b; 3 b, c and f; 5 c, d and f; 6 d; 7 d, e, f, g, h; 8 a, b, c, d, i; 9 a, c, d; 10 a and b.

As regards <u>writing</u>, 1 a, b, d; 2 a and b; 3 c, e and f; 4 a and b; 5 a, c, d; 6 a and d; 7 f, g and h; 8 b, c, d and i; 9 c; 10 a, b maybe c.

In other words, there are plenty of topics within the syllabus that could be focused on, and the suggestions here are not meant to indicate that items omitted from these suggestions would not be helpful in equipping future teachers to meet the requirements of this curriculum. What is also evident from the core syllabus is that, although it is in the form of an itemised list, in fact there are all kinds of overlaps and intersections between the different areas.

5.2.13 Task 8

The willingness and capability of teachers of all subjects to engage in language-sensitive teaching has become a priority in many countries. There may be a number of reasons for this. Which of those mentioned below is most prevalent in a context you are familiar with? How prevalent are the others?

(a) A steady increase in the proportion of students in schools with first languages which are different from the language of schooling.
(b) The growth in the communication options and use of social media that expose students to a wider range of language varieties, (mis)information, opinions and standards of written language.
(c) The intense pressure on young people to achieve a level of functional literacy and oracy that enables them to succeed in employment and continue their education beyond school.
(d) The increasing language- and literacy-related demands that students need to cope with in high-stakes examinations in various subjects.
(e) Feedback from students indicating their need for more support with language and literacy.

5.2.14 Commentary

You may have wanted to say in response that several of these reasons are equally important. However, there are many contexts where there are relatively few students with different language backgrounds, although there may still be wide differences in the breadth of students' language repertoires. Certainly, the huge explosion in the use of social media, including by youngsters, and the likelihood of their having to deal with misinformation, conspiracy theories and other less harmful communications that seek to persuade and influence them mean that there is an onus on all teachers to promote critical language awareness (c.f. Fairclough, 2014). The third reason mentioned is equally crucial, especially because it is all too easy and common for those who struggle with language for whatever reason to give up their effort to attain functional literacy and oracy because they think that it requires effort and engagement with language that is beyond their capabilities. The 'high-stakes' examinations, especially written exams, used in many contexts as a means of enabling students to progress through secondary school, at the end of compulsory schooling or at age 19 for those students who continue beyond school-leaving age often focus students (and teachers) on areas of language and literacy in any subject that can mean that certain students are unable to 'prove' their own potential in the exam, often with significant consequences for their future. The fifth reason mentioned is perhaps less commonly cited, except before an important examination. This is partly because many teachers are not in the habit of finding out which aspects of their lessons and assignments their individual students find difficult. Students need to feel empowered as individuals to bring their language and other learning problems to the attention of their teachers without fearing loss of face with other learners.

You may have also wanted to add as additional reasons the need to develop young people's tolerance of diversity, intercultural awareness and an openness to encounters with people from other language and cultural backgrounds, as well as their need to understand the key relationship between language and power, whether in politics, the workplace, education or commercial transactions.

5.2.15 Task 9

A lower secondary school in a European country for students from ages 12 to 15 has recently undergone a ministry inspection. The head has now received the report. A lot of good points were mentioned, but the three inspectors raised some concerns about the language development and language awareness of students across the school. Based on their observation of 24 lessons and a review of randomly selected written assignments, the inspectors considered that, in general, teachers of all subjects were not providing enough support to students. They were especially concerned about students with disadvantages due to social or linguistic background and special needs. The inspectors recommended a series of in-service workshops on the topic led by specialists in language-sensitive education. The head teacher has now identified some specialists to provide these workshops.

In the first workshop attended by teachers of various different subjects, the moderator begins by eliciting from the participants some examples of students' language and communication difficulties that they have noticed during their own lessons and in students' homework assignments.

Read the transcript of the opening part of the conversation and make a note in your own words of the challenges mentioned. On the evidence of these teachers' remarks, which of the topics in the core syllabus above would it be useful to address in the series of workshops?

Workshop leader: Who wants to get the ball rolling? Say what subject you teach and describe at least one of the language problems you've found it hard to deal with.

(a) *Maria: I teach history in years one and two. Students need to be able to read and understand documents containing historical evidence. Some of them find the reading tasks slow and painful, and that holds things up for the whole class.*
(b) *David: I have a similar problem in geography, but students also have to write about climate or geological phenomena, for example. Often their writing isn't coherent and is much too informal.*
(c) *Dorota: One of my science classes has similar problems. It's a lovely group but half of them are from a migrant background so quite a lot of them don't contribute as much to group or class discussion as the students who don't have other first languages, though some of these also have similar difficulties. And their writing is rather basic with quite a few spelling and other mistakes.*

(d) *Angela: I'm an assistant teacher working in different classes and subjects trying to help individuals with learning or language difficulties. I've noticed quite a lot of students, and not just those with learning difficulties, still don't really understand the difference between the language they use at home or in the playground and the language they need to be able to use in their schooling. When they have to read or listen to something a bit more formal and specialised, they just switch off. It's almost a foreign language for them, although most of them aren't migrants.*

5.2.16 Commentary

This task offers just a few examples of the various language-related problems that teachers of any subject may have to deal with and how training in language-sensitive teaching and learning might help practising teachers to handle their students' language-related difficulties. They include:

(a) Diverse levels of literacy, in this case in reading: depending on their background and the amount of reading they do and what they read at home, some children can quickly adapt to new genres, such as authentic records in this case. Others may have had a much narrower range of reading experience or, if their home language is different from the language of schooling, may read much more slowly in school situations. These issues relate to topics 8a, 8b, 8c and 8i in the syllabus.
(b) Difficulty with another aspect of literacy, the ability to write using more 'academic' language: it is not surprising that in early secondary education, students have problems adapting their writing from the informal style of narration or description that they were used to in primary school to the more formal kind of writing expected in most subjects. This relates especially to the topics under 5 and also topic 6d, as well as the topics under 9.
(c) Lack of confidence in speaking and writing in any subject: many teachers find it challenging to deal with very diverse classes where some students with different language backgrounds are still developing their skills in the language of schooling, and some monolingual students also lack confidence in using language in class that is expected to be clearer and more formal than what they are used to outside school. This lack of confidence due to their limited repertoires can be greater if they feel intimidated by other students in the class who have no problem adjusting to the demands of using more 'academic' language in the various subjects. These issues related to the topics under 3, 6d, 8e, 8f, 8 g and 8i, and the topics under 10.
(d) Lack of motivation and concentration: The assistant teacher mentioning this probably works with individual students who have difficulty keeping up. Their lack of concentration and effort when dealing with the written or spoken language may be due to various factors, including not having had breakfast or a proper night's sleep, but it is usually also to do with their relatively narrow experience of using language other than outside school. It is important that

educators such as this assistant teacher, who are working across subject boundaries with individual students who have difficulties, are also familiar with the range of topics in the syllabus, especially those under 'language and communication in education'.

When guiding teachers in any of these overlapping areas, a first important step is to help them understand the challenges their students face. These teachers have already done this to a certain extent by noticing and reflecting on difficulties their own students are having. During the workshops, the moderators may suggest that teachers do observation of teaching that focuses on language-related issues and how the teachers being observed handle them. This could also include self-observation using video recordings, or observation by a colleague or mentor. Such guided observation can help teachers to define which students are having what kinds of language difficulties, and perhaps to identify the causes of the difficulties in given cases. To do this, it is important for teachers of any subject to have access to or build up a picture of the language repertoires of their students. This will help them to offer better individualised support taking into account the kinds of support—or absence of support—witnessed in the teaching they have observed. They may also be better able to grade tasks to take account within the class of different levels of general proficiency in the language of schooling, and especially of literacy and oracy.

5.2.17 Task 10

Imagine you have been asked to lead a one-hour workshop for teacher colleagues of your own who work at primary or lower secondary level. Prepare an outline plan for a session that would help them to work with students in their classes on one of the issues mentioned in Task 5. Mention some materials and activities you might use.

5.2.18 Commentary

Depending on the focus, adapting task ideas from Units 1–4 of the book could, we believe, be useful for such a one-hour workshop. For practising teachers, another very useful activity, including when the workshop is online, can be to incentivise them to exchange examples of tasks they have given students, and of the difficulties students encountered doing the task, including how each teacher then tried to help students overcome their difficulties. Each workshop participant could, for example, share with the others a range of good and not so good samples of written work. Asking colleagues whether their students have similar problems with that kind of writing and discussing in more detail what the causes of the problems might be can be a useful awareness-raising activity for all. Following this, ideas for addressing the problems identified that have helped students can be exchanged and exemplified.

In certain cases, this kind of collective sharing may lead to an initiative to develop a small bank of shared resources for future use by the group.

5.2 Section 1: Improving the Current Situation in Teacher Education and Training

5.2.19 Task 11

Read the short extracts in Fig. 5.1 from discussions between teachers who have recently been observed and the mentors who observed them. In each case, suggest an answer or comment that you think would be useful and indicate the relevant area of the syllabus in Table 5.1 above that could be relevant in follow-up work.

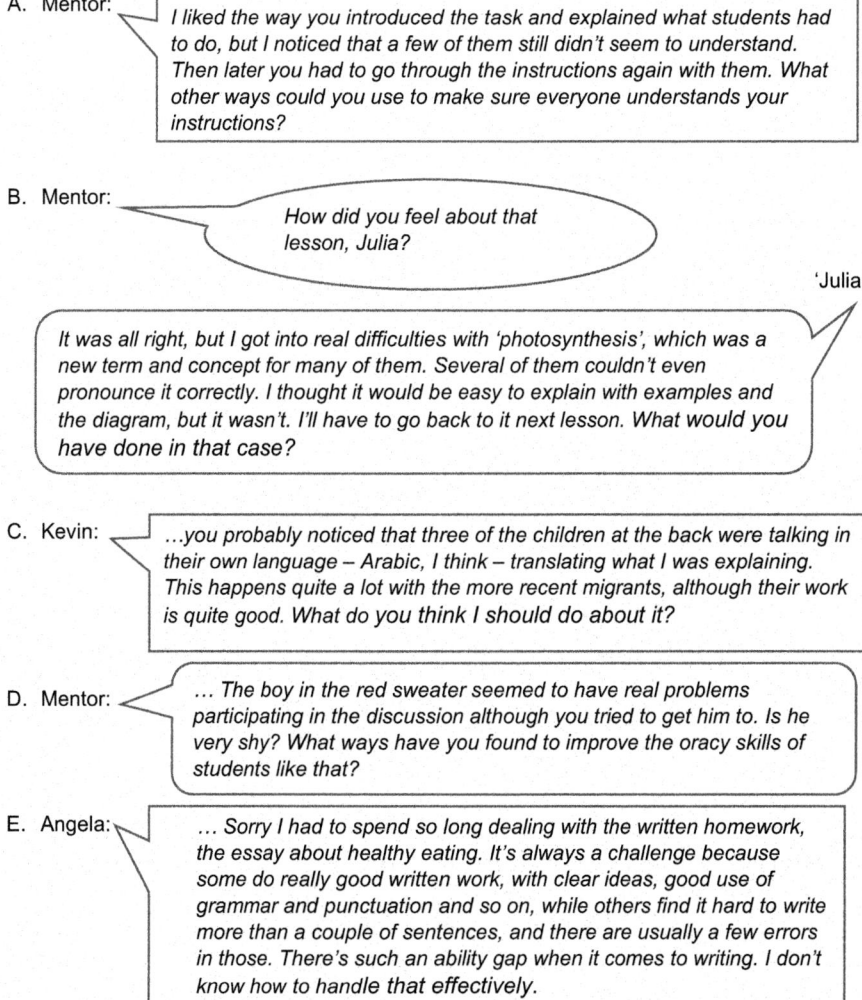

A. Mentor: *I liked the way you introduced the task and explained what students had to do, but I noticed that a few of them still didn't seem to understand. Then later you had to go through the instructions again with them. What other ways could you use to make sure everyone understands your instructions?*

B. Mentor: *How did you feel about that lesson, Julia?*

'Julia': *It was all right, but I got into real difficulties with 'photosynthesis', which was a new term and concept for many of them. Several of them couldn't even pronounce it correctly. I thought it would be easy to explain with examples and the diagram, but it wasn't. I'll have to go back to it next lesson. What would you have done in that case?*

C. Kevin: *...you probably noticed that three of the children at the back were talking in their own language – Arabic, I think – translating what I was explaining. This happens quite a lot with the more recent migrants, although their work is quite good. What do you think I should do about it?*

D. Mentor: *... The boy in the red sweater seemed to have real problems participating in the discussion although you tried to get him to. Is he very shy? What ways have you found to improve the oracy skills of students like that?*

E. Angela: *... Sorry I had to spend so long dealing with the written homework, the essay about healthy eating. It's always a challenge because some do really good written work, with clear ideas, good use of grammar and punctuation and so on, while others find it hard to write more than a couple of sentences, and there are usually a few errors in those. There's such an ability gap when it comes to writing. I don't know how to handle that effectively.*

Fig. 5.1 Issues from lesson observation

5.2.20 Commentary

If well prepared for and well-handled, being observed and having a discussion afterwards can be a means of quickly becoming much more aware of where language and communication issues are aiding or hindering learning, and of identifying ways of overcoming or at least attenuating such issues. In the fictional examples above, the following can be assumed:

- The observations were planned at the request of or with the consent of the teacher.
- Both the teacher and the observer knew beforehand that the focus would be mainly on language and communication (rather than subject knowledge, methodology, behaviour, etc.).
- The mentor had information about the objectives and the plan of the lesson.
- Both were prepared for a discussion afterwards that would focus on problem-solving and support rather than evaluation.

There are various possible suggestions in each case. The following are examples.

(a) Instructions are key, and it is important to ensure they are clearly understood. One way of checking this is to ask one or more students to repeat them or explain them in their own words. In some cases where the task is more complicated it may be helpful to write the steps on the board in a list. Syllabus areas: 7c, 7d and 7e.

(b) This example is about scaffolding, finding ways of helping students to work with the language needed to describe concepts and processes. The mentor might suggest not worrying so much at first about the term 'photosynthesis', which is not that easy to pronounce or spell, but to start by guiding students' understanding of the process by which plants use light, water and carbon dioxide to create oxygen and energy (in the form of sugar). Some of it may be familiar, and questions such as 'how do plants grow?' and 'what happens to plants when there is no light?' may elicit the knowledge students have from their own observations. They may also be aware from their growing interest in climate and global warming that plants, especially forests, play a role in reducing the amount of carbon dioxide in the atmosphere. Clearly, visual aids such as the diagram in Fig. 5.2 below can help clarify the process in student' minds. It may well be that at least some students have heard the term 'photosynthesis' before, and a question such as 'does anyone know what this process is called?' will help to find out. Examining the two main elements in the word, 'synthesis' and 'photo', which are both terms they may already know, may help students to pronounce, write and remember it in future. Syllabus areas: topics under 7, and 9a.

(c) One response from the mentor might be 'don't worry!' Teachers often worry when they hear other languages in the lesson, especially if they are languages they don't understand. However, there is no logical reason why students shouldn't use their first language to 'mediate' to their peers concepts or information in a language that is unfamiliar to them. In the example, it is likely to save everyone including the teacher time and effort. However, Kevin might

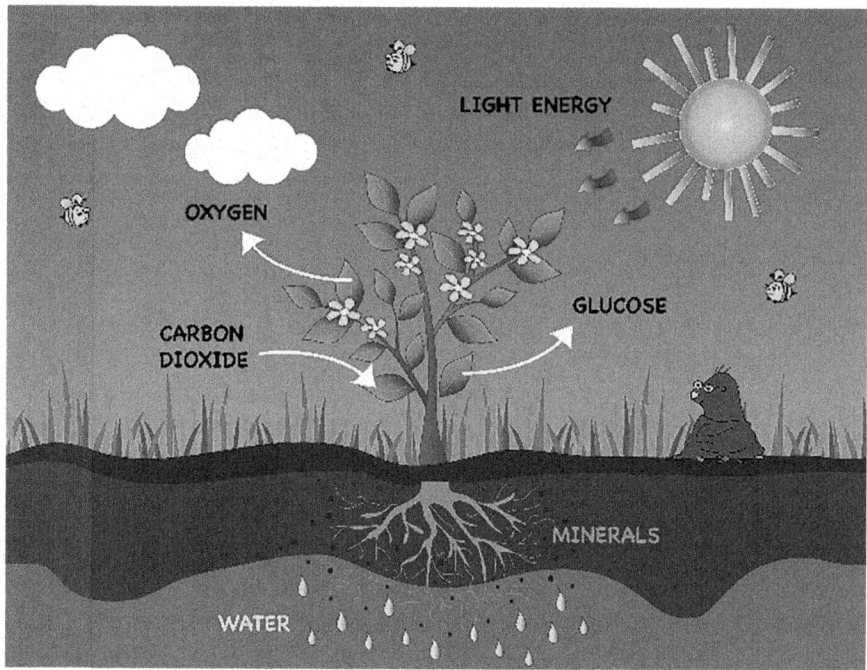

Fig. 5.2 Diagram of photosynthesis

need to check with those students after the lesson or during group work whether they have in fact understood what he was saying. Syllabus areas: topics under 9.

(d) This is a trickier problem because it focuses on an individual student who for whatever reason is inhibited. The teacher may respond that she does not wish to push him too hard or make an example of him and prefers gentle persuasion. She may say that she will continue to try to get him to participate but in pair- or small group work where there is less reason to be inhibited. She may be aware of reasons why he is so shy, such as low-level autism, conditions at home, etc. She may also wish to speak individually to the child to find out whether his language skills are the root of the problem rather than just shyness. Syllabus areas: 3a, areas under 4, 8a, 8e, 8 g, 8i.

(e) Angela clearly finds it hard to deal with mixed writing ability in a class where literacy levels vary greatly. This is a delicate area due to the stigma attached to low literacy. One solution is to use graded writing tasks. Instead of everyone doing the same homework assignment, two or three versions of the task can be organised in which there are different levels of challenge. At the easier level, the assignment can be less challenging in terms of length, e.g. number of words, and more support or scaffolding may be given in the form of leading questions, things to mention, vocabulary to use, etc. At the 'higher' level, the demands can be correspondingly more challenging, and less guidance can be given. If the written work is to be looked at in class it may be important to do this through group work putting students with the same graded task into the same groups so that they can compare their work. Syllabus areas: 1a, 1c, 6d, 7f, 7 g, 7 h, 8a, 8b, 8c. However, as suggested in the commentary, methodological know-how, including especially of the handling of mixed ability and graded tasks, is also relevant to Angela's concerns.

5.2.21 Summary

The purpose of this section was to make the case for including a focus on language-sensitive teaching in pre-service and in-service education, and to give readers the experience of putting together modules or courses that focus on specific aspects of language-sensitive education. Good quality teacher education and training has a powerful multiplier effect, and it is to this we must look if teaching in all subjects is to become more language sensitive in future. This may well require a significant shift in thinking by pre-service curriculum designers wrestling with an already crammed programme of compulsory modules on their courses, and by in-service trainers faced with competing needs and priorities in an educational environment where almost everyone seems to be overwhelmed by the pace of change.

The following section offers further stimuli and support for those interested in taking these challenges on by exploring a range of teacher education task types that can be used in language-sensitive teacher education for teachers of all subjects.

5.3 Section 2: Tasks for Teacher Training

5.3.1 Introduction

In this section, we focus on the practicalities of raising teacher and teacher trainee awareness of the importance of language issues in subjects across the curriculum. We have chosen to do this by presenting a series of tasks. To build on this, we provide in appendix 2 an inventory of task types which may be seen as typical and potentially generative, enabling readers to use them as starting points for the design of tasks for their own contexts and their own training purposes. We also consider the role of classroom observation through three tasks that turn the spotlight on language issues in a teacher's language repertoire. In Section 3, we go on to highlight some existing examples of good practice on teacher education courses.

5.3.2 Task 12

Try the task below and (i) decide whether you would use it with a group of pre-service teacher trainees and (ii) state what students in such a group might learn from it.

Read this lesson transcript of a lower secondary school lesson about bullying. In what ways does the teacher's use of language support or hinder her learners in developing their oracy skills?

> Teacher: *After what happened in the playground last week, we're going to look at bullying today. Let's start by trying to understand what it means. You have two minutes to discuss this in pairs and then I'll ask you to say what it means for you.*
> Class: (discussion)
> Teacher: *OK, time's up. I'm interested to listen to what you've come up with. Please, all of you, listen to your classmates carefully and be ready to add your own views. Cary, what did you and Gemma decide?*
> Cary: *Well, we think it's when someone picks on you and it's unfair.*
> Teacher: *That's a useful way to see it. What exactly do you mean by 'picking on' someone?*
> Gemma: *It can be calling names or maybe just joking about someone's appearance.*
> Teacher: *Those are good examples. Why do you think people do things like that? Anyone?*
> Miriam: *Maybe because they want to show how clever they are?*
> Teacher: *But is it really clever?*
> Jason: *No, it's not. It's actually dumb.*
> Teacher (sharply): *Be careful with your choice of words, Jason!* (more normal tone): *But bullies don't see it like that, do they? You might have experienced name-calling or jokes about your appearance. Does anyone want to share what happened? Yes, Maeve?*
> Maeve: *People make jokes about my name because it's Irish and I feel awful—like I'm the odd one out.*
> Teacher: *That's tough, Maeve. What do your friends think when that happens?*
> Maeve: *Some of them laugh…*(hesitates)
> Teacher: *Go on …. nobody here is laughing.*
> Maeve: *I sometimes laugh too because I don't want to look silly but …* (hesitates again)
> Teacher: *But…..??*
> Maeve: *Inside of myself, I feel awful. I feel angry with the person who joked ….. and angry with myself for … for being too weak to stand up for myself.*
> Teacher: *Maeve, thanks for opening up. So …. anyone…. what can you do to stop someone like Maeve feeling awful? And what can <u>she</u> do?* (Lesson continues) (freely adapted from an online source)

5.3.3 Commentary

If this transcript were used on a pre-service course, it would give trainees evidence of some ways in which a teacher can elicit responses from learners on a topic which isn't always easy to discuss. Trainees might focus on the teacher's use of prompts and direct questions, but also on the way she links ideas together and probes gently for learners to be more precise or to give examples. They might notice that she also gives a very clear signal that she wants to listen to the children's contributions, which inspires trust and encourages them to speak. Trainees might also home in on the exchange with Jason, which probably discourages him, and on the longer exchange with Maeve, where the teacher's carefully expressed empathy draws the girl out to say what is clearly on her mind. A teacher educator might point out that a teacher needs to build up a range of strategies aimed at fostering dialogue in class and confidence in each individual learner.

5.3.4 Task 13

The task below is targeted at teachers of biology attending a short in-service training course, but it may be seen as relevant to other teachers because of the focus on aspects of language that are encountered across discipline areas. What might they learn from it, and how might it change what they do in their classrooms?

Work with a colleague. Read this text about parasites (Fig. 5.3) and:

(i) Identify the terms which will be new to a Year 12 class and state how you would introduce them.
(ii) Identify four prefixes that are common in biology and agree on their meanings.
(iii) Prepare a diagram to use in class to show the six strategy-related ways of classifying parasites, and practise presenting it to each other.
(iv) Agree on any other language features that might cause difficulty for your students

---

Parasites and why we need them

A parasite is best defined as an organism which lives on or in another organism, known as the host. The relationship usually benefits the parasite more than the host, which is sometimes harmed by the parasite. Like many scientific terms, the word 'parasite' is derived from Greek, in this case meaning 'one who eats at another's table'. Parasites occur in all forms of life, even among micro-organisms. Common examples include viruses, mosquitoes, ticks, tapeworms and mistletoe.

Parasites can be classified in different ways. Here are some examples:

1. Classification according to where they live: Ectoparasites such as ticks live on the surface or skin of a host. Endoparasites live inside a host's body, tapeworms for example. Mesoparasites, copepods for instance, penetrate by entering through an opening in the body and find a way of embedding themselves.

2. According to life cycle: An obligate parasite depends on a host in order to live through its life cycle, whereas a facultative parasite can complete its life cycle without a host.

3. According to how they are transmitted: Trophically transmitted parasites, roundworms for instance, are ingested, sometimes with food. Directly transmitted parasites, by contrast, find their own way to a host, e.g. fleas and ticks.

More than 50% of all known species are parasitic in nature, and though they may be regarded as a nuisance or even dangerous by their potential hosts, they do have a role to play in any healthy ecosystem. They help to control dominant species and to ensure diversity. They may also transfer genetic matter between different organisms, meaning that parasitism plays a vital part in natural evolutionary processes.

(text freely adapted from an internet source)

Fig. 5.3 Parasites

5.3.5 Commentary

This task draws the attention of the biology teachers to some of the features of language that are typical of the discourse of their subject. As biologists, they will take these for granted, but as teachers they will need to engage with them and be ready to make them available to their students. In response to question (i), they might home in on highly specialised terms such as compound nouns with prefixes (e.g. 'micro-organism') and this might lead them on to the meaning of prefixes (e.g. 'para-', 'micro-', 'ecto-', 'endo-') addressed in question (ii). As a by-product of this, they may point out that some of the common examples of parasites, such as fleas, lice or roundworms can be defined by reference to the different types of parasite, thus showing why these distinctions are important to biologists. On question (iii), getting the teacher participants to prepare a diagram (it will probably be a typical species classification diagram with a hierarchy) will feed into their lesson preparation, and talking about the diagram will encourage them to think clearly about how to present such relationships to their students. In answer to question (iv) they might pick up on specialised adjectives such as 'obligate' or 'facultative' or maybe suffixes like '-ism' or '-pod'.

The four tasks encourage teachers to see the language of biology from a learner's perspective as well as their own, and to think about language-related ways of bridging the gap from where they are to where their students are. In this way, teachers are encouraged to expand their own pedagogical language repertoires while developing their learners' specialist repertoires. While the original task was aimed at biology teachers, our purpose here is more general: to show how a language focus on a subject text can encourage teachers to see the relationship between content and language and to take it into account when planning lessons. The next task builds on this.

5.3.6 Task 14

The task below is targeted at secondary teachers on an in-service course focused on language issues across subject boundaries. What is the potential value of the task to course participants, and what might they take back from it to their own teaching contexts?

Work in groups of 3 or 4. Read this short transcript of a staffroom conversation in a secondary school and identify the issues it raises and what measures the deputy head might need to take in order to offer support to the teacher and the learners under discussion. Be ready to share your ideas with the whole group. You have 15 minutes.

French teacher: It's a relief to get away from Year 8 and sit down for a few minutes!
Deputy head: Yes, you do look stressed. What's the problem with them?
French teacher: The kids are nice enough, but most of them are just not interested in French. They don't see the point in learning another language.
Deputy head: So they're simply not motivated....

French teacher: Not at all! But it's really tough for them to understand the basics of French when they know so little about their own language. Some of them can't even express themselves in English! And as for grammar.... (shakes head)

Deputy head: What proportion of the class are we talking about here? Maybe they need some support.

French teacher: I'd say more than a quarter of the group. Some of them are recent arrivals from abroad and they are still struggling with English, but some are as British as I am!

Deputy head: It does sound like a bit of a challenge.

French teacher: It is........ and to be honest, I sometimes think I don't have the skills I need to cope with such a mixed group ..... different languages, different cultural backgrounds. I've heard other colleagues talking about the same thing.

Deputy head: I'm glad you opened up about all this. I'll do some asking around and thinking and I'll come back to you.....

5.3.7 Commentary

Teaching can be a pretty lonely profession and teachers don't always talk frankly about the problems they face when they close the classroom door and work with the realities of a difficult class. Some course participants may have experienced similar frustrations with mixed ability, mixed nationality classes, and this task has the potential to give them permission to open up about some of the difficulties they face on a daily basis. The staffroom discussion focuses on language issues, and it reveals on the one hand some basic literacy concerns about the Year 8 students, while on the other hand possibly pointing to shortcomings in the French teacher's own language repertoire. The fact that course participants are asked to offer some responses to these issues allows them to draw analogies with their own situations and possibly to come up with suggestions to take back with them. Participants might note the French teacher's assertion that other colleagues have similar difficulties, and this might inspire the deputy head to plan an in-house training day with a focus on language, or maybe some peer observations; course participants in turn might take similar suggestions back to their own schools after the course.

5.3.8 Task 15

This task might be used with pre-service trainees or in-service teachers at primary level. What might they gain from it?

Look at this text about maps (Fig. 5.4) and (i) identify the language points that a teacher will need to think about in preparing a lesson for upper primary school students, and (ii) prepare questions to draw the attention of teacher participants to these points. Work in pairs and be ready to report back.

5.3 Section 2: Tasks for Teacher Training

> *You probably have an atlas at home, and some of you may also have a globe with a map of the Earth on it. What's the difference? A globe is a three-dimensional representation of the Earth, which is also three dimensional. A map, on the other hand, only has two dimensions. If you were to take a map of the world and wrap it around a large ball.it would not give an accurate view of the world. Mapmakers, more correctly called cartographers, face the challenge of representing the Earth as clearly as possible on paper or in the pages of an atlas. Different cartographers have done this in different ways, known as map projections. Some of these are more accurate than others.*
>
> *On the well-known Mercator projection, for example, the oceans are huge, which makes this kind of map useful for navigation purposes. However, Greenland is shown as bigger in area than South America or Australia, which is clearly a distortion. There are hundreds of different projections. Some try to take account of the curvature of the Earth by showing the North and South Poles in a kind of flattened-out way at the top and bottom of the map, while others simply show the Earth in a way which is easier for intended users, such as navigators or school students like you, even if sizes of land masses are distorted. The projection used in The Times Atlas is an example of this. If you have an atlas at home, take a look and find out which projection it is based on.*
>
> (text from authors' own material)

Fig. 5.4 Making Maps

5.3.9 Commentary

This task is an opportunity to take a language-centred view of a classroom text for upper primary learners. Participants might identify, and prepare questions around, some or all of these features:

- some nouns and associated verbs that might be new but which are keys to understanding (*projection/project, navigation/navigate, distortion/distort*)
- compound nouns and adjectives (*two-dimensional, three-dimensional, mapmaker, well-known, right-hand*)
- the structure and meaning of the 'if' sentences in the first paragraph (quite complicated!)
- a common way of defining and naming (*is known as*)
- ways of giving examples (*'such as...', 'for example'*).

They might also note that the style of the text is more direct and informal than that used in the biology text in Task 13. This is typical of many texts used with this age group, and it is interesting to see how the bar is raised in textbooks for secondary schools, which often make use of more specialised and complex language.

It is likely that participants will 'teach' each other about language while working in pairs, but the task also presents the trainer with an opportunity to summarise and highlight key language issues in the text. The trainer might also ask participants to prepare a lesson based on the text, and to include particular attention to the language issues they have identified.

5.3.10 Task 16

Look at Table 5.4. Consider the list of language-related subskills which a subject specialist teacher will need in order to be able to teach effectively. Divide the list into a maximum of 4 categories based on what the subskills have in common. Give a heading to each of your categories.

Table 5.4 Language-related subskills needed for subject specialist teacher

1. ...... formulate and ask effective questions	12. ...... plan and deliver a clear and accessible presentation using PowerPoint or other media
2. ...... give clear instructions for tasks, experiments or homework	13. ...... simplify language for younger learners
3. ...... reformulate student contributions supportively	14. ...... describe processes in their specialism
4. ...... elicit ideas from students without using questions	15. ...... deconstruct a specialist text to identify key language features
5. ...... define specialist terms in a comprehensible way	16. ...... acknowledge and build on different languages represented in a class
6. ...... paraphrase or reformulate a question or explanation to make it easier to understand	17. ...... write clear handouts and worksheets for class use
7. ...... provide language scaffolding for students' spoken and written assignments	18. ...... give students feedback about their language as well as their subject knowledge
8. ...... distinguish between Basic Interpersonal Communication Skills (BICS) and Cognitive Academic Language Proficiency (CALP) (Cummins, 1979)	19. ...... assess language as well as content
9. ...... offer language support needed by migrant students	20. ...... identify the main specialist text types which students will need to read and/or produce
10. ...... explain a new concept or define a new term	21. ...... take account of the varying levels of literacy and oracy in students in any class that they teach
11. ...... explain the aim of an activity	22. ...... help learners to express themselves

5.3.11 Task 17

Imagine that you are the CPD coordinator in a secondary school. Your colleagues in disciplines across the curriculum have agreed on a programme of peer observation with a focus on how they use language in their classrooms. Draw on the categories you identified in Task 16 to create a short observation checklist to be used in this context, keeping in mind that teachers will be observing reciprocally in 'buddy' pairs and will be discussing their experience after each observed lesson.

5.3.12 Task 18

Consider this transcript of part of an upper primary school lesson. Refer to the list in Task 16 and your checklist from Task 17 and state what advice you would give to the teacher.

> Teacher: *OK, settle down please. What we're going to do is....we're going to work on whales again today. Who can remember the name of the biggest whale?*
> Several pupils: *The blue whale!*
> Teacher: *OK. Don't all shout at once. And where do most blue whales live?*
> Several pupils: *In the Antarctic Ocean!*
> Teacher: *I just asked you not to shout all together. Remember that. And what do blue whales mostly eat? Put your hands up if you know. Martin?*
> Martin: *Some kind of fish, but I forget the word.*
> Teacher: *OK. You're half-way there. Anyone else? Lottie?*
> Lottie: *I think it's called krill.*
> Teacher: *Is she right?*
> Several pupils: *Yes, yes....*
> Teacher: *But it's not really a fish, is it? It's actually a crustacean.*
> Class: (*General muttering and perplexed expressions*).
> Teacher: *OK, that's enough. Settle down. Now I want you to work in groups and write....... let me see ..... three questions you would like to ask about whales, but you can write more if you like*
> Marianne: *Which groups, Miss? I don't want to be with Ellie or Ciaran. They're so bossy.*
> Teacher: *Same groups as yesterday. Move quickly and get started.*
> A different pupil: *What questions should we ask?*
> Teacher: *That's up to you in your group, Jenny. Just brainstorm. And don't waste time because we have a lot to get through today.*

5.3.13 Commentary

In the many observation checklists that we have found and which are in common use, little or no attention is given to the way a teacher uses language, and even less to the way they contribute to their learners' oracy or literacy. This is usually seen as the business of teachers of the language of schooling rather than of subject teachers, who are more likely to be concentrating on subject knowledge in their lessons. While this is to some extent understandable in contexts where teachers are judged by their students' achievements in examinations and the extent to which subject-based curriculum objectives are met, it is also regrettable because well-planned language use contributes so much to any learning experience. Tasks 16 and 17 offer ways in which this imbalance can be addressed, emphasising as they do the notion that every teacher is a language teacher (van der Walt & Ruiters, 2011).

The primary teacher in Task 18 clearly needs advice about some of the ways she uses language, including giving clear instructions, asking and targeting questions, giving clear explanations and supporting pupils when they answer. Some of her pupils clearly feel a bit uncertain about what they should do and she doesn't really pick up on this in the language she uses.

Unless and until we find ways of attending to language in teaching practice and in in-service observations of teaching, it will be difficult address the kinds of weakness that this teacher displays.

5.3.14 Summary

Our purpose in this section has been to engage you as a reader, with some task types that might be appropriate for use in teacher education and training courses. These might be adapted to the context you are working in, drawing on data which you are able to access through your work with teachers and trainees. Data samples may be taken from classroom transcripts, from textbooks, from dialogue in training sessions or just from teachers' stories and experience reports. We know from our own practice that a task-based approach to language issues in teaching and learning is far more likely to engage course participants in thinking and discussion than lectures or pure theory-based inputs, and that following up tasks with reading around relevant theory is often an effective strategy. This is backed up in the literature on task-based learning and task-based teacher training (Padmini Shankar, 2021; van den Branden, 2006, for example). If this section has inspired you to devise your own tasks for use in teacher education or training, it will have served its purpose. An Inventory of many different task types for Teacher Education is offered in the appendix to this book.

5.4 Section 3: Drawing on Good Practice

5.4.1 Introduction

In our research towards this book we looked for examples of good practice in the area of language-sensitive teacher education and found relatively few, either in pre-service or in-service contexts. German-speaking countries in Europe have proved to be an exception to this finding, and it is to them and to the Netherlands that we turn for the material we have selected for inclusion in this section. We will look at curriculum documents, online resources and training materials, interspersed with tasks. We hope that these examples might serve as starting points for innovation and further initiatives in this neglected and rather under-researched field.

5.4.2 Germany

German speakers among you will be interested to look at work that has been carried out in North Rhine-Westphalia in the form of a resource book for teacher educators working in pre-service training institutions (Oleschko, 2017). The book provides a rich and detailed curriculum for language-sensitive teacher education with specialised sections on different areas of school curricula. This is backed up by a section on relevant theory, samples of task types and references to further reading to underpin modules that are taught on teacher education programmes.

5.4.3 Austria

An Austrian teacher educator at the Pedagogical University in Styria, writing about their Bachelor's Degree for Secondary Education, mentions that 'the curriculum contains relatively little focus on language awareness and simply refers to multilingualism in the wider context of diversity and inclusivity' (Boeckmann 2021, personal communication, authors' translation). The situation is different in the curriculum of the Bachelor's Degree for Primary Education, mainly because teachers at primary level are generalists rather than subject specialists. The curriculum contains courses in a number of language-related areas including 'Speaking, Listening and Communicating', 'The Knowledge Base and Methodology of Language-Sensitive Teaching' and 'Language-Sensitive Teaching in Mathematics and Other Subjects'. (Boeckmann ibid.). The recently revised Bachelor's curriculum at another Pedagogical University, in Lower Austria, provides for 'Sprachliche Bildung' (language education) as a cross-curricular issue in more than half of its modules.

5.4.4 Task 19

Who should teach the language dimension on pre-service courses for primary or secondary levels such as those mentioned above? Should it be the responsibility of educators who are specialists in language, or of educators with different subject specialisms? Make a list of arguments for and against in each case.

5.4.5 *Commentary*

Arguments in favour of giving this responsibility to a language specialist might include:

- Knowledge of how language works, its systems and varieties and its terminology
- Pedagogical awareness of how to teach aspects of language
- Familiarity with discourse and genre analysis

Arguments in favour of entrusting it to a subject specialist or a primary education specialist might include:

- Specialist subject knowledge
- First-hand familiarity with subject discourse and common text types (e.g. in historical documents, experimental reports, etc.)
- High levels of familiarity with the main cognitive processes in a subject (e.g. the steps in scientific method, logical connections, etc.)

The arguments in favour of one way are effectively the arguments against in each case. Given this, it is evident that there is scope for cross-disciplinary cooperation between language specialists and subject specialists in the process of planning and teaching courses or modules on language in teacher education. This kind of cross-disciplinary cooperation is still all too rare in higher education institutions, where subject boundaries are clearly delineated and territory often fiercely defended.

The Austrian Language Competence Centre (ÖSZ) offers language support to practising teachers of all subjects, meeting a need that has become more urgent as a result of the large influx of refugees in Austrian schools. Language-sensitive teaching is an important topic area in their catalogue of training materials, which include video inputs by specialists in the area. In one of these videos, Josef Leisen, from the University of Mainz in Germany, draws a distinction between two aspects of a secondary teacher's oral language repertoire: on the one hand, the kind of language which is 'pre-cooked' and appears typically in task instructions and other teaching materials, and on the other hand, the more spontaneous and unpredictable sort of language which is needed to manage or facilitate (German: 'moderieren') a class effectively. He offers a number of examples of good and bad practice in facilitating, and this next task is adapted from one of the scenarios he uses in his talk.

(Original in German available at: https://www.schule.at/bildungsnews/experten-wissen/gespraeche-im-fachunterricht-fuehren accessed 21 January 2022)

5.4.6 Task 20

Look at the examples in Table 5.5 of appropriate and inappropriate teacher language when facilitating different stages in a lesson. What is inappropriate about the language used in the first list and what is appropriate about the other examples? What characterises the language used in each case?

Table 5.5 Appropriate and inappropriate teacher language

Inappropriate language	Appropriate language
Who's confident enough to present?	Present what you've learned and use your mind-map in the presentation.
Which group has found something out?	We're going to listen to ideas from three groups. Your group first, then yours, then yours.
Wrong! Who's got it right?	We're going to look at another example. Please pay attention to similarities and differences.

5.4.7 Task 21

In another video in the same series, aimed at primary teachers, Daniela Rotter offers a sample of dialogic exchanges between teacher and pupils who have just carried out a simple experiment. From this transcript, translated from German, can you identify the main features of the teacher's skill in facilitating this kind of exchange?

> *One of the Pupils: The balloon experiment. First we tipped baking powder into the ... erm ...balloon and then we tipped two centimetres of vinegar into a mineral bottle ... a mineral water bottle ...*
> *Other pupils: poured!..... poured!*
> *Teacher: Stop! You are right. But just the same, try not to interrupt her. 'Tipped' is for powder, 'poured' is....*
> *First pupil: .... poured. And then we put the balloon .... erm....what do we call that bit of a bottle?*
> *Teacher: What do we call that part of the top of a bottle? Where the bottle is open. (pause) Doesn't anyone know? (pause) It's the mouth of the bottle.*
> *First pupil: We fixed the balloon over the mouth of the bottle and then we waited for a bit. And then we put the baking powder from the balloon into the bottle. I mean we moved the balloon so that the powder fell in by itself.*
> *Teacher: And in your group, did you talk about why that happened? Did you guess why?*
> *First pupil: We thinked ... thought ... a bit... but we didn't really find out. We... I.... thought it was something to do with the vinegar and the baking powder. Because when vinegar and baking powder come together, air somehow comes out, or something like that.*
> *That's really a proper research result. When vinegar and baking powder come together.... what's the special word we can use for 'come together'?*
> *Other pupils: combine!*
> Original in German available at: https://www.schule.at/bildungsnews/expertenwissen/gespraeche-im-fachunterricht-fuehren (accessed 6th January 2022)

5.4.8 Commentary

A key reason for including these two tasks is that they focus on oracy which remains relatively neglected in teacher education and training. Leisen addresses the need for teachers to facilitate oral classroom exchanges in an appropriate way, and in doing so, he shifts the emphasis from what teachers *know* about language to what they *do* with it in evolving and dynamic classroom situations. This involves pedagogical as well as linguistic choices. The samples of appropriate language in the right-hand column of the table are underpinned by careful thought about their impact on the learners and their learning. They are detailed and concrete in nature and they are supportive rather than confrontational.

In the second extract, Rotter highlights the following key aspects of the teacher's behaviour and interventions:

- The teacher takes a back seat in order to allow the pupil to report.
- He allows the pupil space and time to formulate her report.

- He asks open, clear questions.
- He clarifies meanings and asks follow-up questions.
- He rephrases the pupil's contributions in order to help her to be more focused.

Here, too, the choices the teacher makes are informed by pedagogy as well as by the language repertoire that he has available. It is very striking that he remains supportive and encouraging throughout, and pupils are quick to pick up on his cues when he asks them for alternative terms to those used by the pupil who is reporting. Thus, there is a clear and positive impact on the development of oracy in the pupils, and clear evidence of expansion in their linguistic repertoires. We also see the beginnings of a bridge towards specialist language, an issue which is taken further in the tasks that follow.

5.4.9 Switzerland

The following statement prefaces a description of a language module on a Pre-Service Teacher Education Course at St Gallen Pedagogical University (Pädagogische Hochschule) in Switzerland.

> *The aim of the module 'Profession-specific language competence for teachers' is to familiarise trainee teachers with language used in professional contexts so that they are able to sensitise their future pupils to the meaning and functioning of language and communication beyond school contexts.* (authors' translation from German)

5.4.10 Task 22

It is plain from this statement that the designers of the module are thinking of the language needs both of the trainee teacher and of their future pupils. What impact would focusing on the language needs of the teacher as well as the pupils have on the language repertoires and awareness of future subject teachers? What are the implications for teacher educators?

5.4.11 Task 23

The St Gallen course team make a distinction between '*Alltagssprache*' (everyday language: EL), '*Bildungssprache*' (the language of schooling: LS) and '*Fachsprache*' (subject specialist language: SSL), seeing '*Bildungssprache*' as a kind of bridge between the other two (Picenoni et al., 2021). The course team consider it essential for trainee teachers to understand this three-way distinction and to be able to work with it, and this is a key area of focus in their language-focused module.

Consider this classroom extract from Unit 3 and find examples of each of the three categories (EL, LS or SSL):

> Teacher: (looking at jars of crystals on a shelf) *OK, well done. The experiment you did last week to grow crystals worked very well. Some of them look beautiful! And in your groups, you've discussed how you did it. Now we need to write up the experiment in more formal scientific language. Can anyone give me some words or expressions you could use in the report?*
> Amy: *'Solution? Saline solution'?*
> Teacher: *What do you mean by 'saline'?* (she writes 'saline' on the board).
> Amy: *Mixed with salt?*
> Teacher: *OK. You said, "we poured lots of salt into warm water". How would you express that in a more formal written description of the experiment? What would you need to change?*
> Ricardo: *Get rid of 'we' to make it more impersonal? and maybe 'lots'?*
> Teacher: *But how can you get rid of 'we'?*
> Isabel: *We could write: "A large quantity of salt was poured into warm water"?*
> Teacher: *What do others think?*
> Jake: *Yes, that's good, and we could add some more detail: "half a litre of water was heated and put into a glass container"—something like that?*
> Teacher: *Wow, that's pretty good, Jake. Do you know the grammatical name for that kind of sentence?*
> Chloe: *I think it's 'passive', whereas 'we poured...' is 'active'?*
> Teacher: *that's right, we called it 'passive voice'. In pairs, can you give me some more examples of sentences in the passive that could go in this written description of your experiment.*

5.4.12 Task 24

Feilke (2012) made an additional distinction between '*Bildungssprache*' and '*Schulsprache*'. He saw the first as the language of *learning* and the second as the language of *teaching* similar to what is often called 'classroom language' in English.

- Please revisit the extract in Task 23 and apply Feilke's further distinction to the language used by teacher and learners.
- How useful are these distinctions to trainee teachers and serving teachers?
- How could the distinctions be addressed in teacher education sessions and/or assignments?

5.4.13 Commentary

Task 22 draws attention to the challenges faced by trainee teachers who are probably thinking for the very first time about the distinctions between the registers they have to operate with in their chosen profession. Trainee teachers are, for understandable reasons, often focused on their own performance at the expense of raising their awareness of how their students are faring in the classes they teach during school practice. This tendency may be reinforced by the process of assessment, when course tutors observe lessons in order to come to a view about a trainee's suitability to enter the profession. The language used by students is not directly up for assessment on such occasions and observation checklists don't take account of it. But there is an added dimension to this, as the extract from the St Gallen document above implies. Students' levels of literacy and oracy are important not only for success at school but also for success in their later working life or in higher academic studies. This places a demand on teacher educators and trainers to build this dimension into their programmes and courses and to themselves become much more sensitive to what it means in practical terms. But the demand extends to the trainees themselves, whether language specialists or not they need a heightened level of awareness of ways of contributing to the development of their future students' language repertoires. To achieve this, they will need support and feedback from teacher educators who have to work out how to build this kind of awareness-raising and practical work on language into their programmes.

The literature in this area is still limited, but Tasks 23 and 24 focus on conceptual frameworks which may be seen as helpful in designing curricula and tasks for trainee teachers to engage with, going beyond Cummins' earlier two-way categorisation of Basic Interpersonal Communication Skills (BICS) and Cognitive Academic Language Proficiency (CALP) (Cummins, 1979). Task 23 includes plentiful examples of both everyday language (used mainly by the learners) and the language of schooling (used mainly by the teacher), and it is interesting to note how the teacher 'nudges' learners towards the more formal, subject-specific language needed to write an experimental report, picked up successfully by Jake towards the end of the extract.

Applying Feilke's distinction to the extract (Task 24) adds an interesting extra dimension. We might classify many of the teacher's interventions as 'Schulsprache', and some of his learners' responses as 'Bildungsprache' as they try out their ideas in order to learn. Teacher-fronted lessons like the one in the extract are likely to feature a lot of 'Schulsprache', whereas a more learner-centred class with groups working together on a task will probably involve learning through the co-construction of ideas, seen by Feilke as 'Bildungssprache'. However, the distinctions should not be seen as mutually exclusive as there is clearly overlap between the categories. A trainee teacher's language repertoire will need to embrace both her own practical language use and an awareness of how and for what purposes learners use language, as well as of the gaps in learners' individual language repertoires. For a serving teacher, being aware of these distinctions may help them to rethink their practice when introducing new concepts or procedures as they teach their own subject.

5.4.14 Netherlands

At the University of Applied Sciences in Utrecht, trainee teachers are required to work on their use of language in their subject areas. One of the lecturers there, Gerald van Dijk, has written extensively about the criteria the course team uses to decide which aspects of language to focus on in Engineering and Technology Education (ETE) in order to raise trainee teachers' language awareness and language knowledge. In designing the programme for these trainee teachers, he and his colleagues have drawn on a strongly linguistic approach based around genre analysis (van Dijk et al., 2020) and working with texts. His inventory of language that needs to be focused on is presented initially, in the task below, in its basic form without examples.

5.4.15 Task 25

1. Which features in the list below:
    (i) are likely to be relevant to future teachers of any subject (not just teachers of Engineering and Technology)?
    (ii) are particularly relevant to future teachers of Engineering and Technology?
    (iii) reflect the St Gallen team's distinction between 'everyday language', 'the language of schooling' and 'subject specialist language'?
    (iv) can be found in the core syllabus we introduced in Table 5.1 above?
2. What are the particular advantages for future teachers of working with texts in the target subject area?
3. What impact might this approach have on the development of a trainee teacher's overall language repertoire?

Functional structure, reasoning, graphic means
A. Text organisation with sub-headings
B. Forms of reasoning
C. Combination of text, graphic representations and formulas
D. General coherence between paragraphs
E. Use of specific devices that make text coherent, such as 'signalling words' (because, therefore, firstly, etc.)
Functional words and tense
F. Use of science and technology concepts
G. Differences between meanings of words in daily life and in ETE
H. Use of verbs that belong to the topic
I. Use of standard word combinations
J. Choice of tense
Functional tone
K. Extent to which the writer makes himself visible in the text
L. Expressing personal, emotions, evaluations and judgements with appropriate strength (van Dijk et al., 2020)

5.4.16 Commentary

1. (i) Almost all of the 12 language categories would be useful for future teachers of any subject to work on. In F and G, a simple substitution of subject areas would make this clear. (ii) F and G, as they stand, are clearly more specialised. (iii) Most of the categories are likely to invite comparison between everyday language and subject specialist language, but F and G are sharply focused on this. Conventions in different subject areas might affect decisions a writer might make about A, B, C, K and L, and highlighting these areas in a teacher education course would probably arouse interest and discussion. (iv) The main overlap is with part 1 of the core syllabus which covers the more formal aspects of language from an analytical perspective.

2. Working with typical texts in a given subject area and focusing on the twelve categories is likely to enhance a trainee teacher's awareness of text conventions and complexity, leading to a greater degree of competence in working with such texts in teaching practice and with their future school students.

3. Subject teachers' own language repertoires will certainly be enhanced by developing an understanding of these aspects of language, thus enabling them to deal with them more effectively in their classes. Of course, this requires a move from knowledge about language towards language pedagogy and towards the development of trainee teachers' language-related strategies to help them to build their students' literacy and oracy.

5.4.17 Task 26

There is an obvious need for teacher educators to work with the real practical implications of a list of categories like the one above, and the extract in Fig. 5.5. is an example of how this might be done on a course for trainee teachers of Engineering and Technology.

1. Which of the twelve categories in the Utrecht model are focused on in this material?
2. Identify at least three important messages for trainee subject teachers in the material.

5.4.18 Commentary

The sequence in Fig. 5.5 illustrates the importance for future teachers to familiarise themselves with language used to express key subject-specific concepts, and also to understand the differences between the way concepts are expressed in everyday language and in the specialised field of Engineering and Technical Education

Characteristics of words and phrases

The frame below shows two sentences from the conclusion of a research report, written by different students. The research question was: What factors play a role in the rusting of iron and how can you explain this?

Jasper: Iron rusts fastest in a warm dark place, where it is a bit wet and salty.

Florien: Factors that play a role in rusting, are a high temperature and the presence of salt and water. Rusting is a form of corrosion or oxidation. The reactants are iron, oxygen, and water. These substances are needed for corrosion.

We see from these examples that it is useful to illuminate language features at word and sentence level. Florien formulates at a higher scientific level than Jasper, through the use of concepts. These concepts come with the theory (…), but they can also be important in order to formulate the test method (the "variables" are kept constant).

The core concepts of science and technology are packed with more and more meanings in the course of a student's education. In the third year, the term 'oxidation' may mean 'reaction with oxygen', but in later years it may be associated with electron transfer. In this way increasingly specific meanings are packed into one word. And those meanings are often different from the meanings that the same word carries in everyday life.

The 'packing of meaning' into concepts is sometimes referred to as 'nominalization'. The box below demonstrates how this works for the concept of refraction.

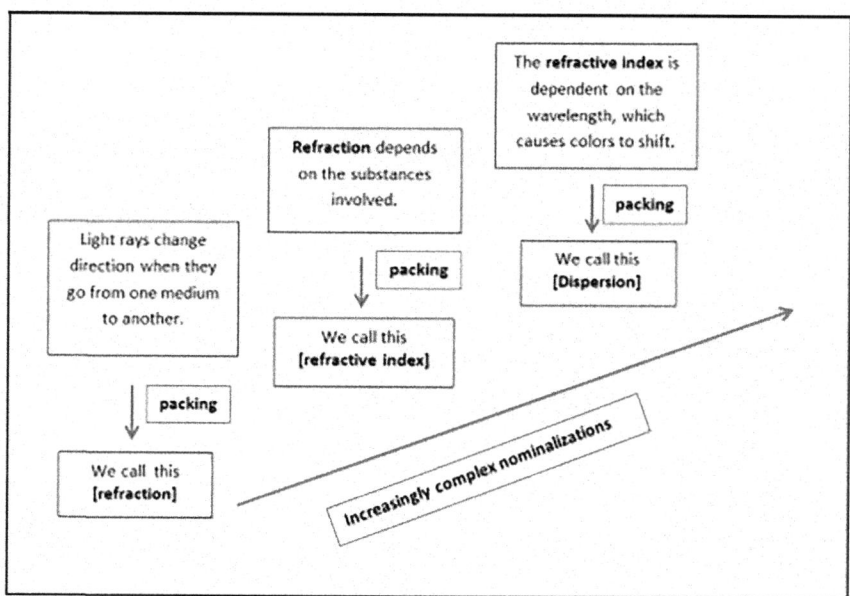

You may not use the word 'nominalization' in class, but rather talk about science words or concepts. It is a word that we use as science educators among ourselves, who want to understand how our science language 'works'.

Fig. 5.5 Characteristics of words and phrases (from van Dijk et al., 2021)

(categories F and G). In the article from which this discussion is drawn, the authors deal with other categories in the list through practical illustrations.

Messages for subject teachers may include:

(i) The need for them to help students like Jasper to start moving from everyday language to more subject-specific language when they speak and write about their subject.
(ii) The importance of developing a basic understanding of core concepts in the subject area.
(iii) The important insight that concepts are not always rigid or static, but that they develop in complexity and meaning as studies of a subject move into greater depth.
(iv) Interestingly, an implicit 'invitation' to aspiring subject teachers, in the final sentence in the extract, to join the discipline community of science educators through the way they use specific terms to define concepts.

5.4.19 Task 27

The Utrecht team use language-related criteria when assessing trainees on teaching practice in vocational schools. They use four different but related observation checklists in order to do this, published as *Kijkwijzer voor taalgericht vakonderwijs* ('Observation guide for language-oriented content teaching') (van Eerde et al., 2006). These checklists are not subject-specific. The criteria used in two of them, dealing with interaction patterns and with language support, are reproduced here in translation from Dutch.

1. What are the implications of the categories in these two instruments for the trainee teachers and for their school students?
2. To what extent do these categories overlap with elements of the core syllabus we offered in Table 5.1 above?

3. Interaction
  Asking questions
  1 • Asks different kinds of questions (descriptive, ordering, explanatory, evaluating)
  2 • Asks open questions
  3 • Asks real questions
  4 • Keeps asking
  5 • Encourages students to ask each other questions
  Generates answers
  6 • Passes on questions and answers to other students
  7 • Attends to turn-taking
  8 • Gives students time to think
  9 • Listens attentively
  Instructions for assignments

10 • *Explains goals*
11 • *Indicates what students should do in a task*
12 • *Explains how students should carry out the task*
Guidance during the execution of assignments
13 • *Gives students time to get going*
14 • *Asks about progress*
15 • *Invites questions*
16 • *Offers support*
17 • *Monitors time and organisation*
Debriefing of assignments
18 • *Refers back to aims*
19 • *Evaluates the process*
20 • *Sums up outcomes*
4. Language support
  Language resources
1 • *Makes the language goals explicit (at the beginning of the lesson)*
2 • *Pays attention to the language goals (during the lesson)*
3 • *Evaluates the language goals (at the end of the lesson)*
  Use of understandable language
4 • *Speaks calmly and articulates clearly*
5 • *Adapts language use to the student (shorter sentences, explaining words, putting emphasis, etc.)*
6 • *Pays attention to difficult words*
7 • *Gives instructions for reading texts*
8 • *Checks own comprehensibility*
9 • *Checks whether students understand text material*
10 • *Provides visual support on blackboard, paper or* via *audiovisual means (schematic, pictures, film, etc.)*
  Feedback on language use
11 • *Provides corrective and explicit feedback on students' language use*
12 • *Repeats examples of good language use by students*
13 • *Helps the students to formulate and reformulate students' language*
14 • *Gives examples of the intended use of language*

5.4.20 *Commentary*

The criteria in both checklists make it very clear that there is a strong pedagogical dimension to the way a teacher understands and uses language in a subject classroom. In the Interaction checklist there is real attention to ways of involving students, to keeping the lesson moving and to the support that should be given to students as they get to grips with the concepts and procedures which are central to the subject. The second checklist makes demands on the teacher's ability to recognise and respond to the language difficulties that students encounter in understanding subject requirements and texts, and in expressing themselves in subject-appropriate ways in speaking and writing.

It is evident from both checklists that the authors have tried to take account of subject-specific language from the students' point of view, and that they see a teacher's role as facilitating students' access to the language and conventions of the subjects they are studying. Reference back to the sample curriculum in Table 5.1 reveals considerable overlap with several of the categories in these two checklists.

5.4.21 Summary

In this section, we have drawn attention to some examples of good practice in approaching the language education of subject teachers in both pre- and in-service contexts. What we have found in our search for such examples is that there is good work going on in this field, and even the beginnings of some cooperation between institutions and wider national contexts. We believe that the work in progress in Germany, Austria, Switzerland and the Netherlands that we have drawn attention to is seminal, and very much worthy of close examination by teacher educators and trainers in other contexts and countries. But, as we hinted in the introduction to this section, these are green shoots rather than a bumper crop, and in some contexts, the UK included, there is still a great deal of work to be done if the role of language in every subject is to be fully understood and to take root in teacher education and training. Two important developments in many countries in Europe and beyond make this even more urgent: (i) the migration of thousands of people into countries where their children have to get to grips with a new language (the language of schooling) in order to take advantage of the educational opportunities offered to them and (ii) the increasing adoption of English as a medium of instruction in secondary and vocational schools as well as in higher education.

5.5 Section 4: Building Language-Sensitive Teaching and Learning Systematically into all Teacher Education

In the previous section, we explored a range of examples that illustrate how the principles, topics and practices of language-sensitive teaching and learning have begun to be addressed in teacher education and the ongoing professional learning of practising teachers. In this section, we lay out a rationale for a systematic approach and suggest ways in which the process of enhancing teacher education and continuing professional development can be carried forward in a much broader range of contexts.

Why is it important to make language awareness and sensitivity to language in teaching and learning more central to teacher education and professional development?

5.5.1 Task 28

Consider the statements in Table 5.6 and indicate whether you agree or disagree with each by putting a number between 0 (disagree strongly) and 5 (agree strongly) in the middle column. Make notes on the reasons for your score in the right-hand column.

Table 5.6 Statements about beliefs

	Score	Reasons
1. Whatever the subject being taught, a majority of students at secondary level need help with understanding and using language well.		
2. By the end of their schooling, students should be able to communicate well in a range of real-life situations such as the following:		
i. Interacting with people from different linguistic and cultural backgrounds.		
ii. Applying for work or further studies and being interviewed.		
iii. Handling situations where they disagree with other language users or are unhappy with their behaviour.		
iv. Being put under pressure to buy something, change their beliefs or political views, for example on social media.		
v. Listening to and showing tolerance of other people's views and beliefs.		
3. Helping students to develop their literacy and oracy and to cope with the various language demands associated with different school subjects should be the responsibility of teachers of the language of schooling.		
4. Teachers of subjects such as science, maths, geography and history need to be aware of and understand the specific language demands related to their subject and be prepared to help students to cope with them.		
5. All pre-service teacher education should include one or more modules or strands that focus on language sensitivity in teaching and learning.		
6. Assessment criteria for successful practice teaching should include some that focus on the (future) teacher's use of language during the lesson and their attention to the language-related needs of learners.		
7. In teacher education modules that focus on methodology and the specifics of teaching a subject, there should also be a focus on how a teacher's use of language can contribute to the effectiveness of a lesson.		

5.5.2 Commentary

These statements cover a range of issues that need to be considered by those designing and implementing curricula for initial teacher education and by teacher educators, whichever subjects the future teachers on their courses are specialising in. In many contexts, the expected outcomes of school education are formally specified in national or state school curricula for the successive levels of education. The design of teacher education courses must first and foremost take account of the needs of students at different levels of education so that future teachers are properly prepared to respond to these needs. However, the social, cultural and language backgrounds of the students in given classes may vary considerably, and teachers can only identify specific individual needs if they know something about students' language background and competences.

As indicated in 1), it is likely that many students, especially those at lower secondary level and in the primary cycle, will need or benefit from language support irrespective of the subject being learned. But, as implied by 2) i. to v. in the list, language and communication are also transversal skills which will be needed in life, perhaps much more so in the current age of globalisation and instantaneous media communications than was the case in the twentieth century. The Council of Europe's *Reference Framework of Competences for Democratic Culture* (RFCDC), for example, recommends that the following 'linguistic, communicative and plurilingual skills' are addressed by teachers:

- *can express his/her thoughts on a problem*
- *asks speakers to repeat what they have said if it wasn't clear to him/her*
- *asks questions that show his/her understanding of other people's positions*
- *can adopt different ways of expressing politeness in another language*
- *can mediate linguistically in intercultural exchanges by translating, interpreting or explaining*
- *can avoid successfully intercultural misunderstandings.* (Council of Europe 2018 vol. 2, p. 20)

It also lists the following areas of 'knowledge and critical understanding of language and communication':

- *can explain how tone of voice, eye contact and body language can aid communication*
- *can describe the social impact and effects on others of different communication styles*
- *can explain how social relationships are sometimes encoded in the linguistic forms that are used in conversations (e.g. in greetings, forms of address, use of expletives)*
- *can explain why people of other cultural affiliations may follow different verbal and non-verbal*
- *can reflect critically on the different communicative conventions that are employed in at least one other social group or culture.* (ibid: 22)

Other frameworks of transversal competences or twenty-first-century skills also include several that relate to language and communication. Such skills and knowledge, and various others listed in the Council of Europe and other frameworks, many of which also have a language dimension, need to be at least partially acquired during childhood and adolescence. It is one of the duties of schools, as well as of parents, to ensure that these transversal competences are addressed. However, we have found little evidence that national curricula include specific attention to them.

It is a truism that all teachers are language teachers, not just the teachers of the language of schooling (i.e. French in France, German in Austria, English in the UK, etc,), as mentioned in statement 3). Some, such as teachers of foreign languages and teachers of the language of schooling, do specialise in language structure, use and meaning during their initial teacher education, although the focus may well be on formal aspects and literature in the language. Teachers working in primary education with children between the ages of 6 and 11 may also pay closer attention to language and communication because of the integrated nature of primary school curricula. However, as young people progress in their schooling each school subject brings with it certain linguistic challenges, and as statement 4) indicates, subject teachers must therefore also take some responsibility for developing their students' language competences and repertoires. Those responsible for teaching the language of schooling cannot alone bear the responsibility for students' literacy and oracy.

The ability to use language effectively as 'social agents' as well as in their education is essential to the development of a young person's potential and to their future role as members of society. For these reasons, as suggested in statements 5) and 6), all future teachers and practising teachers, whatever their subjects, must be fully prepared to teach and support the general development of language and communication skills as well as to teach their subject or range of subjects. Statement 7) points out that there is also a close link between language and teaching methodology: teachers and future teachers need to fully understand and be capable of using effectively, for example, questions, scaffolding and other forms of mediation in their teaching. Thus, as is pointed out in statement 7), the language dimensions of methodology also need to be worked on. This can be greatly aided if there is an explicit focus on the kind of language which teachers use and the sensitivity to language that they show in practice teaching which is observed and assessed by teacher educators (statement 6). We will return to this in Tasks 31 and 32.

What options are available for encouraging practising teachers of all subjects to develop their awareness of and expertise in language-sensitive education?

5.5.3 Task 29

Which of the following measures would help to develop the ability of practising teachers of any subject to ensure that their teaching is language-sensitive?

1. Look back at the core syllabus in Table 5.1 of this unit. Choose two or three of the measures described below which you think would be useful in your context.
2. Give examples in each case of how the academic team (heads of department, coordinators, mentors, etc.) could select language-related issues and organise the action.

   (a) Organise a series of workshops over a month after school hours on issues related to language and literacy development across the curriculum.
   (b) Identify a specialist who could offer individual or small group sessions on such themes for teachers online, for example, in the evening.
   (c) Prepare a questionnaire for teachers asking them to specify language problems that typically arise in their lessons; then analyse the responses to provide individual observation and counselling.
   (d) Organise peer observations between teachers of the same subject in which they each focus on and note down language-related issues that arise in the observed teachers' use of language and in the students' work. Afterwards they exchange ideas about the issues.
   (e) Organise a short 'classroom' research project in which teachers of different subject working in pairs or groups try out specific ways of, for example, using questions, scaffolding learning of new concepts, supporting reading of texts, etc., and report back on this research in a workshop.
   (f) Appoint a teacher with specialist knowledge and experience to observe and respond to individual teachers' needs as a 'language mentor' or language advisor across the curriculum and to lead occasional in-service workshops.
   (g) Set up an online library of video-recorded clips of teaching accompanied by tasks which could be worked on by teachers on a voluntary basis.
   (h) Send one or two teachers on a specialised week-long course and ask them to lead a workshop for the whole teaching team afterwards on the insights they have gained from it.

5.5.4 Commentary

Many factors come into play when considering a new initiative which aims to enhance the quality of teaching and learning in an educational institution: human resources, financial resources, the logistics of timetabling, teachers' attitudes, the established requirements and arrangements for in-service training and continuing professional development, among others. The list of options above is not exhaustive, and each of them can be adapted to respond to the constraints. A common feature, however, is the need for those in management positions to explain to teachers the reasons for any such measures, to try to persuade them of the advantages and to involve them in the decision-making about how best to implement the chosen measure. The questions and notes below may be useful when decision-makers are considering the various options.

5.5 Section 4: Building Language-Sensitive Teaching and Learning Systematically... 169

(a) How many teachers would be free after school hours? How would they feel about a regular after-hours commitment lasting a month? Would there be an option of attending online, for example, via Zoom? Would there be an incentive, such as extra pay or recognition?

(b) An advantage of this option might be that an external specialist would bring in experience and expertise gained outside the school and could act partly as a consultant or critical friend. But where would it be possible to find such a person, and would they be familiar with the pressures of school environments?

(c) If well designed, questionnaires can be a good way of gathering information, although a questionnaire of this kind would require special preparation and would also take some time to complete properly, which hard-pressed teachers may not welcome. Would it be possible to draw up a short list of key questions and, after circulating these, gather the information via individual interviews? This would take the 'researcher' longer but might generate more fruitful answers in a more relaxed way. Most importantly, who would do the survey and analysis work and provide the follow-up support?

(d) Peer observation is often seen by teachers as rewarding and useful because the observer and the observed teacher are usually colleagues and handle the observation and its follow-up in a way that is felt to be mutually supportive (rather than threatening as is sometimes the feeling with management-led observations). However, there are several practical questions to consider, such as: how would peers be given time away from teaching to observe each other? How would they be substituted? How would they react to being asked to focus specifically on the language of teaching and supporting learning? An ideal but rarely applied solution is for teachers to volunteer to record (part of) a lesson on video and, having checked it, to invite one or more peers to comment on it, either privately or in a discussion session. The 'observation' can then be done at any time. This option is referred to and developed in option g.

(e) This next suggestion relates to d. Classroom research projects usually focus on key practical questions. They do not need to be lengthy or involve lots of theoretical reading. The idea is to explore the questions about the importance of language-sensitive teaching and the ways in which it can be done in different subjects, by trying out and/or observing different ways of doing things. Peer observation followed by discussion can be an excellent way of doing this.

(f) It would be ideal if one or more members of the teaching team in a school have the opportunity to develop specialist knowledge and experience in this area and could take the lead and be seen as 'language mentors'. Identifying a person on the teaching team who has the necessary training and experience may not be so easy.

(g) This option may be a less complicated means of supporting option d, but would the various teachers and the students concerned consent to having segments of lessons video-recorded and shared with other teachers? Who would do the recording—the teachers themselves or an observer?

(h) If option f is not feasible, a perhaps more feasible option is to offer willing members of the team the possibility to broaden their awareness and experience of language-sensitive education by attending a specialist course and not just to report back on this but to be given the responsibility of using the insights and expertise gained when supporting colleagues on a planned basis. This could be another way to begin establishing in the school a genuine community of practice to focus on language-sensitive education across the curriculum.

How can we set about strengthening the focus on language-sensitive teaching in initial teacher education?

5.5.5 Task 30

The structure of curricula and courses and those responsible for designing and revising them vary from institution to institution. In your teacher education context, what steps could be taken by those responsible for teacher education curricula to ensure that more attention is paid to language awareness and language-sensitive teaching and learning?

Which of the steps in Table 5.7 would you consider <u>essential</u> and also <u>feasible</u>? If you believe that any of the steps is not essential and/or not feasible give reasons.

Table 5.7 Steps towards language-sensitive teacher education

Possible step	Essential? If not, why not?	Feasible? If not, why not?
1. Review each module/course that is obligatory for all students (e.g. psychology, methodology, etc.) to identify areas and topics where a focus on language and language awareness tasks should or could be added to the course objectives and course content		
2. Review the specific courses that future teachers of each subject are required to complete in order to identify where a focus on language and communication should or could be added or strengthened in the course objectives and the topics covered.		
3. Consider which optional courses could/should also include explicit language-related elements.		
4. Involve lecturers who teach each of the courses reviewed as part of 1, 2 and 3 in discussions and decision making about the strengthening of focus on language and communication. Where possible, ask them to propose ideas of their own.		
5. Having reviewed in this way existing courses and the way they are sequenced over semesters/terms, consider whether there is space in the curriculum for one or more additional obligatory courses or modules on language awareness and language-sensitive teaching and learning.		

5.5.6 Commentary

This task is based on certain assumptions about initial teacher education at bachelor's or diploma level. Most such courses that we know of comprise:

- Certain obligatory courses or modules for future teachers in all specialisms (e.g. educational psychology, sociology, methodology)
- Obligatory subject-specific courses or modules which focus on the background knowledge and teaching of each specific subject or group of subjects
- Optional or elective courses which are more specialised (e.g. educational technology, special educational needs): students are required to take a certain number of these but, depending on the year or semester, they can choose from a menu of courses
- Obligatory supervised teaching practice ('practicum') and observation assignments that take place in one or more partner schools

You will be able to assess the extent to which the teacher education provision that you are involved in fits the above pattern and will be aware of the weighting in terms of credits or numbers of hours applicable to each element. Whatever the situation, it is our belief that an essential aim of teacher education is to ensure that student teachers are keenly sensitive to the role of language and communication in the teaching of any subject and to the linguistic needs of individual students. If teacher educators share our belief but such aims are not yet explicitly spelt out in the course curricula or syllabuses, it will be essential that those responsible for the curriculum and individual course design review each of them and identify the opportunities available to address such aims.

We recommend that subject specialist lecturers from a variety of discipline areas get together with language specialists in order to cooperate in the creation of modules or parts of modules that include a language dimension. They will need to begin by discussing questions such as the following:

(i) Which courses or modules must all student teachers complete, whatever their chosen teaching subject(s)? What aspects of language and communication should/could be included among the learning outcomes of these courses?
(ii) What specific courses are future teachers of each subject (e.g. maths, geography, language of schooling) required to take? How much attention is already given to language and language awareness in these courses and their intended learning outcomes?
(iii) Are any optional courses well suited to include a dimension on language and communication?

Following the review, the team can design from scratch one or more courses or modules, the aims of which are to raise student teachers' language awareness and develop their competences in the area of language-sensitive teaching and learning.

Before embarking on such a review, it is worth establishing certain principles. Here are some that we would recommend:

1. It should be an <u>internal process</u> based on existing documentation and on the evidence of course leaders and lecturers. This is true even if there is a periodic national or regional requirement to review teacher education provision.
2. There should be a <u>consultative approach</u>: as recommended above, those involved in the review should include course leaders and lecturers as well as those responsible for curriculum design and assessment.
3. Essential background to any internal review should include reference to, familiarisation with and discussion of the <u>language competences required of students at different stages of their school education</u>. These are often described in national or state curricula.

Apart from the examples cited in Section 3, mainly from German-speaking countries, we have found few teacher education curricula or course outlines that include a coherent, explicit and incremental focus on issues to do with teachers' language awareness and the ability to deliver language-sensitive education. Language and communication are intricately bound up with almost all aspects of teaching and learning, and they may be difficult to uncouple from methodology, lesson management, the design and running of learning activities, assessment, etc. However, <u>it is essential</u> that all future teachers are given opportunities to—and are required to—focus explicitly on their own and their students' use of spoken and written language and other means of communication in teaching. This need not mean artificially separating language from other aspects of teaching. Rather, it means looking at the normal and varied facets of teaching and learning from a different angle, in the same way that one can, for example, look at driving from the point of view of technical control and knowledge and simultaneously from the point of view of the driver's road sense and alertness to hazards. Similarly, future teachers should become accustomed to assessing the language needs of their individual students and consider how to address these alongside students' cognitive, affective, social and perhaps 'special' needs.

How can student teachers and practising teachers become more sensitive to their own use of language and students' language needs through observation and teaching experience?

5.5.7 Task 31

In the previous section, Task 27 focused on language-related observation criteria used with future subject teachers at the University of Applied Sciences, Utrecht. For this related task, read the following observation guidelines from one of a set that student teachers are asked to use when observing lessons on various subjects in schools. Add three additional guidelines. These could be about introducing a new concept or theory to students, helping them to read a text expressed in subject-specific language, guiding students during a writing activity and so on.

'During your observations in weeks 5 and 6 please focus on the following criteria. In your observation log give evidence to support your findings.

(a) When giving instructions, the teacher's voice is clear and audible for all students, and gestures, drawings etc. are used if necessary. The teacher also checks that students have understood
(b) The questions to students are varied in style and are selected carefully in accordance with what is being taught and the capabilities of individual students
(c) When correcting or giving feedback on individual students' responses phrases such as 'that's not quite right' or 'is that true?' are sometimes used to allow an opportunity for answers to be adjusted.
(d) If one or more students have difficulty understanding, the teacher repeats or rephrases what has been said, or adds an example
(e) If there are students in the class from other language backgrounds who have difficulty understanding, another student who knows the same language may be allowed to translate a term or explanation.
(f) During supervision of group or whole class discussion activities the teacher encourages all students to contribute through invitations and requests and gentle questioning rather than pressure.'

5.5.8 *Commentary*

In initial teacher education, observation of lessons given by experienced teachers in a school setting is a key means of confronting student teachers with the realities of everyday teaching. Many aspects of classroom practice, lesson preparation, methodology, classroom management and subject-related issues can be focused on, but in some observations, it is important that there is an explicit focus on the teacher's and students' use of language and the ways in which this contributes to the effectiveness of the lesson. The criteria above are examples only. Ideally such criteria would be suggested, including by the student teachers themselves, and would be worked on during one of the obligatory courses so that they understand the reasons for looking for evidence of them in observed teaching and learning.

As suggested in the task, the guidelines can be added to and adapted in various ways. Apart from the use of spoken language and the development of students' oracy skills, supporting students in their reading of more complex and longer texts, especially where unfamiliar or subject-related genres and terminology are involved, is one area that deserves attention: how do teachers use language to prepare students to deal with an unfamiliar or challenging text? Various techniques come to mind such as teaching new or difficult vocabulary beforehand, adding headings, highlighting topic sentences, etc., a form of scaffolding which is sometimes called 'easifying'. Students can also be helped if they are asked to read, discuss and ask or answer questions about one section of the text at a time before moving to the next.

Many students find writing particularly challenging, whether in class or as a homework task. Key factors here are the ways in which teachers orientate students to the differences between the kind of writing expected and the everyday language used outside the classroom or in social media exchanges, and guide them in their choice of language forms, use of vocabulary, length of sentences, etc. The way students write and the ways in which teachers support them while they are writing are often rather difficult to observe but can be discussed after the lesson.

In summary, the implication for teacher educators is that it is important to review from time to time the objectives of lesson observation assignments and the orientation of observation schedules and checklists to see whether additions or amendments are needed that focus attention both on the observed teacher's language use and on her sensitivity to the language-related needs of students.

5.5.9 Task 32

Initial teacher education includes one or more periods of practical teaching (practicum) carried out in schools. Depending on the local arrangements, this 'teaching practice' is supported and assessed in some way by teacher educators and/or by teachers in the school who are appointed to be mentors. Experienced teachers may also occasionally be observed by heads of department or other staff responsible for assuring the quality of teaching and supporting ongoing professional development.

In your teacher education and/or teaching context, what criteria and prior orientation guide the assessment of teaching practice or classroom teaching? Is the language sensitivity of student teachers' or experienced teachers' work in the classroom assessed in some way? If so, what criteria are used and how is this aspect of teaching handled?

5.5.10 Commentary

It can be argued that the effectiveness of teachers' or future teachers' work depends at least in part on their ability to use their own language repertoires to match the demands of the subject matter and learning objectives and at the same time to take into account the language awareness and language repertoires of each individual student in the class. This is challenging to say the least, but the teacher competences involved can best be developed through the experience of teaching in real classrooms.

Especially (but not only) in the case of student teachers, the process of developing more and more awareness and skill in this area can be aided through sympathetic guidance and feedback. As illustrated in the task in Section 3 and the checklists used at Utrecht University, the guidance can be in the form of observation and assessment criteria orientated towards language-sensitive education, which should be discussed with those being observed beforehand, and also in feedback afterwards. In some contexts, teaching diaries or logs are used in which the student teacher or experienced teacher may be asked to reflect on their teaching, in this case on the way language-related aspects were dealt with. These diaries can then be referred to in the feedback discussion.

During teaching practice, supervisors should check that trainee teachers are sufficiently focused on language and communication both in lesson planning and in their teaching. In addition, mentors and other assessors of practice teaching need clear criteria for gathering evidence of observed teachers' language-related competences. In the case of observation of experienced teachers, it is useful to ensure that language-related criteria are included in observation checklists and are discussed in feedback.

5.5.11 Task 33

(a) The following are excerpts from a checklist included as an appendix to the Council of Europe's *Handbook for Curriculum Development and Teacher Training—the Language Dimension in all Subjects* (Beacco et al., 2016, pp. 133–138). Which of these selected statements do you find most relevant to the future teachers on your initial teacher education courses? Select four of them and, if you consider that they need to be adapted or simplified, suggest how they could be amended to make them easier for future subject teachers to use.
(b) How could statements of this kind be used in the continuing professional development of experienced subject teachers?

1.2. I make sure that the students have clearly understood what the content and the language goals are, e.g. *by asking questions to check understanding and by encouraging students to ask questions for clarification when they are in doubt. My students can expect that I am willing to rephrase learning goals in a language they can understand.*

1.5. When planning my courses, I take particular care to expand the students' academic language competences. In doing so I consider:

(a) cognitive-linguistic functions: e.g. negotiating, naming/defining, describing / presenting, explaining, arguing, evaluating, modelling, simulating.

(b) genres relevant for my subject area: e.g. description of an experiment, writing minutes, analysing a newspaper article, giving a PowerPoint presentation, retrieving information from factual prose.

(c) communicative skills: listening (comprehension), reading (comprehension), connected speech, talking with one another (dialogue), writing/text production.

2.1. In my teaching, I use linguistic means and strategies in a very reflective way. I choose different language registers that are functional and appropriate for different teaching situations. *I distinguish between an informal, everyday language register (e.g. when the organisation of the learning process is being negotiated), a more formal register of general academic language (e.g. when learning paths and negotiation of meaning are at stake), and a subject-specific register to establish cognitive concepts*, e.g. *by applying subject-specific terminology ("mass" instead of "weight") or by providing collocational expressions ("exerting force on something" in physics).*

2.5. I adapt my speech tempo and the use of language means as far as feasible to the competence level of my students: *simplifications like "motherese" or "teachspeak" do not really help students to develop academic literacy. Therefore, in situations of formal content teaching, I choose expressions slightly above the students' competence level for them to adopt such language patterns. On the other hand, I know which of the students have difficulty following the oral interaction in the classroom. I use simple, short sentences when dealing with these learners and—when necessary—informal, colloquial words.*

2.6. I normally use a broad range of different non-verbal techniques, signalling important aspects of content as well as transitions from one topic to another, or from one phase of teaching to the next, e.g. *by vocal control and modulation, reduced tempo of speech, lowering or raising the voice, and repetition, gestures, and body language.*

2.7. I try to make difficult areas of subject-specific content comprehensible by using redundancy or by intensifying my verbal investment, e.g. *repetition, rephrasing, paraphrasing, extending meaning, exemplifying and/or giving more concrete examples, summarising and repeating the main points.*

2.8. For the cognitive guidance of the students as well as for facilitating comprehension, I often use "announcing" and "discourse-commenting" words and expressions, e.g. *expressions like "and this is particularly important now" or "we will deal with this on Monday in more detail", back- or forward references like "please recall what we said about the structure of a lab report".*

5.5.12 Commentary

In their introduction the authors say '*the checklist is intended for subject teachers who would like to reflect more closely on the language dimension of their own teaching and its implications for their students' development of subject literacy. The checklist can also be used as a tool for mutual classroom observation and discussion among subject teachers within a school.*' (p. 133). In other words, it is not intended primarily for use on pre-service teacher education courses. The way in which the self-assessment criteria are expressed assumes familiarity with certain key language concepts and terminology. This may in some cases be demanding for students on teacher education courses, or indeed for practising subject teachers. Nevertheless, the points covered are highly relevant to everyday practice. As suggested in previous tasks, after discussion and exemplification of the key points in input sessions, it can be very valuable for teachers and future teachers to reflect on such points when observing lessons and when thinking back on their own lessons or teaching practice.

Taking 2.1 as an example, this could be made simpler as follows:

> In my teaching, I think carefully about the language I use. I choose different language registers for different teaching situations. For example, when discussing the learning process with students I use informal, everyday language, but when negotiating the meaning of terms or sentences, I use more formal academic language. But when I am teaching new or recently introduced concepts in my subject, I use subject-related language and, for example, subject-specific terminology and expressions, e.g. in physics: "mass" instead of "weight"; "exerting force on something".

This version of 2.1 assumes less familiarity with terms like 'register', 'functional' and 'negotiation of meaning'. However, it can be argued that understanding such terms is useful as part of teachers' language awareness and understanding of how language works.

As mentioned above, the checklist was originally intended for use with experienced practising teachers and covers the following six areas of teaching (which, in our view, are also areas that need to be focused on in initial teacher education):

1. *Transparency of language requirements in setting up attainment targets and tasks for subject-specific learning;*
2. *Use of language by the subject teacher;*
3. *Classroom interaction and opportunities for the students to speak;*
4. *Scaffolding academic discourse skills, strategies and genres;*
5. *Linguistic appropriateness of materials (texts, different media, teaching/learning materials)*
6. *Linguistic aspects of evaluating academic language and content achievement.*
(ibid: 133)

For practising teachers, it is also important that the areas of language-sensitive teacher behaviour covered by the checklist are first fully understood and discussed in in-service sessions. Teachers need to explore the uses and usefulness of the checklist as a means of reflecting on their use of language in teaching and understand how improving their teaching in the ways indicated will help their students.

5.5.13 Summary

In this section, we have focused on some ways in which language-sensitive teaching can be systematically built into teacher education courses, which all too often do not explicitly address the principles and practice of language-sensitive approaches to teaching. We have suggested undertaking a review of all the obligatory and elective courses and modules that are part of the course in order to check how and where language and communication issues are addressed, and, if they are not addressed, how and in which courses they could be focused on. It may be that a whole new module or course would be the best option.

A similar approach to observation and teaching practice is suggested: teacher educators and those supervising practising teachers need to be satisfied that language-related issues, such as those exemplified in the 'core syllabus' and some of the checklists referred to, are covered by observation checklists that student teachers are asked to use, and in the guidance and assessment criteria for practice teaching. Experienced teachers also need resources and opportunities to reflect and work on the language dimension of their teaching. This may be particularly important for mid-career teachers whose language habits may have become fossilised as they have established tried and trusted classroom routines over the years. Some of the ideas in this section apply equally to in-service or in-house professional development provision.

5.6 Language-Sensitive Education: Taking Action

We believe that all teachers need to be sensitive to the special ways in which language and communication can be used in all subjects and all sectors of education to increase pupils' and students' chances of reaching their full potential in education and as citizens.

In accordance with this belief, we have offered four units in this book containing over 80 tasks for future teachers and practising teachers of all subjects which aim to enhance their awareness of the nature and functions of language in educational settings and beyond, and to familiarise them with some key aspects of language-sensitive teaching and learning. In the fifth unit, we discussed a range of topics and provided additional tasks to stimulate re-examination and design of teacher education courses for future teachers and of in-service provision for practising teachers to ensure that the key roles of language and communication in education are properly explored, and that competences for language-sensitive teaching are developed.

Below we summarise some of the actions that we see as critically important.

1. Those responsible for teacher education, including curriculum designers and teacher educators, should:

   (a) Examine carefully how language-related topics and competences are currently dealt with in degree and diploma courses for future teachers of all subjects and in all sectors (primary, lower secondary, upper secondary and vocational and further education).

   (b) Review the detailed content of obligatory courses to identify opportunities to strengthen content and assignments on language-sensitive practices and the ways in which these practices are focused on in teaching practice.

(c) Go back to the drawing board to redesign course modules and revise assessment requirements to take account of the need for more language sensitivity at classroom level.
(d) Review the criteria used to assess student teachers' knowledge and teaching skills during and at the end of their courses to ensure that criteria related to language-sensitive teaching are included.

2. Those responsible for organising and supporting in-service training and professional development opportunities for teachers working in school and college departments should regularly:

(a) Assess the ways in which individual pupils'/students' language needs are being dealt with and developed.
(b) Propose inter-departmental workshops, short courses, research projects, etc., that reinforce practising teachers' awareness of and competences in language-sensitive teaching.
(c) Include clear language-related criteria in the guidelines and documentation used when observing lessons, including in peer observation.
(d) Encourage staff to establish a community of practice involving teachers from across the curriculum through which insights, experience and advice can be shared.

3. Individual teachers and student teachers of all subjects should independently and with colleagues:

(a) Include explicit attention to the development of pupils' and students' language skills and language awareness in their planning of lessons, however diverse the class is.
(b) Further develop their own language repertoires by trying out various alternative ways of presenting information, giving instructions, asking questions, 'scaffolding' pupils'/ students' learning of new concepts and providing feedback.
(c) Work with colleagues across the institution on ways of systematically developing the oracy and literacy of all pupils/ students, and their ability to use language and communicate effectively in a wide range of educational and general situations.

5.7 Conclusion

The need for a language-sensitive approach to all education is not a new idea, and it is not primarily about innovation. It has, however, become an even more pressing priority than it was in the past when commissions produced lengthy reports (e.g. in the UK in the 1970s and 1980s). Many societies have become even more diverse than they were due to increased global migration and financial and social inequalities. In addition, widespread access to the Internet, the explosion of communication via social media and the immediacy of access to information (whether true or false) have made it essential that more attention is paid to young people's ability to deal with communication and use language effectively, both in their education and beyond.

We wish users of this book every success in their efforts to contribute to this crucial mission.

References

Beacco, J. C., Fleming, M., Goullier, F., Thürmann, E., & Vollmer, H. (2016). *A Handbook for Curriculum Development and Teacher Training—the Language Dimension in all Subjects*. Council of Europe. Retrieved January 21, 2022, from https://rm.coe.int/a-handbook-for-curriculum-development-and-teacher-training-the-languag/16806af387

The Council of Europe. (2018). *Reference Framework of Competences for Democratic Culture* (RFCDC). Retrieved January 2, 2022, from https://www.coe.int/en/web/reference-framework-of-competences-for-democratic-culture/rfcdc-volumes

Cummins, J. (1979). Cognitive/Academic Language Proficiency, Linguistic Interdependence, the Optimum Age Question and Some Other Matters. *Working Papers on Bilingualism, 19*, 121–129

Feilke, H. (2012). Bildungssprachliche Kompetenzen—fördern und entwickeln. *Praxis Deutsch, 233*, 4–13

Oleschko, S. (Ed.). (2017). *Sprachsensibles Unterrichten fördern*. Landesweite Koordinierungsstelle Kommunale Integrationszentren (LaKI) Nordrhein Westfalen. Retrieved January 26, 2022, from https://sprachsensibles-unterrichten.de/wp-content/uploads/2017/12/Buch_Sprachsensibles-Unterrichten-foerdern.pdf

Padmini Shankar, K. (2021). Implementing Task-Based Teacher Training: Narratives from Language Classrooms. *Journal of Modern Languages, 31*(2). https://doi.org/10.22452/jml.vol31no2.225

van den Branden, K. (2006). Training Teachers: Task-Based as Well? In K. Van den Branden (Ed.), *Task-Based Language Education: From Theory to Practice* (pp. 217–248). Cambridge University Press.

van der Walt, C., & Ruiters, J. (2012). Every Teacher a Language Teacher? Developing Awareness of Multilingualism in Teacher Education. *Journal for Language Teaching, 45*

van Dijk, G., et al. (2020). Design Principles for Language Sensitive Technology Lessons in Teacher Education. *International Journal of Technology and Design Education*. Retrieved January 6, 2022, from https://doi.org/10.1007/s10798-020-09622-w

van Dijk, G., Hajer, M., Kuiper, H., & Eijkelhof, H. (2021). *A Language Sensitive Pedagogy for Science and Technology: Reading, Talking and Writing About Practical Work*. Hogeschool Utrecht. Retrieved January 21, 2022, from https://elbd.sites.uu.nl/wp-content/uploads/sites/108/2018/06/Van-Dijk-et-al-2015-A-pedagogy-for-writing-practical-reports-15-juli.pdf

van Eerde, D., Hacquebord, H., Hajer, M., Pulles, M., & Raymakers, C. (2006). *Kijkwijzer voor taalgericht vakonderwijs*. SLO/Platform Taalgericht Vakonderwijs.

All References in Units 1-5

Alexander, R. J. (2013). Improving Oracy and Classroom Talk: Achievements and Challenges. *Primary First.*, 22–29.

References

Alexander, R. J. (2018). Developing dialogic teaching: genesis, process, trial. *Research Papers in Education.* Retrieved June 8, 2022, from http://robinalexander.org.uk/wp-content/uploads/2019/12/RPIE-2018-Alexander-dialogic-teaching.pdf

Anderson, L. W., Krathwohl, D. R., Airasian, P. W., Cruikshank, K. A., Mayer, R. E., Pintrich, R., Raths, J., & Wittrock, M. C. (2001). *A Taxonomy for Learning, Teaching, and Assessing: A Revision of Bloom's Taxonomy of Educational Objectives.* Longman.

Barnes, D. (1976). *From Communication to Curriculum.* Penguin.

Barnes, D. (2008). Exploratory Talk for Learning. In N. Mercer & S. Hodgkinson (Eds.), *Exploring Talk in Schools.* Sage.

BBC. (2005). Online Poll on Regional Accents. http://www.bbc.co.uk/voices/yourvoice/poll_results.shtml

BBC. (2009). News Report on Survey of Accents by Bury Technologies. http://news.bbc.co.uk/1/hi/business/7843058.stm

Beacco J.C., Fleming M., Goullier F.,Thürmann E., Vollmer H (2016). *A Handbook for Curriculum Development and Teacher Training—The Language Dimension in all Subjects.* Council of Europe. Retrieved January 21, 2022, from https://rm.coe.int/a-handbook-for-curriculum-development-and-teacher-training-the-languag/16806af387

Bearne, E. (Ed.). (1999). *Use of Language Across the Secondary Curriculum* (pp. 26–37). Routledge.

Blommaert, J., & Backus, A. (2011). Repertoires Revisited: "Knowing Language" in Superdiversity in *Working Papers in Urban Language & Literacies, 67.* Retrieved January 27, 2022, from https://www.academia.edu/6365319/WP67_Blommaert_and_Backus_2011_Repertoires_revisited_Knowing_language_in_superdiversity

Bloom, B. S. (Ed.). (1956). *Taxonomy of Educational Objectives—The Classification of Educational Goals.* McKay.

Brau, B. (2018). Constructivism. In R. Kimmons (Ed.), *The Students' Guide to Learning Design and Research.* EdTech Books. Retrieved June 3m 2022, from https://edtechbooks.org/studentguide/constructivism

Campbell, A. (2014). The Effects of Text Messaging on Students' Literacy. Retrieved April 15, 2020, from https://thescholarship.ecu.edu/handle/10342/4582

Carter, A. (1997). *Shaking a Leg: Collected Writings.* Penguin Group USA.

Christensen, M., & Kirby, S. (Eds.). (2003). *Language Evolution.* Oxford University Press.

Council of Europe. (2001). *A Common European Framework of References for Languages.* Council of Europe. Retrieved Jaune 3, 2020, from https://www.coe.int/en/web/portfolio/the-common-european-framework-of-reference-for-languages-learning-teaching-assessment-cefr-

Council of Europe. (2020). *CEFR Companion Volume with New Descriptors.* Council of Europe. Retrieved May 23, 2022, from https://rm.coe.int/common-european-framework-of-reference-for-languages-learning-teaching/16809ea0d4

Council of Europe. Linguistic Integration of Adult Migrants Website on Language Profiles. Retrieved May 23, 2022., from https://www.coe.int/en/web/lang-migrants/profile-language-/-profiling

Council of Europe. (2018). *Reference Framework of Competences for Democratic Culture* (RFCDC). Retrieved January 2, 2022, from https://www.coe.int/en/web/reference-framework-of-competences-for-democratic-culture/rfcdc-volumes

Cummins, J. (1979). Cognitive/Academic Language Proficiency, Linguistic Interdependence, the Optimum Age Question and Some Other Matters. *Working Papers on Bilingualism, 19,* 121–129.

Crystal, D. (1995). *The Cambridge Encyclopaedia of the English Language.* Cambridge University Press.

Dawes, L., Dore, B., Loxley, P., & Nicholls, L. (2010). A Talk Focus for Promoting Enjoyment and Developing Understanding in Science. *English Teaching: Practice and Critique, 9*(2), 99–110.

Derewianka, B., & Jones, P. (2016). *Teaching Language in Context* (2nd ed.). Oxford University Press.

Essays, UK. (2018, November). Attitudes Towards Accents: The Scouse Accent. https://www.ukessays.com/essays/languages/liverpool-accent.php?vref=1

Fairclough, N. (2014). *Language and Power* (3rd ed.). Longman.

Feilke, H. (2012). Bildungssprachliche Kompetenzen—fördern und entwickeln. *Praxis Deutsch, 233,* 4–13.

Gardom Hulme, P., Locke, J., & Reynolds, H. (2017). *AQA Activate for KS3: Student Book 1.* Oxford University Press.

Hammond, J. (2001). Scaffolding and Language. In J. Hammond (Ed.), *Scaffolding: Teaching and Learning in Language and Literacy Education* (pp. 15–30). Primary English Teachers' Association. https://files.eric.ed.gov/fulltext/ED456447.pdf

Hammond, J., & Gibbons, P. (2001). What Is Scaffolding? In J, Hammond (Ed.), *Scaffolding: Teaching and Learning in Language and Literacy Education* (pp. 1–14). Primary English Teaching Association. Retrieved August, 2021, from https://files.eric.ed.gov/fulltext/ED456447.pdf

Heugh, J, French, M, Armitage, J, Taylor-Leech, K, Billinghurst, N, & Ollerhead, S (2019). *Using Multilingual Approaches: Moving from Theory to Practice—A Resource Book of Strategies, Activities and Projects for the Classroom.* British Council https://www.teachingenglish.org.uk/article/using-multilingual-approaches-moving-theory-practice

Hofstede, G. (2012). Hofstede's fifth dimension: New evidence from the World Values Survey. *Journal of Cross-Cultural Psychology, 43*(1), 3–14.

Krathwohl, D. R. (2002). A revision of Bloom's Taxonomy: an overview. *Theory into Practice, 41*(4), 212–218.

Lessons in Observation. (2013). Evaluating Teaching and Learning: Early Years Foundation Stage (EYFS) Reception Numeracy (Excerpts). Retrieved April 30, 2020, from https://www.youtube.com/watch?v=WwUCufOeOdE

Levine, N. *How to search the internet.* wikiHow, ("a wiki building the world's largest, highest quality how-to manual. Please edit this article and find author credits at wikiHow.com. Content on wikiHow can be shared under a Creative Commons License"). Available at https://www.wikihow.com/Search-the-Internet. Accessed 28 August 2022.

Little, D (2010). *The-Linguistic-and-Educational-Integration-of-Children-and-Adolescents.* Retrieved October, 2010, from Council of Europe https://rm.coe.int/the-linguistic-and-educational-integration-of-children-and-adolescents/16805a0d1b

McConachie, S. M., & Petrovsky, A. R. (2010). *Content Matters: A Disciplinary Literacy Approach to Improving Student Learning.* Jossey Bass.

Manzoni, C., & Rolfe, H. (2019). *How Schools are Integrating New Migrant Pupils and Their Families.* National Institute of Economic and Social Research.

Mercer, N. (2000). *Words and Mind—How we Use Language to Think Together.* Routledge.

Mercer, N. (2014). *Why Teach Oracy?* University of Cambridge. Retrieved July 28, 2021, from https://www.cam.ac.uk/research/discussion/why-teach-oracy

Mercer, N., & Dawes, L. (2018). *The Development of Oracy Skills in School-Aged Learners. Part of the Cambridge Papers in ELT Series.* [pdf] Cambridge University Press. https://languageresearch.cambridge.org/images/CambridgePapersInELT_Oracy_2018_ONLINE.pdf

Montoya, S (2018). *Defining Literacy.* Presentation at 5th GAML (Global Alliance to Monitor Learning) Meeting. UNESCO. Retrieved May 29, 2020, from http://gaml.uis.unesco.org/wp-content/uploads/sites/2/2018/12/4.6.1_07_4.6-defining-literacy.pdf

Morgan, N., & Saxton, J. (1991). *Teaching, Questioning and Learning.* Routledge.

Nicholson, H. (1999). Talking in Class—Spoken Language and Effective Learning. In E. Bearne (Ed.), *Use of Language across the Secondary Curriculum* (pp. 26–37). Routledge.

Oleschko, S. (Ed.) (2017). *Sprachsensibles Unterrichten fördern* Arnsberg: Landesweite Koordinierungsstelle Kommunale Integrationszentren (LaKI) Nordrhein Westfalen. Retrieved January 26, 2022, from https://sprachsensibles-unterrichten.de/wp-content/uploads/2017/12/Buch_Sprachsensibles-Unterrichten-foerdern.pdf

Oracy Cambridge. Retrieved May 5, 2020a., from https://oracycambridge.org/

Oracy Cambridge. (2020b). *Prof Neil Mercer's Evidence to the Oracy APPG.* Retrieved July 28, 2021, from https://oracycambridge.org/prof-neil-mercers-evidence-to-the-oracy-appg/

References

Padmini Shankar, K. (2021). Implementing Task-Based Teacher Training: Narratives from Language Classrooms. *Journal of Modern Languages, 31*(2). https://doi.org/10.22452/jml.vol31no2.225

Picenoni, M., et al. (2021). *Skript zum Modul Berufsspezifische Sprachkompetenzen*. Pädagogische Hochschule.

Pinker, S. (2003). Language as an Adaptation to the Cognitive Niche in Christensen. *M. and S. Kirby, 2003*, 16–37.

Rao, K. (2016, January 4). Don't Prepone It—Do the Needful. 10 Indianisms We Should All Be Using. *The Guardian*. https://www.theguardian.com/commentisfree/2016/jan/04/indian-english-phrases-indianisms-english-americanisms-vocabulary

Sealy, A. (1996). *Learning About Language*. Open University Press.

Sharpe, T. (2001). Scaffolding in Action—Snapshots from the Classroom. In J. Hammond (Ed.), *Scaffolding: Teaching and Learning in Language and Literacy Education* (pp. 1–14). Primary English Teaching Association. Retrieved August, 2021, from https://files.eric.ed.gov/fulltext/ED456447.pdf

Slone, I. B. (2013). "Who Survives, Who Doesn't?" An Interview with Margaret Atwood. Retrieved April 15, 2020, from https://hazlitt.net/feature/who-survives-who-doesnt-interview-margaret-atwood

The Guardian. (2005). Michael Howard's Newsnight Interview. Retrieved April 2, 2020, from https://www.theguardian.com/politics/2005/apr/22/election2005.uk6

van Dijk, G., Hajer, M., Kuiper, H., & Eijkelhof, H. (2021). *A Language Sensitive Pedagogy for Science and Technology: Reading, Talking and Writing About Practical Work*. Hogeschool Utrecht. Retrieved January 21, 2022, from https://elbd.sites.uu.nl/wp-content/uploads/sites/108/2018/06/Van-Dijk-et-al-2015-A-pedagogy-for-writing-practical-reports-15-juli.pdf

van den Branden, K. (2006). Training Teachers: Task-Based As Well? In K. Van den Branden (Ed.), *Task-Based Language Education: From Theory to Practice* (pp. 217–248). Cambridge University Press.

van der Walt, C., & Ruiters, J. (2011). Every Teacher a Language Teacher? Developing Awareness of Multilingualism in Teacher Education. *Journal for Language Teaching, 45*(2).

van Dijk, G. et al. (2020). Design Principles for Language Sensitive Technology Lessons in Teacher Education. *International Journal of Technology and Design Education*. Retrieved January 6, 2022, from https://doi.org/10.1007/s10798-020-09622-w

van Eerde, D., Hacquebord, H., Hajer, M., Pulles, M., & Raymakers, C. (2006). *Kijkwijzer voor taalgericht vakonderwijs*. SLO/Platform Taalgericht Vakonderwijs.

Voice 21. (2019). *The Oracy Benchmarks*. Voice 21. Retrieved May 29, 2020, from https://voice21.org/wp-content/uploads/2019/11/Benchmarks-report.pdf

Vygotsky, L. (1978). *Mind in Society*. Harvard University Press.

Wilkes, A. (2014). *KS3 History: Renaissance, Revolution and Reformation: Britain 1509-1745 Student Book*. Oxford University Press.

Wilkinson, A. (1965). The Concept of Oracy. Retrieved January 27, 2022, from https://onlinelibrary.wiley.com/doi/abs/10.1111/j.1754-8845.1965.tb01326.x

Woods, D., Bruner, J. S., & Ross, G. (1976). The Role of Tutoring in Problem Solving. *Journal of Child Psychology and Psychiatry, 17*(1976), 89–100.

Appendix: Inventory of Task Types for Teacher Education and Training

Introduction

This inventory contains some of the task types that can be used in teacher education and professional learning. They are listed by various different kinds of 'focus'. For each type, some possible task activities are suggested, and illustrative examples are provided taken mainly from Units 1–4 of the book. Most of the examples could easily be adapted by teacher educators and others working with teachers, and they may suggest alternative and/or additional follow-up tasks with a focus that is relevant to the specific local context.

In a book of this kind, it is important that the task types can be used by individual teachers working alone, but we believe that most of them could also be useful in group situations during face-to-face or online courses. Of course, when people are working in a group all sorts of other types of focus provided by the course leader or the participants can be used, including examples of live teaching, role-play, simulations, online apps and learning platforms. In certain training situations, teacher educators may wish to draw parallels between the task types in this inventory and the kinds of activities that teachers could do with their own students.

1. **FOCUS: written dialogue or transcript of a lesson**

    TASKS: analyse, describe, compare, explain
    Examples:

(a). Infer the roles/ages of the speakers	Unit 1, Task 5, Task 11
(b). Explain the reason for the misunderstanding	Unit 1, Task 4
(c). Describe the relationship between the speakers	Unit 1, Task 25
(d). Explain why A says this/uses this phrase. Comment on the way B uses language	Unit 1, Task 3, Task 9, Task 11

(*continued*)

© The Author(s), under exclusive license to Springer Nature Switzerland AG 2022
R. Bolitho, R. Rossner, *Language-Sensitive Teaching and Learning*,
https://doi.org/10.1007/978-3-031-11339-0

(continued)

(e). Describe the kind of language X uses in order to do Y	Unit 1, Task 13
(f). Explain/make inferences about interactions x, y, z in the lesson. Describe how students use language when responding to the teacher	Unit 2, Tasks 6, 15
(g). Categorise (in a table) different kinds of language used for different purposes	Unit 2, Tasks 9, 10, 16
(h). Find examples of/ identify different kinds of learner (or teacher) talk	Unit 2, Task 17, Unit 3 Task 4
(i). Identify and analyse a teacher's language issues	Unit 5, Task 9, 11
(j). Identify and analyse learners' language issues in transcripts of lessons	Unit 2, Task 6, Unit 3, Task 4

2. **FOCUS: spoken interaction or lesson segment in audio or video recording**
   TASKS: as for 1 above.
   Examples:

(a). Analyse pronunciation (and/or stress, intonation, body language, facial expression, etc,)	Unit 1, Task 15
(b). Describe the speaker's/ teacher's objectives	Unit 2, Task 12
(c). Describe the teacher's difficulties and attitude to them	Unit 2, Task 13
(d). How does the teacher elicit information? What language does he/she use to help them understand?	Unit 2, Tasks 2, 4
(e). Compare the teacher's (speaker's) approach in segment A with the approach of the teacher in segment B	Unit 2, Task 14

3. **FOCUS: written and/or illustrated texts**
   TASKS: reflect, analyse, link, compare
   Examples:

(a). Read the information, and find an example	Unit 1, Task 16
(b). Explain the differences between the written and oral descriptions	Unit 1, Task 14
(c). Identify differences between one variety of a language and others	Unit 1, Task 18
(d). Reflect on the writer's attitude/ feelings, opinions	Unit 1, Task 21
(e). Explain the power or purpose of the text	Unit 1, Tasks 24, 26
(d). Identify the likely source(s) of the text(s)	Unit 1, Task 22
(e). Deconstruct and analyse specialist texts from textbooks and the Internet (basic discourse analysis)	Unit 2, Tasks 1 and 2
(f). Identify potential difficulties in a text and simplify/easify it to make it suitable for class use	Unit 5, Task 6

4. **FOCUS: spoken text**
   TASKS: as for 3 above but with attention to features of spoken language

5. **FOCUS: list of situations or contexts, or self-selection of a situation or context**

   TASKS: reflect on how language is used and how language use varies according to situation, category or context, decide on or select the best or most important option, match language examples with categories or situations

   Examples:

(a). Consider 4 learning situations and the different ways communication is used. What other means are used?	Unit 2, Tasks 1, 3, 5
(b). Explain the different options available (to the teacher) and the likely effect	Unit 2, Task 8
(c). Give examples of different kinds of language that could be used in different (teaching) situations	Unit 2, Task 11
(d). Which questions are in which category?	Unit 3, Tasks 21–22
(e). Indicate what literacy or oracy skills you consider to be most essential in the following situations	Unit 4, Task 11

6. **FOCUS: list of features or phenomena in an interaction or lesson**

   TASKS: explain the reasons, effects, implications
   EXAMPLE: Unit 2, Task 7

7. **FOCUS: questions for reflection and further exploration**

   TASKS: think about and select options, write notes, relate to your own context
   Examples:

(a). What might a teacher do to consolidate textbook work?	Unit 3, Task 3
(b). In the light of your experience, find examples of good practice	Questions for reflection at the end of sections

8. **FOCUS: definitions or explanations**

   TASKS: comment, choose the 'best' version, use the definition to provide examples
   Examples:

(a). As defined, what forms can X take? Give examples	Unit 3, Task 5
(b). In your view, which is the best definition?	Unit 4, Task 7
(c). What extra dimension does this other definition add?	Unit 4, Task 8

9. **CONTEXT: teaching practice of student teachers or experienced teachers' observed lessons**

   TASKS: plan, practise teaching-related language skills, identify and respond to students' needs, reflect on opportunities for improvement in language use

(a). Practise key skills such as explaining, defining, giving instructions, formulating questions, offering support/scaffolding, paraphrasing

(b). Identify and respond to learners' literacy and oracy needs (in the context of teaching practice)

(c). Record and reflect on your own lessons and identifying language issues that need attention

(d). Identify and respond to language needs of students with migrant background

10. **CONTEXT: observation of real teaching (live or recorded)**

TASKS: notice and reflect, assess, comment, suggest alternatives

Examples:

(a). Use a checklist to gather evidence of effective and less effective uses of language by the teacher

(b). Identify causes of problems and critical incidents in classroom communication and suggest ways they could have avoided or overcome

(c). Assess and comment on the ways in which the teacher handles students' language difficulties and helps them to choose good language options

(d). Assess the teacher's and students' choice and use of language during tasks focused on intercultural issues

Index

A
Academic language, 67–69, 96, 100, 132, 139, 175–177
Accent, 14, 15, 17, 58, 59, 131
Acquisition (*vs.* learning), 32
Alexander, R. J., 44–47, 49, 125
Alliteration, 81–83, 102, 103
Alltagssprache, 156
Anderson, L.W., 92
Assessment, 67, 75, 94, 111–115, 124, 129, 158, 172, 174, 178, 179
Atwood, Margaret, 7
Austria, 60, 61, 131, 153, 164, 167
Austrian Language Competence Centre (ÖSZ), 154

B
Backus, A., 68, 69
Barnes, D., 49, 53
Basic interpersonal communicative skills (BICS), 132, 158
Beacco, J.C., 120, 175
Bearne, E., 106, 107, 116
Bildungssprache, 156–158
Bilingual, 60, 65, 66
Biology, 86, 89, 103–105, 146, 147, 149

Blommaert, J., 68, 69
Bloom's *Taxonomy*, 94, 95, 97
Body language, 31, 32, 43, 82, 96, 131, 132, 166, 176
Boeckmann, 153
Brau, B., 32
British English, 17
Brummie, 15

C
Campbell, A., 6, 7
Carter, Angela, 21
Classroom research, 168, 169
Co-construction, 53, 121, 158
Code-switching, 69
Cognition, 32, 94
Cognitive Academic Language Proficiency (CALP), 132, 158
Common European Framework of Reference (CEFR), 39, 44
Community of practice, 130, 170, 179
Constructivism, 32, 80
Continuing professional development (CPD), 150, 164, 168, 175
Core syllabus, xxii, 127, 130–133, 135, 136, 138, 159, 160, 162, 168, 178

Council of Europe, 39, 44, 67, 166, 167, 175
Critical awareness, 27, 116, 132
Critical discourse analysis, 24
Critical literacy, 116
Critical thinking, 92, 116, 118
Crystal, D., 107, 116–118
Culture/cultural, 2, 4, 5, 14–21, 44, 59, 60, 62–67, 92, 106, 131, 133, 138, 148, 166
Cummins, J., 132, 158
Curriculum, xxi, 8, 24, 40, 41, 67, 69, 70, 75, 91, 107, 108, 114, 116, 119, 121, 122, 127–130, 133, 135, 136, 144, 150–153, 164, 168, 170–172, 178, 179

D
Dawes, L., 34, 48, 52, 125
Deconstruction, 120, 121
Derewianka, B., 118
Dialect, 15–17, 131
Dialogic teaching, 44–46, 124, 132
Discourse, 68, 94, 103–105, 120, 123, 132, 147, 153, 154, 177
Discourse community, 103, 104
Diversity, 62, 106, 133, 135, 138, 153
Domain (of language use), 39
Dyslexia, 65, 135

E
Easification, 88
Elicitation, 97, 132
Empathy, 62, 63, 124, 145
Engineering and Technology Education (ETE), 159
Ethnicity, 14, 16, 19
European Language Portfolio, 67
European Union, 24
Everyday language (EL), 156–160, 162, 174, 175, 177
Exploratory talk, 49, 101, 109

F
Fairclough, N., 23, 24, 137
Feilke, H., 157, 158
Floyd, George, 22, 23
Four Sides Model, 3, 4
French, 17, 46, 77, 93, 115, 147, 148, 167
Function, 62, 91, 131, 175, 178

G
Gardom Hulme, P., 70
Genre, 72, 73, 77, 99, 116, 118–122, 131, 133, 139, 153, 159, 173, 175, 177
Geordie, 15
Germany, 20, 128, 129, 131, 152–154, 164
Gettysburg Address, 23
Gibbons, P., 76
Google, 86

H
Hammond, J., 76, 120
Heugh, J., 66
Historical enquiry, 83
Hofstede, G., 19

I
Identity, 1, 8, 14–21, 131
Inculcation, 25
Indian English, 17, 68
Initial teacher training/education, 127–129, 166, 167, 170, 171, 173–175, 177
In-service teacher training, 60, 105, 127, 129, 131, 134, 146–148, 152, 164, 168, 178, 179
Instrumental/integrative, 62
Interaction, 3, 4, 6, 32, 34–36, 43, 46, 47, 49, 50, 52, 53, 73, 80, 88, 90, 91, 96, 103, 105, 122, 132, 133, 162, 163, 176, 177
Intercultural awareness, 67, 138
Interlocutor, 10

J
Jones, P., 118
Joyce, James, 25, 26

K
Krathwohl, D.R., 93

L
Language and power, 21–26, 138
Language awareness, 96, 124, 131, 137, 138, 153, 159, 164, 170–172, 174, 177, 179
Language of schooling, xxi, 41, 57, 64, 67, 69, 108, 114, 115, 117, 121, 130, 133,

135, 137, 139, 140, 151, 156–159, 164, 167, 171
Language pedagogy, 160
Language profile, 64, 65
Language register, 131, 175, 177
Language-related criteria, 162, 175, 179
Language repertoire, 53, 54, 57–69, 75, 96, 97, 99–106, 108, 121–126, 130–132, 135, 137, 140, 144, 147, 148, 154, 156, 158–160, 174, 179
Language-sensitive, xxi, 127, 129–132, 137–139, 144, 153, 154, 164–179
Language variety, 17, 65, 67, 68, 137
Learning talk, 45–53, 132
Leisen, Josef, 154, 155
Lesson observation, 134, 141, 174
Life skills, 107, 117
Lincoln, Abraham, 23
Literacy, xxi, 6, 7, 68, 83, 87, 97, 99, 101, 103, 105–119, 121–129, 132, 133, 135, 137, 139, 140, 143, 148, 151, 158, 160, 167, 168, 176, 179
Little, D., 68
Lower order/higher order thinking skills, 94

M
Malaysian English, 15
Manglish, 15, 16
Manzoni, C., 62, 63
McConachie, S.M., 108
Mediation, 10, 44, 45, 50, 52, 53, 88, 90, 97, 132, 167
Mentor, 140–142, 168, 174, 175
Mercer, N., 49, 53, 109, 125
Metalanguage, 100
Migrant students, 63, 64, 69
Minority language, 14
Miscommunication, 3, 9, 131
Modal verbs, 23
Monolingual, 63–66, 139
Montoya, S., 106
Morgan, N., 91, 97
Multilingual, 61, 66, 69, 133
Multiplier effect, 115, 118

N
National Council of Teachers of English (NCTE), 111, 112
Native speaker, 2, 13, 20
Negotiation of meaning, 176, 177

Nicholson, H., 74
Northern Ireland, 19, 119, 135
North Rhine-Westphalia, 128, 152

O
Oleschko, S., 152
Online chat, 6
Onomatopoeia, 102, 103
Open questions/closed questions, 90, 91
Oracy, 68, 97, 99, 101, 105–119, 121–126, 129, 132, 133, 135, 137, 140, 145, 151, 155, 156, 158, 160, 167, 173, 179
Oracy Benchmarks, 117
Oracy Cambridge, 109, 114
Oracy Framework, 114, 117

P
Padmini Shankar, K., 152
Pedagogic/pedagogy, 44, 58, 156, 160
Peer observation, 130, 148, 150, 168, 169, 179
Petrosky, A.R., 108
Photosynthesis, 124, 142, 143
Picenoni, M., 156
Pinker, S., 14
Piribauer, Gerda, 61
Plenary teaching, 45–47, 53, 75, 109
Plurilingual, 65, 66, 69, 166
Practicum, 171, 174
Pre-service teacher education, 61, 128, 134, 136, 176

R
Rao, K., 17
Rolfe, H., 62, 63
Rotter, Daniela, 155
Ruiters, J., 151

S
St Gallen Pedagogical University, 156
Saxton, J., 91, 97
Scaffolding, 57, 76–84, 87–89, 97, 120, 132, 142, 143, 167, 168, 173, 177, 179
Schulsprache, 157, 158
Schulz von Thun, Friedemann, 3, 4
Scouse, 15
Sealy, A., 2
Self-assessment, 67, 176

Sharpe, T., 83, 84, 88
Sharpton, Al, 22
Slone, I. B., 7
Social agent, 1–8, 44, 131, 167
Subject discipline, 104, 120, 121
Subject specialist language (SSL), 156, 157, 159, 160
Subject teacher, xxi, 105, 108, 135, 151, 156, 160, 162, 164, 167, 172, 175–177
Switzerland, 17, 131, 156, 164

T
Taxonomy, 92, 94
Taxonomy of Educational Objectives, 92
Teacher education, xxi, xxii, 61, 120–122, 124, 126–180, 185–188
Teachers' questions, 90, 91
Teaching Standards for England, 128
Teaching talk, 45, 46, 50, 53, 54, 132
Teenage culture, 18
Textbook, 41, 54, 70–77, 84, 86, 88, 94, 100, 103, 119, 120, 132, 149, 152
Textism, 7
Transferable/transversal skills, 107, 108, 166, 167
21st century skill, 8, 167
Twitter, 7

U
UNESCO, 116, 118
University of Mainz, 154
University of Oldenburg, 128
University of the Highlands and Islands, 94
Urban accent, 15
Utrecht University of Applied Sciences, 158

V
van den Branden, K., 152
van der Walt, C., 151
van Dijk, G., 149, 158, 159
van Eerde, D., 162
Varieties, 15–17, 20, 65, 67–69, 88, 119, 121, 129, 131, 135–137, 153, 171
Vernacular, 16
Vocabulary building, 82
Voice 21, 109, 117
Vygotsky, L., 32, 79, 80, 97

W
Wilkes, A., 72
Wilkinson, A., 116–118
Woods, D., 78

Z
Zone of proximal development (ZPD), 79, 97

Printed by Printforce, United Kingdom